T0319436

Financial Liberalization and Economic Development in Korea, 1980–2020

This volume is part of the multivolume study
Rising to the Challenges of Democratization and Globalization in Korea

Harvard East Asian Monographs 440

Financial Liberalization and Economic Development in Korea, 1980–2020

Yung Chul Park,
Joon-Kyung Kim,
and
Hail Park

Published by the Harvard University Asia Center
Distributed by Harvard University Press
Cambridge (Massachusetts) and London, 2021

Printed in the United States of America

The Harvard University Asia Center publishes a monograph series and, in coordination with the Fairbank Center for Chinese Studies, the Korea Institute, the Reischauer Institute of Japanese Studies, and other facilities and institutes, administers research projects designed to further scholarly understanding of China, Japan, Korea, Vietnam, and other Asian countries. The Center also sponsors projects addressing multidisciplinary, transnational, and regional issues in Asia.

Library of Congress Cataloging-in-Publication Data

Names: Pak, Yŏng-chʻŏl, 1939- author. | Kim, Joon-Kyung, 1956- author. | Park, Hail, author.
Title: Financial liberalization and economic development in Korea, 1980-2020 / Yung Chul Park, Joon-Kyung Kim, and Hail Park.
Description: 1 Edition. | Cambridge : Harvard University Asia Center, 2021. | Series: Harvard East Asian monographs; 440 | Includes bibliographical references and index. | Summary: "Analyzes the deepening of and structural changes in Korea's financial system since the early 1980s and presents the empirical results of the effects of financial development on economic growth, stability, and the distribution of income. Finds that, contrary to conventional wisdom, financial liberalization has contributed little to fostering the growth and stability of the Korean economy and has exacerbated income distribution problems"—Provided by publisher
Identifiers: LCCN 2020043112 (print) | LCCN 2020043113 (ebook) | ISBN 9780674251281 (cloth) | ISBN 9781684176304 (adobe pdf)
Subjects: LCSH: Financial institutions—Government policy—Korea (South) | Economic development—Korea (South) | Korea (South)—Economic policy. | Income distribution—Korea (South)
Classification: LCC HG187.K6 P35 2021 (print) | LCC HG187.K6 (ebook) | DDC 332.095195—dc23
LC record available at https://lccn.loc.gov/2020043112
LC ebook record available at https://lccn.loc.gov/2020043113

Index by Alex Trotter

♾ Printed on acid-free paper

Last figure below indicates year of this printing

30   29   28   27   26   25   24   23   22   21

Contents

Tables and Figures

Tables

Figures

Acknowledgments

This volume on financial development is one in the series of studies on economic, social, and political changes over the past four decades in Korea organized by the Korea Development Institute (KDI) and the Harvard University Asia Center. The finance volume has taken much longer to complete than others in the series. All three of us have changed our institutional affiliations since the project started. These changes have made it challenging to work together during our transition periods. We set out to delve into developments in different financial industries and the transformation of financial and regulatory policy during the course of financial liberalization in Korea. This approach has required gathering a large amount of microfinance data, including from household surveys, needed to conduct a set of panel estimations and has taken much more time than expected.

In writing the book, we have received valuable suggestions for improving our analysis from Thorsten Beck at the Cass Business School, London, and Ugo Panizza at the Graduate Institute, Geneva. We also appreciate the comments by and encouragement of our colleagues working on other volumes. We are grateful to Barry Eichengreen, who was the coordinator of the project, and Dwight Perkins, who assisted us in preparing a draft for review by the Asia Center.

We have learned a great deal from comments by a large number of people who participated in various conferences and discussion meetings organized by the KDI and the Asia Center. We would like to thank many fellows at the Korea Institute of Finance, who read an earlier draft of the book. Their comments helped us clarify many of the arguments we make in various chapters and tighten our analysis overall.

At Korea University, Yung Chul Park thanks Dean Sung-han Kim and Professor Innwon Park, director of the Center for East Asian Studies (CEAS) of Graduate School of International Studies, for providing excellent research support. At the CEAS, Dr. Jung Hwan Park worked with Hail Park in conducting most of the empirical examinations for the study. Two research fellows at the CEAS, Jinhee Lee and Heon-il Lim, took over the demanding task of providing research assistance. All of them were our valued associates. Without their devotion, we would not have completed the book. The CEAS also thanks Kookmin Bank for its financial support of the study. We were also fortunate to enlist Larry Meissner for editorial assistance. He helped us to not only improve our writing but also to sharpen our analysis. At the KDI School of Public Policy and Management, Joon-Kyung Kim owes a debt of gratitude to Jun Il Kim and K. S. Kim for their valuable comments and input. At Kyung Hee University, Wenbo Wang provided excellent research assistance for Hail Park.

In Cambridge, we are grateful to Gretchen O'Connor for editing a preliminary draft. We are also grateful to Robert Graham at the Asia Center for guiding us in submitting a final draft for publication. Most of all, we would like to thank him for graciously enduring the long delay in completing the study. Finally, we wish to thank KDI and its management for continuously supporting this study and bringing it to fruition.

Contributors

Yung Chul Park, Distinguished Professor, Division of International Studies, Korea University.

Joon-Kyung Kim, Professor, KDI School of Public Policy and Management.

Hail Park, Department Chair/Associate Professor, Department of International Business and Trade, Kyung Hee University.

List of Abbreviations

ABS	Asset-backed security
BAI	Board of Audit and Inspection
BIS	Bank for International Settlements
BOK	Bank of Korea
BOT	Bank of Thailand
CAMELS	Capital adequacy, asset quality, management, earnings, liquidity, and sensitivity to market risk
CBO	Collateralized bond obligation
CD	Certificate of deposit
CDS	Credit default swap
CI index	Chinn-Ito index
CLFC	Consumer loan finance company
CMCA	Capital Market Consolidation Act
COVID-19	Coronavirus disease 2019
CP	Commercial paper
CPI	Consumer Price Index
CRC	Corporate Restructuring Company

CRS	Currency swap
DEA	Data envelopment analysis
DFY	Ratio of direct finance to GDP
DR	Depositary receipt
DTI	Ratio of debt to income
ECB	European Central Bank
ECOS	Economic Statistics System of the Bank of Korea
EFSO	Establishment of Financial Supervisory Organizations
FAY	Ratio of total finance to GDP
FDI	Foreign direct investment
Fed	Federal Reserve Board
FHC	Financial holding company
FHCA	Financial Holding Company Act
FISIS	Financial Statistics Information System
FIU	Financial intelligence unit
FSC	Financial Services Commission or Financial Supervisory Commission
FSI	Financial soundness indicator
FSS	Financial Supervisory Service
GDP	Gross domestic product
HHI	Herfindahl-Hirschman Index
HPI	House price index
IDFY	Ratio of indirect finance to GDP
IFC	International finance center
IMF	International Monetary Fund
ITC	Investment trust company

KDB	Korea Development Bank
KDI	Korea Development Institute
KFCC	Korean Federation of Community Credit Cooperatives
KHCB	Korea Housing and Commercial Bank
KIS	Korea Information Service
KIS VALUE	Database of NICE Information Service Co. Ltd.
KLIPS	Korea Labor and Income Panel Study
KOFEX	Korea Futures Exchange
KONEX	Korea New Exchange
KOSDAQ	Korea Securities Dealers Automated Quotations
KOSIS	Korean Statistical Information Service
KOSPI	Korea Composite Stock Price Index
KRX	Korea Exchange
KSE	Korea Stock Exchange
MSB	Mutual savings bank
MSFC	Mutual savings and finance company
NACF	National Agricultural Cooperative Federation
NBFI	Nonbank financial institution
NFBO	Nonfinancial business operator
NFFC	National Federation of Fisheries Cooperatives
NPL	Nonperforming loan
ROA	Return on asset
ROE	Return on equity
RP	Repurchase agreement
SFC	Short-term finance company

SHFLC	Survey of Household Finance and Living Conditions
SMEs	Small and medium enterprises
SPC	Special-purpose company
TFP	Total factor productivity

Introduction and Overview of Financial Development

An extensive literature on financial development and economic growth contends that, in theory and according to empirical work, the transition to a liberal financial system spurs growth by increasing productivity and allocative efficiency of the economy and improves income distribution through various channels while mitigating the risk of financial instability. However, the experiences of many emerging economies do not necessarily support these beneficial effects. Depending on the level of financial development, financial liberalization may not help sustain financial stability or achieve a more desirable income distribution.

Korea embarked on a sweeping liberalization of its financial system in the wake of the 1997 Asian financial crisis. The reform has served as the primary driver of financial growth and diversification in the country. But it has been far from trouble-free. Korea endured a series of episodes of financial turbulence, including the 2008 global financial crisis. The reform has been inimical to growth and stability but has had little bearing on financial deepening. What is puzzling about Korea's experience is that financial deepening has had little or no impact on industrial efficiency or improving distributive equity.

There is also evidence that the deregulation of capital account transactions was, in part, responsible for precipitating the two major crises in 1997 and 2008. This experience underscores the need to rethink the conditions under and the speed at which financial liberalization could proceed with minimum adverse consequences.

Intermediated credit provision fluctuates substantially with the business cycle (Bernanke and Gertler 1989). The short-term variations in intermediated credit to gross domestic product (GDP) are, therefore, unlikely to reflect the changes in the efficiency and development of financial markets and institutions. Many episodes of financial crisis demonstrate that credit and asset price cycles often move together, suggesting that rapid increases in credit relative to GDP could reflect credit bubbles rather than rapid improvements in the efficiency and development of financial systems.

The causal nexus between financial development on the one hand and real sector developments and financial stability on the other hand is multifaceted and varies from country to country. For this reason, empirically identifying and gauging the significance of the causal relations has been a challenging task. This study analyzes the background and consequences of financial market deregulation and opening since the early 1980s to assess its effects on growth, efficiency, equity, and stability in the Korean economy.

We begin with an overview of financial development during the past four decades, starting in the early 1980s. The overview is followed in chapters 1–5 by an analysis of the growth and structural changes in the financial system, the effects of financial liberalization on financial institutions and markets, and the financial behavior of households and firms. Chapters 6–9, which constitute the core of this study, present the empirical results of the effects of financial development on economic growth, stability, and distribution of income.

Chapters 10–12 cover the reform of the financial regulatory system and its efficiency in preserving financial stability. Chapters 13–15 analyze the causes, resolution, and consequences of the 1997 and the 2008 financial crises. Chapter 16 discusses the potential effects of the COVID-19 pandemic on the financial turmoil. A summary and conclusions are presented in chapter 17, the final chapter.

The Evolution of a Market-Oriented Financial System before the 1997 Crisis: An Overview

The defining feature of Korea's financial development since the early 1980s has been a tale of liberalization and opening. After the 1997 crisis, great strides were made in building a market-oriented financial system through sweeping reforms for the deregulation and opening of financial markets and intermediaries. But the new system failed to steer the country away from a credit card boom and bust in 2003, a liquidity crisis in 2008, and a run on its savings banks in 2011. Clearly, financial liberalization is no panacea.

Economists disagree on the causal connections between financial liberalization on the one hand and savings and investment, consumption smoothing, financial stability, and income distribution on the other hand. While some predict that financial liberalization will spur growth by increasing savings and investment and improving the efficiency of the latter, evidence from country studies does not always support this view.[1]

What effect of financial liberalization has on real sector variables is an empirical question. This study endeavors to answer it, at least in part, by assessing the impact of such liberalization on Korea. Our conclusions are broadly negative. In Korea's case, it would appear, financial liberalization and opening have delivered less than promised.

The sections that follow, therefore, examine the causes and consequences of those disturbances with the goal of gaining insights into the causal connections between financial liberalization and financial stability. The sections also attempt to address the question of whether a well-functioning financial system should be complemented by an efficient system of financial regulation to safeguard against financial instability—and if so, by what kind of financial regulation.

Financial Liberalization in the 1980s: The First Wave of Liberalization

It has long been an accepted economic tenet that a market-oriented financial system is more efficient than a repressive government-controlled system in allocating resources. Yet during the 1960s and 1970s, like many other countries with developing or emerging economies, Korea did not establish a financial market infrastructure or a policy regime appropriate for reaping the benefits of financial liberalization. In reality, politicians and policy makers were unable or unwilling to steer the economy toward a more liberal regime due to a fixation on controlling the financial system as an instrument for supporting industrial policy—more precisely,

---

1. Levine (2005), Bekaert et al. (2006), and Galindo et al. (2007) provide positive assessments of the impact of financial liberalization on real variables.

the export-led development strategy. Another justification for financial control may have been the belief that at the early stages of financial development, financial markets are prone to failures. It was not until the early 1980s that structural changes were initiated to lay the foundations for a market-oriented financial system. Since then, the process of deregulating financial markets and institutions has moved forward through four stages of reform. However, each stage lacked a comprehensive and consistent strategy regarding the pace, scope, and sequence of reform, resulting in intermittent financial restructuring marred by relapses and regressions—at least until after the 1997 financial crisis.

It would hardly be an understatement to argue that during much of the postwar period up to the late 1970s, Korea's financial system was one of the most repressive regimes in the developing world. Asset liability management at banks and nonbank financial institutions (NBFIs), interest rates, and capital account transactions were all under tight government control. The control system was geared to support an industrial policy regime directed toward export promotion. In particular, export performance was one of the essential criteria for credit allocation for bank borrowers in the 1960s and 1970s.

During the latter part of the 1970s, economic growth slowed, while inflation accelerated at an annual rate of 20–30 percent. Increases in real wages in the manufacturing sector rapidly outpaced productivity growth. And the wage increases, combined with a real appreciation of the exchange rate, resulted in a sharp decline in export earnings in real terms, as well as a widening current account deficit. To make matters worse, the growing political uncertainty triggered by the October 1979 assassination of President Park Chung Hee narrowed options for short-run macroeconomic policy management, as it severely curtailed Korea's access to foreign borrowing.

By the early 1980s, when the economy was deep in recession, it became evident that the root causes of the economic malaise were not cyclical but structural. The collusive arrangement among the government, the chaebol, and the banks, which were the main players of Chalmers Johnson's developmental state, was coming apart at the seams with mounting inefficiencies in resource allocation, internal and external imbalances, and cronyism bred by the mismanagement of industrial policy.[2] Realizing

---

2. There is no official definition of a chaebol. However, Korea's Fair Trade Commission defines a "large corporate group" as a business entity with total assets (including

the limitations of the developmental state, and no doubt swept up by the liberal ideology that permeated the global economy at the time, the government of President Chun Doo-hwan, which came to power in 1980, sought to find a way out of the difficulty by espousing market orientation and economic opening.

The shift in the development strategy launched the first wave of economic liberalization. The planned liberalization included general financial deregulation and opening in the early 1980s, which highlighted bank privatization, entry relaxation, interest rate deregulation, the removal of directed lending to strategic industrial sectors, and preferential interest rates on policy loans. However, many of these measures were not implemented, as Korea's policy makers were unprepared to forsake their penchant for interventionism. Backing out of the reform pledge, they continued to dither about the timing and scope of liberalization throughout the 1980s. As a result, only cosmetic changes were achieved during this period, and the country held fast to its dirigiste policy regime of the past. In the end, the initial tide of reform failed to make much progress in removing many of the features of a repressive financial system.

BANK PRIVATIZATION

The privatization of government-owned or -controlled banks is a good example of how reluctant the Korean government was to relinquish its grip over finance despite its avowed objective of pursuing liberal reform. The government did denationalize commercial banks. But this change was only superficial, as the banks continued to be subject to direct and

---

those of its affiliates) that exceed 5 trillion won (about $4.3 billion at 1,163 won/dollar), involves at least two companies, and is effectively controlled by the same individual or corporate entity. As of May 2019, there were fifty-nine such groups in Korea. These groups are subject to restrictions on the cross holding of shares of their affiliates. Thirty-four of the groups had total assets of more than 10 trillion won. They are required to disclose their management performance. The chaebol is somewhat similar to the pre-war Japanese zaibatsu, as they are family owned and managed. Three of the four largest—Samsung, Hyundai Motor, and LG Group—are well-known global brand names. SK Group, focused on telecommunications and information technology services, has been increasing its number of affiliates and is now the third largest. Small and medium enterprises (SMEs) are firms with total assets of less than 500 billion won. In between there are a large number of what this study calls "other large firms." For brevity, the chaebol and other large firms are classified into a single category of large firms.

indirect administrative controls, which made internal governance as ineffective and weak as ever.

For example, even after the avowed deregulation, the government continued to influence bank management through various channels. It was not even discreet about appointing bank CEOs and other senior executives, and the boards of directors had neither a clearly defined role nor any statutory power to resist the government control. The stated objective of privatization was to create private banks with public-minded owners and managers.[3] The government wanted to prevent the chaebol from monopolizing financial resources through bank ownership to avoid a repeat of the chaebol domination of privatized banks in the 1950s.

The first privatization, in June 1981, was of Hanil Bank, the best managed and most profitable among all commercial banks. Against the government's wishes, however, two major chaebol acquired a controlling interest in the bank. This takeover provoked subsequent policy debates on whether there was any need to impose a ceiling on the equity share that a single individual or entity could hold, but the problem of mounting nonperforming loans at the banks earmarked for privatization shelved the ownership reform until mid-1982.

Toward the end of 1982, the government amended the General Banking Act to impose an 8 percent ceiling on the individual ownership of any nationwide commercial bank's voting stock. Around the same time, two more banks—Korea First and Seoul Banks—were privatized, and a third, Chohung Bank, followed in 1983. After that, it took seven years before the government put on sale another bank, Citizens Bank. The ownership ceiling did not succeed in barring the industrial groups from controlling privatized banks, however, as a group could acquire a controlling interest in a bank by having the NBFIs they owned hold the shares or by colluding with other stockholders in a de facto takeover of a bank.

For this reason and because of its adherence to industrial policy, the government continued to intervene in the allocation of loans at these supposedly privatized commercial banks. It put pressure on the banks to bail out firms in troubled industries such as the overseas construction,

---

3. Other considerations were also at play: the proceeds from the sale of government shares were expected to help ease the government budget constraint in a period of fiscal austerity and the supply of "good stocks" would stimulate the stock market (B. Choi 1993).

shipping, textile, machinery, and lumber industries, which were especially hard hit during the global recession in the early 1980s.

ENTRY DEREGULATION

As part of the financial reform, the government loosened the regulations on entry into the banking sector, but this was hardly opening up the industry. The move was initially motivated by the need to charter two new joint-venture banks with Korean and foreign capital and was followed by the establishment of two new commercial banks in 1991.[4] The Korea Investment and Finance Company obtained a banking license to restructure itself as Hana Bank. The merger of two other investment and finance companies created another new bank, Boram Bank. The entry relaxation also facilitated the opening of foreign bank branches. By 1987, the number of such branches had reached fifty-four, and they accounted for more than 10 percent of the total commercial bank assets and 63 percent of foreign currency–denominated loans in Korea.

The 1982 financial scandal involving commercial paper fraud in the informal curb market underscored the urgency of integrating that market into the organized financial system, as it was entrenched as a viable source of informal finance outside the purview of financial supervision. To this end, Korea's policy makers allowed curb market lenders to organize themselves into short-term finance companies (SFCs) and mutual savings and finance companies (MSFCs) in 1982. Within a year, twelve new SFCs and fifty-seven new MSFCs had opened their doors.

THE SHIFT IN THE COMPOSITION
OF POLICY LOANS

It was clear from the beginning that the process of financial liberalization would not be complete unless the government lowered the number of policy loans that supported exporters and firms in heavy and chemical industries to the maximum allowed by the World Trade Organization. In phasing out policy loans, the subsidy elements in the interest rates for

---

4. One was Shinhan Bank, which was established mainly by Korean residents in Japan in July 1982. The other was KorAm Bank, a joint venture between the Bank of America and several major Korean corporations that was established in March 1983.

Table I.1. Interest Rate Differentials between Export Loans and General
Loans (percent)

	1961–65	*1966–72*	*1973–81*	*1982–86*	*1987–91*
Export loan interest rate (A)	9.3	6.1	9.7	10.0	10.0–11.0
General loan interest rate (B)	18.2	23.2	17.3	10.0–11.5	10.0–11.5
Difference (B—A)	8.9	17.1	7.6	0.0–1.5	0.0–0.5

Source: Y. Cho and Kim 1995.

Table I.2. Deposit Money Banks' Required Ratio of Loans to SMEs to Total
Lending (percent)

	1965	*1976*	*1980*	*1985*	*1986*	*1992*
Nationwide commercial bank	30	30	35	35	35	45
Local bank	30	40	55	55	80	80
Foreign bank branch	—[a]	—[a]	—[a]	25	25	25

Source: Y. Cho and Kim 1995.
Notes: For 1965, the ratio is in terms of total loans (including those in US dollars). For 1976, the ratio is in terms of an increase in total loans. And for 1980, the ratio is in terms of an increase in loans in won only. SMEs are small and medium enterprises.
[a] Not available.

many types of export financing were eliminated. For example, the difference between the average interest rate for export loans and that for general commercial and industry loans, which was as large as 17 percent in the late 1960s, almost completely disappeared after 1982 (see Table I.1), and the number of eligible firms for policy loans sharply declined.

However, the impact of such a cutback was offset to some extent by new subsidized loan programs for small and medium enterprises (SMEs) (see Table I.2). Much of the increase in bank loans to SMEs was at the expense of lending to the chaebol (see Table I.3).

In 1987, the government imposed a maximum of 4 percent on the share of loans to the nation's thirty largest chaebol at each bank. At the same time, the government also tried to reduce bank financing by those chaebol by forcing them to repay their bank debts with funds raised on the stock market. As a result, the share of bank loans extended to those chaebol fell from 23.7 percent in 1988 to 20.4 percent in 1991, while that of

Table I.3. Share of Loans to SMEs and the 30 Largest Chaebol by Deposit Money Banks (percent)

	1988	*1989*	*1990*	*1991*
Loans to SMEs	48.1	50.1	55.5	56.8
Loans to the 30 largest chaebol	23.7	20.7	19.8	20.4

Source: Y. Cho and Kim 1995.
Note: SMEs are small and medium enterprises.

loans to SMEs rose from 33.1 percent in 1983 to 56.8 percent in 1991. The reduction in the relative share of policy loans through such measures was almost negligible. And contrary to the government's proclamations, there was little change until the early 1990s. Instead, what changed was just the composition of policy-directed lending by reallocating some of the subsidized loans from the chaebol and export-oriented firms to SMEs.

INTEREST RATE DEREGULATION

The year 1984 was a milestone in Korea's history of financial liberalization, as the government took the first step toward interest rate deregulation. For the first time in Korea's postwar history, banks and NBFIs were allowed to set their lending rates within a given range adjusted for the creditworthiness of borrowers. The government complemented this partial interest rate liberalization with a host of other measures: the lifting of the upper limit on call rates in 1984, decontrol of yields on convertible bonds and debentures with bank payment guarantees in 1985, freeing of interest rates on certificates of deposit (CDs), and issuing rates for financial debentures marketed by deposit money banks in 1986. This series of interest rate deregulations culminated in the decontrol of bank and nonbank lending rates toward the end of 1988—the first year of the government of President Roh Tae-woo, which had succeeded the Chun regime in February 1988.

The Roh government was as committed as the previous regime to deregulating and opening financial markets. It began by lifting myriad remaining restrictions on asset management at banks and NBFIs. It also eased control of the foreign exchange market and current and capital account transactions. However, a surge in unemployment and widespread labor disputes delayed the implementation of the Roh government's new plan for the full liberalization of interest rates in August 1991. The plan envisaged completing the deregulation of interest rates in four stages, starting with the freeing of long-term interest rates and then freeing short-term and other interest rates, including deposit rates, by the end of 1997.

REFORM OF FOREIGN EXCHANGE CONTROL

During the second half of the 1980s, export earnings continued to outstrip import payments. The ensuing current account surplus between 1986 and 1989 gave the Roh government policy makers room and confidence to remove many of the import restrictions and lower the average tariff rate to 15 percent from 20 percent. With this change, Korea was able to meet the obligations of the International Monetary Fund (IMF) Article VIII—including the level of current account liberalization—in 1988.

Despite the surplus in the current account, the Korean government was not prepared to dismantle an array of controls over capital account transactions for fear of destabilizing the domestic financial market. But these controls made it increasingly more challenging to manage the US dollar peg. This difficulty led to the adoption in March 1990 of the variant of the managed floating exchange rate regime known as the market average rate system. The new system increased the flexibility of the exchange rate by allowing intra-day fluctuations of the won-dollar exchange rate within the range of 0.40–2.25 percent over the 1990–95 period.

CAPITAL MARKET OPENING

Throughout the 1980s, control over capital flows was managed as a way to balance the current account. When the current account was in deficit, the government took measures to induce capital inflows. It did this by, for instance, allowing domestic banks to borrow more from abroad. At the same time, the authorities tightened regulations on capital outflows, mainly by restricting residents' foreign investments—as it did during the first half of the 1980s. When the current account continued to register a sizable surplus between 1986 and 1989, the government reversed the policy to reimpose direct controls on capital inflows while easing restrictions on capital outflows.

Although the increase in the current account surplus generated pressure to open the capital market, the Roh government was far from prepared to remove all controls on capital movements, inflows as well as outflows. As in the case of interest rate decontrol, the government chose a gradual approach to be carried out over four stages, starting in 1989. The plan allowed foreigners limited access to the stock market (they could first invest in domestic stocks through equity funds and later directly in a limited number of shares) and permitted foreign securities firms to open branches in Korea by 1992.

This plan initially led to a partial relaxation of capital outflows, opening new avenues for Korean corporations to make limited portfolio investments in foreign securities. Only a year later, however, the government had to reverse its policy, as the current account started to deteriorate due to rising inflation, a real appreciation of the won, and a global recession. Facing difficulties in financing the mounting current account deficit, the government removed some of the restrictions on capital inflows in the hope of attracting foreign investments in domestic securities.

The Kim Young-Sam Government and the Second Wave of Liberalization in the 1990s

Kim Young-sam defeated two other candidates in the December 1992 presidential election and was inaugurated on February 25, 1993, ending a long period of authoritarian or quasi-democratic governments. The Kim government placed economic globalization at the fore of its economic policy priorities.

The globalization agenda set the stage for the second wave of financial market liberalization and opening that began in June 1993 by creating a blueprint for phasing out the regulatory system controlling capital account transactions over three years. The plan was one of the main components of the government's globalization strategy. It also proposed relaxing the requirements for foreign exchange transactions, widening the daily won-dollar trading margins, increasing the limits on foreign investment in the stock market, and taking out long-term loans from global financial markets.

Despite a series of capital account liberalizations that had begun in the late 1980s, firms—especially the large industrial groups—demanded the removal of remaining restrictions. They contended that the rigid control over capital inflows kept domestic interest rates high, which undermined their relative competitiveness in world markets. In response to this and mounting international pressure for further deregulation, the government unveiled its new Foreign Exchange System Reform Plan in December 1994. The plan envisaged an almost complete liberalization of current and capital account transactions and the development of an efficient foreign exchange market in three stages over five years.[5]

In moving forward with deregulating capital inflows, the government removed restrictions on short-term external borrowing but planned to retain control over the domestic long-term bond market and long-term foreign financing until much of the interest rate differentials between local and international capital markets had disappeared. The rationale behind this asymmetry was that short-term external borrowing, the majority of which was for trade financing, would not add to the foreign debt as much as long-term borrowing would.

Because of the considerable interest rate differentials between foreign and domestic financial markets, lifting many of the restrictions on capital flows in a managed floating exchange rate regime induced a massive increase in external financing. Banks obtained much of the increase from the international wholesale funding market to re-lend to chaebol and large firms for their funding of long-term investments. This created mismatches on the bank and corporate balance sheets. The maturity mismatch was more severe for merchant bank corporations. Practically all of these were heavily engaged in offshore operations, borrowing short and lending long. According to one estimate, they invested 80 percent of their short-term debts, which amounted to 70 percent of their long-term assets.

The rate at which short-term foreign liabilities were piling up was alarming. Korea's debt-servicing capacity was limited, and its foreign exchange reserves were dwindling. The increase in short-term foreign loans rendered the economy highly vulnerable to a sudden reversal of capital inflow.

Korea was unable to defend itself against the onslaught of currency speculation that led to a drought of US dollar liquidity. Unable to acquire what was needed in liquidity from international financial markets, Korea had to approach the IMF for rescue financing. The IMF-organized liquidity injection spared Korea from declaring a debt moratorium. How-

---

5. The plan included a few exceptions and stipulated a gradual and staged liberalization process, with the speed of liberalization to be adjusted depending on the state of the economy.

ever, the support required an extensive array of reforms for market liberalization and opening that Korea was hardly prepared to undertake.

There is no denying that the financial vulnerabilities of highly leveraged financial institutions and large industrial groups were the immediate triggers of the crisis, exacerbating it and making it more difficult to manage. However, if the chaebol were irresponsible and reckless borrowers, why would international lenders voluntarily lend them so much money? Were the lenders misled by falsified data and misinformation propagated by the Korean government? Or did they each assume that they would be the first out the door if things went wrong or collectively believe there would be a bailout? That is, were they merely speculators moving in for short-term gains and moving out with a moment's notice at the first sign of distress?

The 1997 Financial Crisis and the Third Wave

The 1997 financial crisis has served as a reminder of the limitations and risks of a government-led growth strategy powered by exports and massive investment, much of which was undertaken by large firms with funds borrowed from international wholesale funding markets. It also brought home the urgency of restructuring all sectors of the Korean economy, including strengthening the resilience of the corporate and financial sectors to external shocks. In the aftermath of the crisis, Korea was told time and again that there was no alternative but to embrace market deregulation and opening if the country was serious about curing its economic malaise.

It took Korea a year and a half to recover from the crisis, which was much faster than expected. The swift recovery has raised the question of whether Korea could have avoided the crisis had it been able to mobilize a sufficient amount of liquidity at the onset to assure panicking international lenders that their loans would be repaid in full. Indeed, the liquidity crisis that Korea suffered in 2008 may support the view that the leading cause of the 1997 crisis was not insolvency risk but rather overreaction to a short-term balance of payments problem.

In contrast to this revisionist view, many would argue that the crisis had a silver lining: Korea would have never made the gains in efficiency, soundness, and stability of its financial industries that it has achieved without the reforms imposed by the crisis. This study examines the extent to which Korea has been able to reap these benefits through reform.

The reforms mandated by the IMF ushered in the third wave of economic liberalization. Corporate restructuring was brutal. A large number of insolvent firms, including sixteen chaebol, were liquidated or merged with other firms. The survivors were forced to streamline their businesses and investment activities to specialize in sectors where they had a competitive edge and to improve their balance sheets by lowering the debt-equity ratio to less than 200 percent from more than 300 percent before the crisis.

The IMF, other international financial institutions, and members of the Group of Seven all argued that the reform would transform Korea's financial system into a regime as free and open as those of advanced economies. The crisis also gave the opposition party, led by Kim Dae-jung, an opportunity to consolidate its power base by campaigning to rein in the chaebol. Kim, who had won 34 percent of the vote in the 1992 election, won the December 1997 election by half a percentage point and was inaugurated president in February 1998. The new administration took bold steps to restructure the chaebol in ways that had been unthinkable under previous governments.

During the three years following the crisis, most of the controls on market interest rates and the foreign exchange rate were lifted. So were the regulatory restrictions on asset and liability management at banks and other financial institutions and on capital account transactions. The fourth phase of the interest rate liberalization that had begun in 1991 was completed in February 2004, with the freeing of interest rates on all deposits to be determined by individual financial institutions.

The Fourth Wave: An Aborted Attempt and the 2008 Liquidity Crisis

Following the recovery from the 1997 crisis, Korea began running large and persistent surpluses on its current account. These were driven by weak domestic demand and soaring exports based on a massive depreciation of the won. The monetary authorities continued to sterilize current and capital account surpluses to accumulate foreign exchange reserves. By the end of 2004, the level of reserves had reached $199.1 billion. This was more than 25 percent of GDP, compared to less than 14 percent at the end of

1998. The sterilization eased the pressure for a currency appreciation against the US dollar and other major international currencies. But it was becoming costly.

As in the 1980s, the persistent surplus in the current account provided a rationale for further financial market opening. Thus, the fourth wave of financial liberalization set out to make Seoul an international finance center (IFC).

The concept of an IFC is related to the view that the financial system is an export sector. Thus, a full-fledged IFC performs both traditional intermediation activities and fee-generating activities. To be successful, an IFC has to host markets for international debt, mergers and acquisitions, derivatives, and private equity financing, as well as the professional services (legal, accounting, consulting, and the like) that tend to cluster in a financial center. This was not easy to do.

Advocates focused on financial services as a growth sector, one that seeks to build a nationally based financial center premised on relative comparative advantages such as skill base, favorable regulatory policies, and subsidies (see Kose, Prasad, and Terrones 2009). The road map proposed in 2003 set 2020 as the target date for the completion of the plan. In 2005, the timeline was revised to bring the target year forward to 2015.

Korea's policymakers were overwhelmed by the daunting tasks of creating a successful nationally based financial center. These tasks included the complete liberalization of capital account transactions, full convertibility and internationalization of the won, and allowing offshore trading in the won. The plan was too ambitious and unrealistic. Among the short-term roadblocks that the Roh Moo-hyun administration, which took office in February 2003, had to face were a credit card loan crisis, a nascent real estate market boom, and an increase in the strength of the won caused by large capital inflows. Not surprisingly, the fourth wave never even hit the shore.

The mounting pressure for a currency appreciation still needed to be dissipated. However, a series of measures to relax the outflow of portfolio capital did little to subdue the pressure. This was because external borrowing financed much of domestic residents' portfolio investments in foreign securities, in particular at the short end of global financial markets. The surge in portfolio investments resulted in a substantial increase in short-term foreign liabilities. In the eyes of international lenders, the investments had reached an unsustainable level, akin to the run-up to the 1997 crisis.

Soon after coming into power in February 2008, the government of President Lee Myung-bak had to clean up the debris from the bursting of the 2007 real estate bubble. The government was then swept up by the global liquidity crisis that was aggravated by the September 2008 collapse of Lehman Brothers.

The 2008 crisis was rooted in the sudden reversal of capital inflow, which dried up the availability of reserve currency liquidity. Korea could not hold currency speculators at bay on its own. Although more than $250 billion was held in foreign exchange reserves, Korea had to secure external liquidity that would be sufficient to convince foreign creditors of its debt servicing capabilities, while at the same time preventing capital outflows. Korea was unwilling to approach the IMF for precautionary liquidity. Instead, it negotiated a $30 billion currency swap with the U.S. Federal Reserve Board, and that was enough for international creditors.

It took a year and a half for the Korean economy to recover. This swiftness was in part because of the strength of Korea's economic fundamentals. However, the recovery has not put the economy back on the precrisis path toward robust growth and stability. Korea has been unable to escape from what appears to be a low-growth trap while grappling with mounting household debt. That debt was larger than nominal GDP at the end of 2014 and could pose systemic risks to the financial system.

Build-Up of a Financial Crisis: The Collapse of the Park Geun-hye Government and the Rise of Moon Jae-in's Progressive Regime

By the early 2010s, the inefficiency of the financial system and the loss of global competitiveness by Korean banks and NBFIs had become evident. Therefore, it is not surprising that the government of President Park Geun-hye, who was inaugurated in February 2013, laid out a three-year plan for structural reform in 2015 to improve competitiveness and innovation in the financial industry.

The reform had three main components: (1) the deregulation of the financial market; (2) enhancement of the stability of the financial system; and (3) protection for consumers of financial services. The reform measures were also deemed critical for assisting the financial industry in adapting to the changes driven by digital transformation in the global financial landscape.

The three reform objectives required the implementation of a large set of specific measures. Among them were the elimination of many outdated financial laws and regulations (211 out of 1,064) and incidences of administrative or regulatory window guidance (650 out of 700); the reform of the pervasive practice of requiring collateral or cosigners for loans; and the introduction of crowdfunding and internet-only banks. However, except for the creation of two internet banks in 2007, little was accomplished before a political crisis erupted in 2016 that eventually led to Park's impeachment early in 2017.

The presidential election held in May 2017 ushered in the progressive government of Moon Jae-in, which was deeply committed to introducing a populist regime of economic policy. The new government had no interest in pursuing the financial reform laid out by the previous administration, with the exception of reforming the supervision and regulation of digital transformation in finance and fostering the fintech industry.

Instead, the administration has been preoccupied with reviving the sagging economy through the implementation of an income-led growth strategy. The scheme is based on the hypothesis that an increase in the minimum wage rate will expand household incomes, which will, in turn, boost consumer spending. The rest of the plan is based on the simple multiplier effect. Three years after the inception, however, there is no evidence suggesting that the new strategy has been effective in reversing the downturn of the economy.

In retrospect, the lack of interest in addressing the erosion of efficiency and stability of the financial system has made Korea's policymakers complacent about the growing distortions and disarray in the private equity industry. In 2015, the Park Geun-hye government undertook an extensive reform to deregulate the entry and operations of hedge fund firms without putting in place any prudential supervision on the private equity industry that would have provided a safety net for investors.

At the end of 2013, there were 7,734 hedge funds (see FSC 2020a). Six years later, the number rose to 11,734 (see FSC 2020a). During the same period, the number of hedge fund management firms had risen almost fourfold to 213 (see FSC 2020a). A growing number of these hedge funds have made fraudulent investments and amassed large losses. As a consequence, they have been unable to make redemptions. This failure has triggered a flood of outflows of funds, rippling through other financial markets to threaten systemic risk at a time when Korea has had to battle the twin crises of recession and the COVID-19 pandemic.

Perspectives on Financial Deepening and Real Activity

Casual observers who review the economic developments in Korea since the 1997 crisis struggle to make a proper assessment of the benefits and costs of financial reform and liberalization. They see that Korea emerged from the depths of the crisis to build many of the market-supporting institutions that play an essential role in successful market economies. But they also see crises and other outcomes that were arguably exacerbated, if not caused, by the liberalization. On the benefits of reform, citing some of the financial indicators, advocates of financial liberalization can argue that Korea's experience is a success story, a feat that is impressive by any standard. In their view, the reform has set in motion fundamental changes that have been pivotal in the creation of a deeper, more stable, and more diversified financial system with new institutions and financial products.

There is no doubt that financial reform has led to a dramatic change in the ownership structure of many banks and NBFIs. In particular, foreign investors hold controlling interests in some institutions. Mergers with and the consolidation of banks and other financial institutions into financial holding companies have created megabanks. Six are large enough to make S&P Global's 2019 list of the hundred largest banks in the world, as measured by assets.

Compared to the sophisticated financial systems of advanced economies, advocates will find that the problem confronting Korea's financial system is not too much financial liberalization, but too little.

They will also note that financial and corporate reforms have effectively broken up the collusive ties between the government, banks, and chaebol. That had been the institutional basis for the export-led growth strategy launched in the early 1960s and relentlessly pursued afterward. They will assert that a free and open financial system would be more effective than a collusive system in realizing growth potential through efficiency gains, innovation, and productivity growth. However, this is not necessarily what has transpired in Korea.

In contrast to this positive assessment, skeptics of unfettered finance will focus on a series of financial excesses and market failures since the 1997 crisis. These include a credit card crisis in 2003, a real estate market bubble that burst when Korea succumbed to another debilitating liquidity crisis in 2008, and the subsequent near-collapse of the savings banking system in 2011. Indeed, this series of financial crises may provide clear evidence that earlier expectations of the positive effects of financial market deregulation have not been realized. These expectations include bringing corporate governance and transparency up to international norms and practices, as well as a significant improvement in asset-liability and risk management.

Nor has the deregulation helped financial institutions gain economies of scale and scope. A large number of new financial instruments have appeared, but such practices as making loans based on collateral rather than assessments of the borrower's ability to repay continue. In a service-oriented economy with low capital intensity, this can lead to underfunding growth businesses.

Skeptics recognize that the inherent weaknesses of a liberal financial regime were further aggravated by a spate of regulatory malfeasances resulting from an inefficient financial supervisory system. However, the skeptics assert that although bad regulation is a problem, too little control is a more serious one.

Assessing the many costs and benefits of financial liberalization and balancing them against each other are daunting tasks. Ultimately, however, the liberalization needs to be judged based on its effects on the performance of the economy. As shown in chapter 6, there is no clear evidence of efficiency gains from financial liberalization. There may have been too much finance relative to real sector activities. The financial deepening may have resulted in a decline in the overall productivity of the economy and may not have had any measurable effect on macroeconomic stability. It may also have reduced distributive equity.

The mainstream view is that in a financially open economy with capital mobility, a flexible exchange rate system serves as a buffer against external shocks, helping preserve the stability of domestic financial markets. As shown in chapter 8, this study finds no strong evidence supporting this conventional wisdom. On the contrary, although Korea has had a free-floating economy since 1998, it has been among the most vulnerable to external shocks emanating from international financial markets. Compared to other emerging economies in Asia, for example, Korea's stock and foreign exchange markets have displayed a much higher degree of volatility since 2008.

The near-collapse of the financial system during the 2008 global financial crisis exacerbated the domestic slowdown in growth. This occurred with a deterioration in income and wealth distribution that hit the middle class, causing a polarization among income earners.

To what extent, if at all, should the relative decline in economic performance be attributed to the liberal financial reform? At this stage of development, those proponents who see a need for further financial deregulation would argue that it is premature to evaluate the economic liberalization correctly or play down its benefits. Korea may still have some distance to travel before completing a trouble-free transition to a full-fledged free-market system. Proponents would also point out that the slowdown in potential growth was bound to occur. After all, the economy has become large, and Korea faces low fertility rates and a rapidly aging population. It is per capita growth and better living standards that matter.

These are valid arguments. However, there is one element of the fallout of the 1997 crisis that has been ignored by both supporters and detractors of liberalization. This element has fused itself to the financial reform to affect a significant behavioral change in the private and public sector, with the consequence of undermining growth momentum.

The crises of 1997 and 2008 have sent a clear warning to financial and nonfinancial firms that, in a liberalized financial environment, the government can no longer bail them out, and that foreign currency liquidity can vanish at a moment's notice. To stay clear of financial turmoil, therefore, firms have had to be much more prudent in managing risk than they were in the past.

This greater prudence has resulted in dampening the risk tolerance of households, financial and nonfinancial firms, and the government alike. This may be a new normal for a relatively small economy with open trade and financial regimes. But it has had the downside of diminishing much of the precrisis spirit of economic drive and vigor. In turn, that has dampened investment in innovative future industries. And that may precipitate a growth outcome worse than expected.

CHAPTER I

Growth and Structural Changes in the Financial System

Measure of Financial Growth

A country's financial development or financial deepening is often measured in terms of the sum of private credit supplied by banks and non-bank financial institutions (NBFIs) and the market value of money and capital market instruments relative to gross domestic product (GDP).[1] In the empirical literature, private credit relative to GDP is commonly used as a proxy for financial development, but there is no common definition for or measure of private credit. The measure varies greatly across countries, and different authors use different measures in their empirical analyses, which makes it difficult to compare and assess their results.[2]

This study uses total finance to GDP, which encompasses both indirect and direct finance, as a measure of financial depth.

Ratna Sahay and coauthors (2015) developed a financial development index that is more comprehensive than the ratio of total assets to GDP, as it covers the size and liquidity of financial institutions and markets, accessibility to financial services, and efficiency of financial institutions.

---

1. This section draws on J. Park et al. 2018.

2. The World Bank's Global Financial Development Database introduces total banking assets to the GDP as a measure of financial deepening that offers an alternative to private credit to GDP. The database includes credit not only to the private sector but also to the government, as well as bank assets other than credit. See World Bank 2019 for further observations on this issue.

However, it is not clear whether the index is a better indicator of financial development because the subcomponent indices are based on just a few indicators—which may not adequately cover the relative importance of the different dimensions of financial development.

For example, in the study by Sahay and coauthors, the efficiency of Korea's banking sector is measured by a composite index of six subindicators of the four largest commercial banks in the country.[3] The index could be used to measure profitability but not necessarily efficiency, when the "Big Four" (Woori Bank, KB Kookmin Bank, Shinhan Bank, and KEB Hana Bank) are engaged in oligopolistic competition for market share in Korea's banking market. The International Monetary Fund index developed by Sahay and coauthors and the total finance to GDP ratio defined and estimated in chapter 1 are highly correlated to each other: the correlation coefficient between the two for 1985–2015 is 0.95 in Korea. It is therefore not surprising that as far as the causal nexus between finance and growth is concerned, Sahay and coauthors found results similar to those of other studies that use private credit to GDP as a measure of financial development.

For these two reasons, the total finance to GDP ratio is used here as a proxy for financial depth—which in turn is defined as the sum of indirect and direct finance.

INDIRECT FINANCE

Private credit is a measure of indirect finance, which excludes credit issued by the central bank. In the context of the Korean economy, indirect finance is the total amount of loans and discounts extended to the private sector by deposit money banks (that is, commercial or specialized banks that take deposits and provide loans) and NBFIs. The latter consist of two types of financial intermediaries. The first is nonbank depository institutions (which, along with deposit money banks, are classified by the Bank of Korea as depository corporations)—that is, mutual savings banks; credit unions; mutual credits at the National Agricultural Co-

---

3. The subindicators are net interest margin, lending-deposits spread, noninterest income to total income, overhead costs to total assets, return on assets, and return on equity. Meanwhile, efficiency of the financial market is measured by the stock market turnover ratio (the value of stocks traded divided by capitalization).

operative Federation, the National Federation of Fisheries Cooperatives, and the National Forestry Cooperative Federation; and community credit cooperatives. The second (more fully described in chapter 2) is other financial intermediaries, which include life insurance companies, merchant banking corporations, asset management companies (investment trusts), and trust companies.

DIRECT FINANCE

Direct financing refers to financing through two channels:

- Capital markets, where size is measured by the total par values of listed private bonds issued by nonfinancial corporations and the stock market capitalization of KOSPI (Korea Composite Stock Price Index), the Korea Securities Dealers Automated Quotation, and the Korea New Exchange.
- Money markets for commercial paper, certificates of deposit, repurchase agreements, and cover bills.

Government and public bonds, as well as call loans and monetary stabilization bonds are excluded from the list because they are not instruments of intermediation between financial institutions and the markets on the one hand and the private sector (which includes nonfinancial firms and households) on the other hand.

As seen in Figure 1.1 and Table 1.1, phenomenal growth and extensive diversification of markets and institutions have occurred in Korea's financial sector since 1975. The growth increased the total finance to GDP ratio to 307 percent in 2019 from 46 percent in 1975. The most striking development has been the expansion of direct finance since the mid-1980s. This has led to much of the growth of the financial system. However, the path of financial deepening has been far from monotonic and has been marked by a great deal of variability.

As an alternative to GDP, this study also uses real or tangible assets as a scale variable for financial deepening.

Figure 1.2 presents the ratios of total financial assets to both GDP and the nominal value of tangible assets (which is approximated by the sum of nominal values of capital stock and land). As expected, the ratio of financial assets to GDP was much higher than that of financial to tangible assets throughout the period. At the end of 2013, the former was eight times higher than the latter.

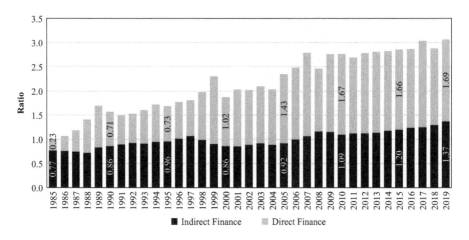

Figure 1.1. Total Finance to GDP Ratio
Source: Economic Statistics System of the Bank of Korea.
Notes: Total financial assets are defined in the text.

Table 1.1. Total Finance and Relative Size of Financial Markets (trillion won, percent, and times)

	1975 (A)	1980	1990	2000	2010	2019 (B)	2019 (B/A)
Total finance	4.9	27.1	314.7	1,221.2	3,655.6	5,882.3	1,200.5
	(46.3)	(68.7)	(159.2)	(192.3)	(288.9)	(306.5)	
└Indirect finance	4.2	21.1	172.0	558.4	1,447.0	2,629.8	626.1
	(85.6)	(78.0)	(54.6)	(45.7)	(39.6)	(44.7)	
└Direct finance	0.7	5.9	142.7	662.8	2,208.6	3,252.5	4,646.4
	(14.4)	(22.0)	(45.4)	(54.3)	(60.4)	(55.3)	
└Money markets	0.1	1.1	23.2	92.3	213.8	395.5	3,955.0
	(11.9)	(18.2)	(16.2)	(13.9)	(9.7)	(12.2)	
└Capital markets	0.6	4.9	119.5	570.5	1,994.8	2,856.9	4,761.5
└Bonds	0.1	2.3	40.5	353.5	755.0	1,134.4	11,344.0
	(13.5)	(46.5)	(33.9)	(62.0)	(37.8)	(35.5)	
└Equities	0.5	2.6	79.0	217.0	1,239.9	1,722.6	3,445.2
	(86.5)	(53.5)	(66.1)	(38.0)	(62.1)	(64.5)	

Source: The sources are identified in the text.

Notes: The percentages represent the percent of gross domestic product for "total finance," the percent of total finance for "indirect finance" and "direct finance," the percent of direct finance for "money markets," and the percent of capital markets for "bonds" and "equities."

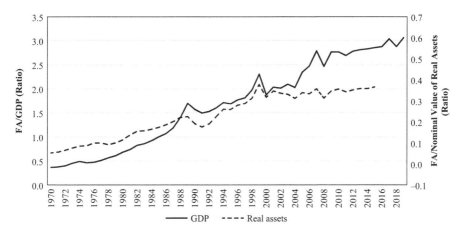

Figure 1.2. Alternative Measures of Financial Deepening
Source: Economic Statistics System of the Bank of Korea.
Notes: The figure shows the ratios of total financial assets to gross domestic product (GDP) and to tangible assets, which consist of the nominal values of capital stock and land. Capital stock is the sum of construction assets, including residential and nonresidential buildings and other real estate; facility assets, including transport equipment, machinery and other equipment, and cultivated biological resources; and intellectual property, including research and development. FA = Financial assets.

The two ratios show a similar trend and degree of fluctuation until 1998. Since then, they have diverged: the growth of financial assets has surged relative to GDP while only keeping pace with the growth of tangible assets. This divergence primarily originated from the sustained rise in the prices of tangible assets—in particular, housing and land. In view of the fact that financial growth helps ease the exchange not only of goods and services, but also of real assets, the divergence raises questions as to whether financial depth has become as deep as it is depicted by the rise in the total finance to GDP ratio in Figure 1.1.

Changes in Financial Structure

The pace of growth in direct finance as a share of total finance began to accelerate in the mid-1980s. By the mid-1990s, the proportion of indirect finance surpassed that of direct finance. Ever since, both money and capital markets have been the dominant source of domestic financing, driving Korea's financial depth.

In the 1990s, nonfinancial firms relied heavily on bank loans for working capital and fixed investment. Although corporations were able to raise more funds on the booming stock market, the share of equity financing was less than 20 percent throughout the decade. After the 1997 crisis, equity financing's share began to soar, peaking at 47 percent in 2007 before plummeting to below 30 percent in 2008 and inching back up to approximately 35 percent after that.

Two market developments are attributable to the expansion of direct finance: the migration of households to money and capital markets in search of higher yields, and a large influx of foreign investment in local bonds and stocks.

Corporate restructuring after the 1997 crisis entailed a reform that required large firms and the chaebol to reduce their ratios of debt to equity to about 200 percent (from more than 500 percent before the crisis). This deleveraging created strong incentives for firms to rely more on equity and internal financing (net savings, net capital transfers, and capital consumption allowances). The share of internal financing, which had been below 40 percent on average in the 1990s, began to surge after the 1997 crisis, rising to 74 percent in 2018 (see chapter 3).

1975–89: RAPID GROWTH OF CAPITAL MARKETS AND NONBANK FINANCE

The ratio of total finance to GDP soared to 172 percent in 1989 from about 46 percent in 1975. During this fifteen-year period, capital markets and NBFIs displayed a spectacular expansion as domestic sources of financing. The increase in direct finance as a share of GDP was impressive, surging to 87 percent in 1989 from about 7 percent in the mid-1970s (Figure 1.3 and Table 1.1). This was accompanied by a sixfold increase in nonbank financing as a share of GDP over the same period, mostly at the expense of lending by commercial and specialized banks (Figure 1.4).

The rapid expansion of these two subsectors of the financial system reflected the government's sustained efforts on three fronts of market deregulation: broadening and deepening capital markets, embarking on a gradual liberalization of financial intermediation industries, and drawing private moneylenders into the regulated and supervised financial system. This last was done in 1972 by allowing the lenders to establish two new types of NBFIs: short-term investment finance companies and mutual savings and finance companies.

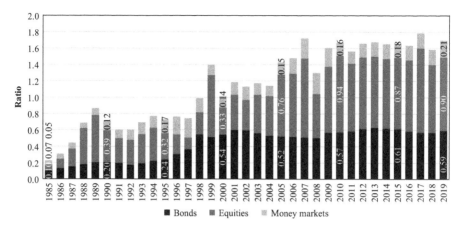

Figure 1.3. Components of Direct Finance as a Share of GDP
Source: Bank of Korea and Financial Statistics Information System of the Financial Supervisory Service.

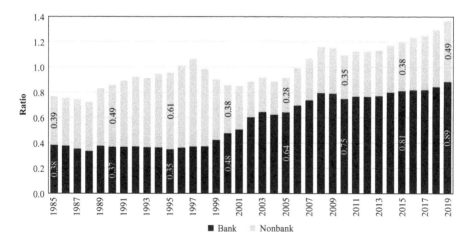

Figure 1.4. Components of Indirect Finance as a Share of GDP
Source: Bank of Korea.

Four years later, the government chartered three merchant banking corporations to diversify the channels of external borrowing. Compared to commercial banks, these institutions had enjoyed greater leeway in setting their borrowing and lending rates in supplying short-term financing. The three institutions grew rapidly because they were able to carve out an increasingly large share of the bank loan market—so much so that the share of commercial and specialized banks as a share of indirect finance plummeted to less than 35 percent from 77 percent in 1970, before rising again in 1998.

1990–99: UNBRIDLED EXPANSION AND THE COLLAPSE OF NONBANK FINANCE

After a lengthy period of rapid expansion, the growth of the financial sector began to slow significantly, with bank financing displaying little growth. This was combined with a drop of 42.2 percent in the KOSPI in 1997, resulting in a deceleration of the growth in direct finance.

Much of the expansion during this period came from the nonbank financial sector, the rampant lending of which sowed the seeds of the 1997 financial crisis. Unable to withstand the liquidity crisis in 1998, many of the short-term finance companies went bankrupt, thereby touching off the sustained decline of the nonbank finance sector. Excluding the crisis years of 1997 and 1998, the ratio of total finance to GDP rose 12 percentage points to 184 percent in 1997 over the preceding ten years.

2000–07: FINANCIAL LIBERALIZATION AND THE RESUMPTION OF FINANCIAL GROWTH

Capital market liberalization and opening in the wake of the 1997 crisis brought about a massive increase in foreign investment in Korean equities, which ignited a recovery and the subsequent expansion of the stock market, as shown in Figure 1.5. By 2004, foreign investors accounted for more than 40 percent of Korea's stock market capitalization. The banking sector also grew rapidly, filling the vacuum created by the failure of many short-term investment finance companies. Powered by the large capital inflows and resurgence of bank financing, total finance jumped to 282 percent of GDP at the end of 2007, up from 192 percent in 2000. The financial restructuring also saw a sharp increase in bond market financing in 1998 and 1999, and its share in direct financing has since remained stable at around 40 percent on average.

Figure 1.5. Share of the Stock Market in Direct Finance
Source: Bank of Korea and Korea Exchange.

2008–17 GLOBAL FINANCIAL CRISIS, RECESSION, AND THE DECELERATION OF FINANCIAL GROWTH

By the time the 2008 global financial crisis erupted, Korea had amassed large foreign exchange reserves. Together with liquidity support from the US Federal Reserve Board, these reserves allowed Korea to ward off what could have been another devastating liquidity crisis. But the recession resulting from the global financial crisis slid the economy into a slump. This in turn weakened demand for external financing in the nonfinancial corporate sector, hamstringing overall financial growth. Overall, in the decade beginning with 2008, the growth of the money and capital markets slowed. This was due in part to a relative fall in foreign equity investment that was not quite counterbalanced by the recovery of lending by banks and NBFIs.

2020: COVID-19 PANDEMIC AND A LOOMING FINANCIAL CRISIS

The coronavirus pandemic broke out in February 2020 when there were already signs that the Korean economy was heading into a slowdown. The impact of the pandemic, as it has required lockdown and social distancing, has been severe, with mounting job losses and the failure of numerous small and medium-sized businesses.

As part of the effort to mitigate the adverse effects of the pandemic, policymakers have injected a vast amount of liquidity into the economy and supported financial institutions through fiscal and monetary channels. Inevitably, the ample liquidity flowing into the market has stoked speculation in housing, stock, and other real asset markets and has inflated their prices.

The full effect and duration of the pandemic are still unknown. As long as this uncertainty remains, Korea's policymakers will have to struggle to manage a trade-off between keeping credit allocated to the most vulnerable sectors and sustaining financial stability. But if the easy stance of monetary and fiscal policy weighs against stability, the bubble in the housing and equity market is bound to expand and eventually burst, setting off another financial crisis, which is likely to be much more enduring and costly than that of 2008.

CHAPTER 2

Financial Liberalization and Structural Changes in Financial Institutions and Markets

Diversification and Changes in the Relative Size of Financial Institutions and Markets

Over the past four decades, Korea's financial sector has made great strides not only in growth but also in diversifying institutions, markets, and instruments. Since the launching of financial liberalization in the early 1980s (and particularly since the 1997 crisis), a host of new financial institutions have come into existence. Table 2.1 lists the types of institutions. Table 2.2 shows the shares of these institutions in terms of total assets.

By 2018, nine financial holding companies were in operation. Of these, the Bank of Korea classifies seven as bank holding companies and two as nonbank holding companies. These firms dominate Korea's financial industries.

Reflecting the rapid growth of direct finance, an increasing number of capital market institutions—dealers, brokers, futures companies, investment intermediaries, and investment advisory entities—have succeeded in enlarging their market share to emerge as credible competitors to banks and other NBFIs.

Table 2.1. Financial Institutions

Classification		1999	2018
Banks	Commercial nationwide banks	11	8[a]
	Commercial local banks	7	6
	Commercial branches of foreign banks	50	38
	Specialized banks[b]	6	5
Nonbank deposit institutions	Mutual savings banks	203	79
	Credit cooperatives	5,584	3,571
	Postal savings system	1	1
	Merchant banking corporations	11	1
Financial investment business entities	Securities companies and futures companies	66	60
	Collective investment business entities[d]	64	215
	Investment advisory and discretionary investment business entities	32	179
	Trust business entities[e]	3	56
Insurance companies	Life insurance companies	29	25
	Non-life insurance companies	17	32
	Other entities[f]	1	4
Other financial institutions	Bank holding companies	—[g]	7
	Nonbank holding companies	—[g]	2
	Credit-specialized financial companies[h]	49	97
	Venture capital companies[i]	—[g]	162
	Securities finance companies	1	1
Financial auxiliary institutions[j]		14	54

Source: Bank of Korea (2018) and Economic Statistics System of the Bank of Korea (https://ecos
.bok.or.kr/EIndex_en.jsp).

Notes: Data for 2018 are as of the end of February 2018.

[a] Includes two online banks established in 2017.

[b] Korea Development Bank, Export-Import Bank of Korea, Industrial Bank of Korea, National Agricultural Cooperative Federation (NACF), and National Federation of Fisheries Cooperatives (NFFC).

[c] Credit unions, community credit cooperatives, and mutual banking.

[d] Asset management companies.

[e] Bank, securities, insurance, and real estate trust.

[f] Postal insurance, mutual aid services of NACF, NFFC, Korean Federation of Community Credit Cooperatives, and National Credit Union Federation Korea.

[g] Not available.

[h] Leasing, credit card, or installment financing companies and new technology venture capital companies.

[i] Includes companies for new technology development and establishing small and medium enterprises.

[j] Securities finance companies, credit guarantee institutions, credit information companies, Korea Housing Finance Corporation, Korea Asset Management Corporation, and financial brokerage companies.

Table 2.2. Total Assets of Major Financial Institutions (billion won, percent)

	2000	*2010*	*2019*
Deposit money banks[a]	829,338	1,841,707	3,419,327
	(72.8)	(65.5)	(60.8)
Mutual savings banks	21,351	86,814	77,160
	(1.9)	(3.1)	(1.4)
Credit unions	20,469	47,783	102,373
	(1.8)	(1.7)	(1.8)
Credit-specialized financial companies[b]	62,351	120,774	161,701
	(5.5)	(4.3)	(2.9)
Credit card companies	35,411	54,461	130,211
	(3.1)	(1.9)	(2.3)
Life insurance companies	120,509	408,495	918,161
	(10.6)	(14.5)	(16.3)
Non-life insurance companies	29,031	99,009	320,652
	(2.5)	(3.5)	(5.7)
Securities companies	52,171	199,805	482,674
	(4.6)	(7.1)	(8.6)
Futures companies	526	1,794	3,158
	(0.0)	(0.1)	(0.1)
Asset management companies	1,273	3,670	7,409
	(0.1)	(0.1)	(0.1)
Merchant bank corporations	21,273	1,752	3,339
	(0.2)	(0.1)	(0.1)
Total	1,158,291	2,811,604	5,626,165
	(100.0)	(100.0)	(100.0)

Source: Financial Statistics Information System of the Financial Supervisory Service (http://www.fss.or.kr/fss/eng/main.jsp).

Note: The numbers in parentheses are percentages of total assets.

[a] Includes domestic commercial banks and specialized banks.

[b] Leasing companies, installment financing companies, and venture capital companies.

Between 2000 and 2019, the banking sector, which consists of commercial and specialized banks, lost market share in terms of assets by 12 percentage points—mostly to insurance companies, both life and non-life, and other capital market institutions. As new institutions, futures and asset management companies have yet to gain a strong foothold.

Structural Changes in Financial Intermediaries

DEPOSIT MONEY BANKS

Deposit money banks—that is, commercial and specialized banks—are the backbone of Korea's financial intermediation industry. Commercial banks include nationwide banks, local banks, and domestic branches of foreign banks. At the end of 2018, there were fifty commercial banks, including six nationwide banks (Woori, KEB Hana, Shinhan, Kookmin, Citibank Korea, and Standard Chartered Bank Korea), six local banks (Daegu, Jeju, Jeonbuk, Kwangju, Kyoungnam, and Pusan), and the domestic branches of thirty-eight foreign banks. The combined assets of these banks amounted to 3,419 trillion won, equivalent to 178 percent of nominal GDP, and made up almost 61 percent of indirect finance in 2019.

Until the 1970s, Korea had had only five nationwide banks: Chohung, Jaeil, Hanil, Seoul, and the Commercial Bank of Korea. In the 1980s, however, there was an explosion of commercial banking resulting from financial reform and the subsequent restructuring of the banking industry. That led to the creation of eleven more nationwide commercial banks. With the resolution of the 1997 crisis, many of these sixteen banks were liquidated or merged with healthy institutions, reducing their number to six at the end of 2018.

The government created local banks to disperse and improve access to financial services geographically by allowing a single bank operate within the boundary limited to each of the country's nine provinces. Of the eleven local banks that were established between 1967 and 1971, five were either liquidated or merged with other banks after the 1997 crisis. This left six local banks, whose combined assets were less than 11 percent of the assets of all commercial banks at the end of 2019.

At the end of 2018, thirty-eight foreign bank branches were in operation, accounting for less than 15 percent of the total assets of commercial banks. Initially, foreign branches were limit to providing foreign financing and foreign currency trading. Liberalization has enabled them to operate within nearly the same regulatory confines of other Korean commercial banks.

There are five specialized banks owned by the government. These banks specialize in supplying policy-directed financing and financial services that commercial banks are unable to provide. The specialized banks' services include long-term financing for infrastructure development and loans, guarantees, trade finance, and financing for foreign investments provided to exporters and importers. The banks also lend to SMEs and farming and fishing communities with limited access to commercial banking.[1]

Because of their specific loan portfolios, specialized banks depend heavily on government funds and bond issuance rather than deposits for funding. However, with the continuous decline in the demand for policy loans, the difference in the structure of assets between commercial and specialized banks has become less pronounced, making them almost indistinguishable.

NONBANK FINANCIAL INSTITUTIONS

As explained in chapter 1, NBFIs consist of nonbank depository institutions taking deposits and providing loans and other nonbank intermediaries that do not have banking licenses. The former include mutual savings banks, credit cooperatives (such as credit unions and community credit cooperatives), mutual banking at agricultural, fishery and forestry cooperatives, postal savings accounts,[2] and merchant bank corporations. The latter include life and non-life insurance firms, financial investment business entities, and other financial institutions (see Table 2.1).

There were seventy-nine mutual savings banks (MSBs) in operation at the end of 2019. They held total assets amounting to 77.15 trillion won, a little over 2.9 percent of total indirect finance at the end of 2019. They were formerly known as mutual savings and finance companies (MSFCs), which were created in 1972 by the Mutual Savings and Finance Company Act.

The MSFC act was one of three laws that provided the legal basis for the implementation of the August 3 Emergency Economic Measures of 1972. Another act created short-term investment and finance companies. The objective of the two laws was to draw informal lending facilities that served the credit needs of households and SMEs into the organized financial system to make them more formalized credible financial institutions.

---

1. All of the specialized banks, except for the NACF and the NFFC, were established as state-owned enterprises under specific specialized banking acts.

2. The Postal Savings and Insurance Act stipulates that the government will manage postal savings accounts as a form of public finance and will take responsibility for making postal savings payments (including interest).

In the early phases of development, many MSFCs could not compete with deposit money banks for customers. With the rise in bankruptcy filings, the Korean government introduced a raft of measures designed to bolster public confidence in MSFCs, including the introduction of a risk-based capital requirement, governmental guidance and supervision, and higher interest rates on deposits.

By the middle of the 1990s, the progress in financial liberalization and market opening had eroded MSFCs' competitive edge. After the 1997 crisis, a massive increase in insolvencies of SMEs exacerbated managerial difficulties, resulting in a large number of bankruptcies.[3]

In an effort to revive public confidence, the financial authorities amended the Enforcement Decree of the Mutual Savings and Finance Company Act in June 2000 and the act itself in March 2001, which eased restrictions on business areas and requirements for opening branch offices, as well as increasing the scope of lending and raising single-borrower credit ceilings. With the amendment of the act in March 2001, mutual savings and finance companies were renamed MSBs. These measures were supplemented by doubling the capital requirement, adding outside directors to the board, and creating audit committees. In May 2006, an additional amendment of the enforcement decree further eased regulations on single-borrower credit ceilings for healthy savings banks.

For all practical purposes, merchant bank corporations have disappeared from the financial scene in Korea. However, their history of growth and demise deserves a careful review, as it provides an important lesson about the perils of a pell-mell liberalization of financial markets. Merchant banks provide various types of corporate financing, including short-term financial services such as the issuance, underwriting, and guarantees of bills expiring within one year, as well as trading in those bills; borrowing and relending of long- and short-term foreign capital; investment in foreign currency securities; and trading in foreign exchanges.

In an effort to increase Korea's access to international financial markets after the 1973 first oil crisis, the country's policymakers sought to diversify channels of foreign capital inflows. They also saw the need to establish new financial institutions that could provide consolidated financial services to complement the financial system, which was then domi-

---

3. For more on their demise, see chapter 12.

nated by banks. Creating merchant banks structured in joint ventures with foreign partners seemed to be the answer.

The first merchant bank, the Korea Merchant Banking Corporation, was established in April 1976. By 1979 an additional five merchant banks had opened. There were no further openings until the early 1990s. Short-term investment and finance companies then restructured themselves as merchant banks in the 1990s, as part of the restructuring of the financial sector. With this change, nine local companies in 1994 and fifteen more in 1996 were converted into merchant banks. By the end of 1997, there were thirty merchant banks in all.

In the run-up to the 1997 crisis, these banks took advantage of the regulatory freedoms accorded them, and with no efficient risk management systems in place, they were reckless in investing in a variety of dicey foreign assets and lending to risky borrowers with funds raised on the short end of the global funding market. When the 1997 crisis broke out in Thailand, they began amassing a large amount of nonperforming assets and loans in both domestic and foreign currency, as many of their borrowers were falling behind on their repayments. When these banks were cut off from international financial markets, they could not roll over their short-term liabilities. Unable to secure liquidity, many merchant banks had to close their doors.

The unexpected demise of the merchant banks shocked many foreign lenders and hastened their departure from Korea, worsening the market turmoil and expanding the 1997 financial crisis to that country. The government had to liquidate sixteen insolvent merchant banks in 1998 and thirteen more in 1999–2005. At the end of 2018, there was only one merchant bank in operation, along with three banks and two securities companies providing merchant banking services.

Insurance companies—both life and casualty—accounted for the largest share of the nonbank financial sector in terms of assets (22 percent of the total assets of major financial institutions as of the end of 2019). Since the start of financial reform in 1998, their growth has outpaced that of any other institution among the NBFIs. As of 2018, there were fifty-seven insurance companies. Life insurers had assets of 918 trillion won ($788 billion), and non-life insurers had 320 trillion won ($274 billion) at the end of 2019.[4]

---

4. In addition to private insurance firms, the state-run postal savings system and the four mutual associations (operated by the NACF, NFFC, National Credit Union

With the deregulation and opening of the insurance industry during the second half of the 1980s, fifteen life insurance companies began operations between 1988 and 1994. After the 1997 crisis, many insurers could not withstand the increase in the number of contract rescissions and had to dissolve their operations or merge with other firms. This trend continued into the 2000s, when larger life insurance companies acquired or merged with smaller ones to strengthen their competitiveness—causing a further decrease in their numbers.

The size of the life insurance industry increased dramatically, surging from 35 trillion won ($45 billion) in annual premium income in fiscal 1995 (the year that ended in March 1995) to 110.7 trillion won ($100 billion) in fiscal 2018. The ratio of paid benefits to premium income ratio rose to 76 percent at the end of fiscal 2000, fueled by growing insurance contract rescissions after the 1997 financial crisis. The rate subsequently dropped to 62 percent at the end of fiscal 2009, before rising to 78 percent in fiscal 2018. This was mainly due to the decrease in surrender value amounts; the development of various insurance products, including variable and annuity insurance; and an increase in subscriptions to long-term insurance coverage.

By the end of 2018, life insurance companies were securing 79.5 percent of their operating funds from premium income and policy reserves, much of which was invested in bonds, equities, and other securities. Of their total assets, 74 percent was in securities, while loans accounted for 20.1 percent—a steep decline from 45.3 percent in 1995.

Structural Changes in Financial Markets

OVERVIEW

Financial markets consist of money, capital, and financial derivatives markets. The capital market is made up of stock and bond markets. Listed stocks are traded on the Korea Exchange (KRX) and the Korea New Exchange (KONEX), while unlisted shares are traded on an over-the-counter market created in 2017.

Various fixed-income products issued by central and local governments, public and private corporations, and financial institutions are widely traded in the bond market. As shown in Table 2.3, the growth of

---

Federation of Korea, and Korean Federation of Community Credit Cooperatives, respectively) also provide insurance services.

Table 2.3. Financial Market Size (trillion won, percent)

	1980 (A)	1990	2000	2010	2018 (B)	B / A
Money markets	1.5	44.3	138.8	264.8	457.2	304.8
Capital markets	5.0	114.0	638.8	2,352.7	3,247.1	649.4
Bonds	2.5	35.0	423.6	1,112.9	1,674.9	670.0
Stocks	2.5	79.0	215.2	1,239.9	1,572.2	628.9
Total	6.6	158.3	777.6	2,617.5	3,704.3	561.3
	(16.7)	(80.1)	(122.4)	(206.9)	(195.6)	

Source: Bank of Korea (2018) and Economic Statistics System of the Bank of Korea (https://ecos
.bok.or.kr/EIndex_en.jsp).

Notes: Financial market size is based on outstanding balances at the end of the period. Money
markets include call, repo, certificates of deposit, commercial paper, electronic short-term bonds,
cover bills, monetary stabilization bonds with one-year maturity or less, and treasury bills. Data
on bond markets are based on figures for bonds in the Korea Securities Depository (excluding
short-term monetary stabilization bonds with one-year maturity or less and treasury bills). Data
on stock markets are based on the market capitalization of listed stocks on the Korea Composite
Stock Price Index and the Korea Securities Dealers Automated Quotations markets. The numbers
in parentheses are percentages of nominal GDP.

the financial market has been phenomenal. The size of the market was
561 times larger in 2018 than it was in 1980, reaching 196 percent of nominal GDP. Among the submarkets, the bond market registered the fast-
est growth during the 1980–2018 period, increasing its size by a factor of
670.[5] Since the 1997 crisis, Korea has also seen the rapid growth of structured and derivative products. These include futures, options, and swaps
for interest rates, foreign exchange, credit, and equities.

MONEY MARKET

Money markets include call markets, as well as a wide range of short-term
financial markets for such instruments as repurchase agreements (RPs),
commercial papers (CPs), financial debentures, certificates of deposit
(CDs), cover bills, the Bank of Korea's monetary stabilization bonds, treasury bills, and electronic short-term bonds. As shown in Table 2.4, the

---

5. Figures for the money and bond markets in Table 2.3 are higher than those estimated for analysis in this chapter, because they include money market instruments and
bonds issued by the central and local governments, central bank, and public institutions. These nonprivate instruments are excluded in the analysis in chapter 1.

Table 2.4. Money Market Size (trillion won, percent)

	1980	1990	2000	2010	2018
Call	0.2	3.4	16.1	22.5	13.2
	(12.0)	(7.7)	(11.6)	(8.5)	(2.9)
Repurchase agreements	0.1	3.4	26.1	78.8	158.3
	(8.0)	(7.6)	(18.8)	(29.7)	(34.6)
Commercial papers	1.1	12.7	44.7	76.4	158.8
	(72.7)	(28.8)	(32.2)	(28.9)	(34.7)
Asset-backed short-term bonds	—ª	—ª	—ª	—ª	45.8
					(10.0)
Certificates of deposit	—ª	6.8	14.2	44.5	34.5
		(15.4)	(10.2)	(16.8)	(7.5)
Cover bills	—ª	0.3	11.2	1.6	0.3
		(0.7)	(8.1)	(0.6)	(0.1)
Monetary stabilization bonds	0.0	15.2	26.5	41.1	46.2
	(0.2)	(34.4)	(19.1)	(15.5)	(10.1)
Treasury bills	0.2	2.5	0.0	0.0	0.0
	(10.0)	(5.6)	(0.0)	(0.0)	(0.0)
Total	1.5	44.3	138.8	264.8	457.2
	(100.0)	(100.0)	(100.0)	(100.0)	(100.0)

Sources: Bank of Korea (2017) and Economic Statistics System of the Bank of Korea (https://ecos.bok.or.kr/EIndex_en.jsp).

Notes: Market size is based on the outstanding balance at the end of the period, excluding call and repo. The numbers in parentheses are the share of the total. Call and repurchase agreement data are based on daily average balances.

ª Not available.

growth of the money market has been remarkable. In 1980, the total amount of funds raised through money markets was a negligible 1.5 trillion won ($2.46 billion). Ten years later, the amount had shot up to more than 44.3 trillion won, representing 22.4 percent of GDP.

Growth continued into the 1990s. Between 1990 and 2000, the money market recorded more than a threefold increase, as did the volumes of CPs and monetary stabilization bonds. CDs, which had come on the market in 1984, became one of the most widely used means of short-term financing for the next three decades.

Since 2000, growth has been moderate, although at the end of 2018, the size of the market by par value had risen to 457.2 trillion won ($381.6

billion), three times higher than the value eighteen years earlier. Among the short-term instruments, RPs—used as the main instrument of open market operations and diversification of households' asset portfolios—have been the main driver of the growth.

STOCK MARKET

A small, rudimentary stock market came into existence when the Korea Stock Exchange (KSE) opened its doors for trading in 1956. For the next two decades, the market barely functioned as a source of equity capital. It remained shallow, brittle, and highly speculative, with a limited number of listed firms. It was not until 1977 that it acquired some of the features of a more formally organized exchange, with the creation of the Securities Supervisory Board and Securities Commission.

Thereafter, a series of institutional reforms built up the KSE's infrastructure and improved its efficiency. However, these reforms did little in the way of expanding the share of equity financing or moderating volatility. This was because large firms and the chaebol, which were the most qualified issuers of equities, were unwilling to dilute their ownership stakes. A decade later, the government concluded that the time had come to set up both a second stock market and an over-the-counter market for medium-size and venture firms. Thus, in 1997, the government reorganized the over-the-counter market into the Korea Securities Dealers Automated Quotations (KOSDAQ), which was independent of the KSE. In 1999 the Korea Futures Exchange (KOFEX) was created.

It was the resolution of the 1997 crisis and attendant reforms, which reduced the level of government regulation of the stock market, that brought about a massive increase in equity financing. In 1996, market capitalization amounted to a mere 117.4 trillion won, 24.4 percent of GDP and a fraction of indirect financing. The market collapsed in 1997, but two years later, market size had almost tripled—reaching 448.2 trillion won, or 77.7 percent of GDP.[6]

After the 1997 crisis, there was an increasing need to expand the sources of financing for SMEs by increasing their access to equity financing. To

---

6. For the next two years, the stock market suffered from the bursting of the global information technology bubble in 2000.

that end, in April 2005, a third stock market, the Korea Over-the-Counter Bulletin Board, was established for small firms unable to obtain a listing on the KSE or KOSDAQ. Contrary to initial expectations, the market languished. There was little increase in trading volume until the market was reorganized again as the Free Board in July 2005.

The KSE, KOSDAQ, and KOFEX merged in January 2005, becoming the Korea Stock and Futures Exchange—renamed the KRX in 2009.[7] This was followed in 2013 by the creation of a third stock exchange, KONEX, exclusively for SMEs and venture capitalists prior to their listing on KOSDAQ.

FOREIGN EQUITY INVESTORS

In 1981, the government began gradually opening its stock market to foreign investors. As the first step, foreign investors could invest indirectly in the form of beneficiary certificates and country funds established exclusively for them. In 1992, for the first time, foreign investors were allowed limited direct investment in listed stocks.[8] Thereafter, the government raised the ceilings several times before removing them in 1998, with the exception of public corporations.

Driven by a massive increase in foreign investments, the stock market has posted extraordinary growth since the early 2000s. The market saw an almost sixfold increase in size (market capitalization), surging from 215.2 trillion won in 2000 to 1,239 trillion won, or more than 97.9 percent of nominal GDP, in 2010 (Table 2.5).

The number of listed firms also rose, reaching 794 on KOSPI, and 1,569 on KOSDAQ and KONEX, for a total of 2,363 at the end of 2020—up from 1,526 (683 on KOSPI) fifteen years earlier.

With a large influx of foreign capital following the complete opening of the market, the share of foreign investments in Korean stocks jumped to a record high of 45 percent in March 2004. Thereafter, it declined to a

---

7. The KRX was created through the integration of the KSE, KOFEX, and KOS-DAQ under the Korea Stock and Futures Exchange Act. The securities and derivatives markets of the former exchanges are now business divisions of KRX: the Stock Market Division, KOSDAQ Market Division, and Derivatives Market Division.

8. The government stipulated an overall limit for all foreign investors of 10 percent of the total outstanding stocks for each individual issue and a ceiling of 3 percent per issue for a single foreign investor.

Table 2.5. Stock Market Size (trillion won, percent)

	1980	1990	2000	2010	2018
KOSPI	2.5	79.0	186.2	1,141.9	1,344.0
	(100.0)	(100.0)	(86.5)	(92.1)	(84.8)
KOSDAQ	—[a]	—[a]	29.0	98.0	228.2
			(13.5)	(7.9)	(15.2)
KONEX[b]	—[b]	—[b]	—[b]	—[b]	—[b]
Total	2.5	79.0	215.2	1,239.0	1,572.2
	(100.0)	(100.0)	(100.0)	(100.0)	(100.0)

Sources: Bank of Korea (2017) and KOSIS (http://kosis.kr/index/index.do).

Notes: The numbers in parentheses are the share of the total. Data for KONEX since 2013 are available, but the amounts are so small that they are not shown here.

[a] Not available.

[b] Figures for the KONEX area available since 2013, but so small that they are not shown here.

monthly average of below 30 percent in 2008 and 2009, before rising to 33 percent at the end of 2019 (Figure 2.1).

BOND MARKET

Korea's bond market was a minor source of financing throughout the 1960s and 1970s. It was dominated by government bonds that were limited in variety, illiquid, and heavily regulated. The Korean government issued the first of its bonds in 1950 to finance the wartime fiscal deficit. Issuance, underwriting, and pricing were subject to government control. The bond market was small relative to the intermediated credit market because the government, following the cherished tradition of fiscal frugality, was averse to running a large fiscal deficit even when economic growth was weak and the supply of private bonds insignificant. The yields on new issues of government bonds were set at such low levels that there was no private demand for them. Rather, financial institutions controlled by the government were forced to hold most of the issues.

Under these circumstances, the amounts of government and other public bonds with government guarantees were not large enough to create primary and secondary markets or strengthen the market infrastructure—including agencies for the rating and valuation of bonds, underwriters, and dealers—needed to support the bond market. In the early 1970s, in

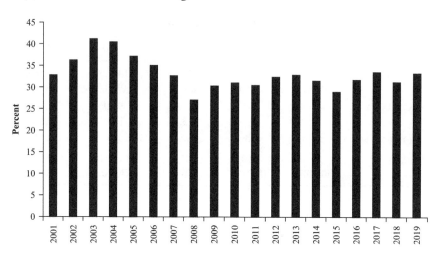

Figure 2.1. Share of Foreign Ownership in Korea's Stock Market
Source: Financial Statistics Information System of the Financial Supervisory Service.

an effort to establish the market infrastructure, the government allowed the public offering of the corporate bonds and began promoting a three-year corporate bond market as the benchmark debt instrument. However, corporate bonds were almost entirely guaranteed by banks, making it difficult to distinguish bond issuance from bank loan financing.

The bond market grew to 17.5 percent of GDP at par value by 1990 (from 6.3 percent in 1980). Much of the growth was spurred by the increase in the supply of corporate bonds. In 1990, the corporate bond share of overall bond markets was 63 percent (Table 2.6). Still, the corporate bond market remained a relatively small source of business financing, with a lack of liquidity and a limited menu in terms of maturity and credit quality. The remainder of the bond markets in 1990 consisted of bonds issued by the government (18 percent of overall bond market) or by government-controlled banks such as the Korea Development Bank and Korea Industrial Bank (19 percent of overall bond market).

Because of the large interest rate differential between domestic and international financial markets, the government delayed opening the bond market until 1997. In that year, the ceiling on foreign investment in listed bonds was abolished. Despite the complete opening, foreign demand remained weak, with a market share of around 0.5 percent until 2005.

Table 2.6. Bond Market Size (trillion won, percent)

	1980	1990	2000	2010	2018
Government and public bonds	0.5	6.3	246.7	705.0	1,161.3
	(20.0)	(18.0)	(58.2)	(63.3)	(62.4)
Financial bonds	0.4	6.6	49.1	217.3	445.2
	(15.4)	(18.9)	(11.6)	(19.5)	(23.9)
Corporate bonds	1.6	22.1	127.9	190.6	253.8
	(64.6)	(63.0)	(30.2)	(17.1)	(13.6)
Total	2.5	35.0	423.7	1,112.9	1,860.4
	(100.0)	(100.0)	(100.0)	(100.0)	(100.0)

Sources: Bank of Korea (2017), and Korea Financial Investment Association (http://eng.kofia.or
.kr/index.do).
Notes: "Government and public bonds" include government, municipal, monetary stabilization, and special bonds. The numbers in parentheses are percentages of total bonds.

The 1997 crisis devastated the corporate bond market, with the demise of many large firms—including some of the chaebol. This was exacerbated by the mandate for chaebol to lower their debt-equity ratios. The number of credible issuers fell dramatically, reducing the share of corporate bonds in the overall bond market to below 31 percent in 2000. But the collapse of corporate debt financing was more than made up for by the massive increase in government bonds issued for financing the bank and corporate restructuring, fiscal deficit, and foreign exchange sterilization fund.

The restructuring of the banking industry, which entailed a great many mergers and acquisitions, resulted in a severe contraction of the lending capacity of banks. In an effort to ease the financing constraint, the government allowed corporations to issue bonds up to four times their capital and also to issue asset-backed securities (ABSs).[9]

All this, coupled with postcrisis reforms, contributed to the expansion (and improvement in the efficiency) of the bond market infrastructure. In 1999, reform led to the creation of the primary dealer system, an interdealer market for government bonds and high-yield collateralized bond obligation funds. These changes were followed by additional

---

9. ABSs include collateralized bond obligations, collateralized loan obligations, mortgage-backed securities, and asset-backed commercial papers.

reforms in 2000 that established private bond evaluation companies and the Dutch-auction system for government bonds, in addition to introducing fungible issues and the mark-to-market fair value accounting system. The limited menu of bonds with different maturities meant the absence of a yield curve, which deprived financial institutions and nonfinancial firms of its use as an important guide for forecasting interest rates, pricing bonds, and creating strategies for boosting returns and minimizing risks.

Since 2005, the government has taken steps to diversify the maturity structure of bonds by fostering the market for bonds with maturities longer than five years. The government increased its own issues of twenty-year bonds in 2006 and of ten-year treasury inflation-protected securities in 2007. However, the supply of these long-term bonds has remained relatively small compared to that of other public bonds.

Overall, the deepening and diversification of the bond market have been as impressive as those of the stock market. During the 2000–18 period, the size of the market (excluding government bonds) almost quadrupled. At the end of 2018, government and public bonds accounted for almost 62.4 percent of the outstanding amount of bonds, while the share of corporate bonds was only 13.6 percent. (Government and public bonds include public enterprise and monetary stabilization bonds, as well as special bonds issued by funds for deposit insurance and nonperforming loan management.)

In the run-up to the 2008 financial crisis, the yields on short-term government bonds rose above the dollar-won currency swap (CRS) rate. This differential created opportunities for arbitrage, causing a sharp increase in the foreign demand for short-term government and monetary stabilization bonds in 2007.

The crisis of 2008 weakened foreign demand, but the persistent positive differential between the short-term government and CRS interest rates, together with the economic recovery thereafter, restored foreign demand, raising its market share to a period high of more than 7 percent at the end of 2012 (see Figure 2.2).

Foreign investors held mostly short-term treasury bonds and monetary stabilization bonds as instruments for arbitrage transactions, holding 25.7 percent and 19.6 percent, respectively, of these instruments. Together, the instruments accounted for more than 45.3 percent of foreign ownership of Korean bonds outstanding at the end of 2019.

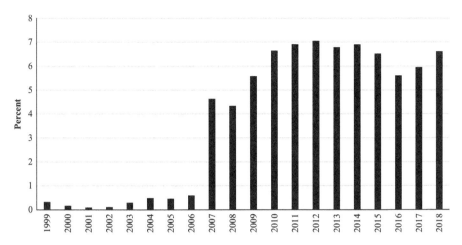

Figure 2.2. Foreign Ownership of Domestic Bonds
Source: Financial Statistics Information System of the Financial Supervisory Service.
Note: The data are based on listed bonds.

MARKETS FOR STRUCTURED FINANCIAL INSTRUMENTS

Financial reform has also set off a flurry of financial innovation, bringing into the markets a large number of products designed to facilitate the diversification of funding and risk management at both financial institutions and nonfinancial firms. The increase in the supply has been matched with an equally strong demand for a variety of instruments—including ABSs and derivatives—as a means of hedging market risk stemming from greater volatility in financial asset prices.

The markets for derivatives appeared on the financial scene with the issuance of stock price index futures in 1996 and options in 1997. However, it was the inception of KOFEX in 1999 that boosted the issuance and trading of a host of new derivative products. These included KOSDAQ 50 index futures and options; CD interest rate futures; and currency futures, swaps, and options.

Between 2001 and 2018, the market for derivative instruments saw a massive increase in trading volume. The total volume of trade in derivatives for underlying assets such as foreign exchange, bonds, equities, and money market instruments amounted to 21,965 trillion won in 2018, more than 4.8 times the level of 2001 (see Figure 2.3).

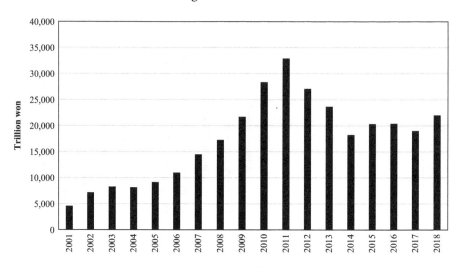

Figure 2.3. Value of Annual Transactions of Financial Derivatives
Source: Financial Statistics Information System of the Financial Supervisory Service.

Between 2001 and 2008, the amount of currency-related derivative transactions grew more than tenfold, while the transaction volume for interest rate derivative products was almost thirty-five times higher. Trading in stock derivative products was almost twelve times greater in 2008 than in 2003.

During the first phase of post-1997 financial and corporate restructuring, which ended in 2003, the government issued large amounts of ABSs to turn nonperforming loans at financial institutions into marketable securities. With the enactment of the law on asset securitization in 1998, the demand for ABSs exploded in 1999 and 2000, and they were also widely used to recapitalize, secure liquidity, and deleverage at banks and other financial institutions. In 2001, credit card companies began securitizing their card loans and other receivables as a means of new financing.

After the completion of the restructuring, the need for new ABS issuances for that purpose declined. However, restructuring ABSs was supplanted by new issuances of mortgage-backed securities and ABSs for the financing of large long-term infrastructure projects. The market for ABSs was highly unstable. Beginning in 2007, sluggishness in the housing and other real estate markets slashed demand so much that, in 2011, the amount of new ABSs issued fell to one-third of the volume a decade earlier.

CHAPTER 3

Financial Behavior of Households and Nonfinancial Firms

Households

ASSET MANAGEMENT

The changes in asset composition shown in Figure 3.1 demonstrate that households have become more risk averse in managing their wealth portfolios since the 1997 financial crisis. Indeed, despite the growth of bond and equity markets and the proliferation of new capital market products, the shares of risk-free deposits, insurance products, and pension funds in household asset portfolios have been on the rise.

The collapse of the capital market during the 1997 crisis reduced the combined share of bonds and equities in household asset portfolios from an average of 25 percent in the early 1990s to below 20 percent by 2005. After a period of stagnation, the combined share jumped to 34 percent in 2007, due largely to a booming stock market, before falling back to 22 percent in 2019. In contrast, the share of risk-free assets such as currency and deposits rose to more than 60 percent in 2000 from less than 50 percent on average in the 1990s. Since 2005, this share had declined gradually, reaching 45 percent in 2019. Reflecting the risk averseness, insurance and pension reserves also recorded a sustained gain, from about 18 percent in the early 1990s to more than 33 percent in 2019.

As shown in Figure 3.2, there was a sharp increase in the holdings of real assets during the rampant housing market boom in 2002–08. A

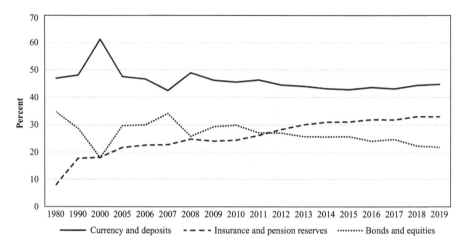

Figure 3.1. Shares in Total Financial Assets of Households and Nonprofit
Institutions
Source: Economic Statistics System of the Bank of Korea.

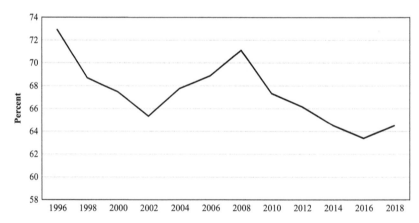

Figure 3.2. Share of Real Assets in Total Assets of Households and
Nonprofit Institutions
Source: Bank of Korea.
Note: Real assets include construction assets, facility assets, intellectual property products, inventories, land, mineral and energy resources, and standing timber assets. Data on real assets are from the national balance sheets, and those on financial assets of households and nonprofit institutions are from BOK Financial Transactions table.

large expansion of household loans combined with lower interest rates supported an age-old belief that real assets were safer and had higher yields than financial instruments and inflamed housing demand. The sluggishness of the economy following the 2008 global financial crisis has weakened the demand for housing and other real properties. The resurgence of the housing market boom in some metropolitan areas during 2017 and 2019 suggests that it is too early to judge whether there has been a fundamental shift toward financial instruments for holding wealth.

LIABILITY MANAGEMENT

On the liability side, the most conspicuous development since 1997 has been a large increase in household loans, defined as the sum of consumer loans and debt of self-employed individuals. In 2001, the volume of household loans from banks and other financial institutions began increasing rapidly. Household loans totaled less than 30 percent of GDP in 1994 and had risen to 40 percent six years later.

By the end of 2019, however, the total had soared to 1,505 trillion won, equivalent to 78.4 percent of GDP and 190.7 percent of household disposable income. Such a level was feared to endanger the soundness and stability of the financial system (see Table 3.1).

The massive increase in household loans after the 1997 crisis was set off by two changes in bank lending, both related to postcrisis reforms. One change was the eased restrictions on consumer loans, including mortgages, which released a huge pent-up demand for bank loans by households. In 2001 and 2003, household borrowing soared by more than 56 percent. The other change was a massive fall in demand for bank loans by the chaebol and other large corporations, which came under heavy pressure from the government to improve the soundness of their balance sheets by curtailing debt financing. In response, banks and NBFIs set out to attract household borrowers.

In the face of a real estate boom, in September 2002 regulatory authorities imposed a loan-to-value capping on mortgage loans to avert the acceleration of housing prices. The regulation did not achieve the desired goal: mortgage loans continued to grow by an average of 13 percent annually until 2006.

Table 3.1. Household Loans and Credits by Financial Institutions (2001–19) (trillion won, percent)

	2001	2003	2005	2007	2009	2011	2013	2015	2017	2019
Loans from depository corporations (A)	206.0	322.0	393.2	474.1	549.8	639.6	687.2	812.4	974.6	**1,084.0**
Deposit money banks[a]	156.7	253.8	305.5	363.7	409.5	455.9	481.1	563.7	660.7	**767.7**
Mortgage loans	86.5	152.5	208.4	245.8	273.7	308.9	328.9	401.7	464.2	**534.0**
Nonbank depository institutions[b]	49.3	68.3	87.7	110.4	140.3	183.7	206.1	248.6	313.9	**316.3**
Mortgage loans	—c	—c	—c	46.6	64.8	83.1	89.2	89.1	114.1	**99.8**
Loans from other financial institutions (B)	97.5	98.9	100.2	121.3	184.5	221.8	273.4	325.6	395.5	**420.5**
Insurance companies[d]	32.6	42.9	48.2	55.9	66.1	74.7	86.4	98.8	114.8	**119.0**
Pension funds[e]					8.6	13.6	14.0	12.8	13.6	**14.8**
Credit-specialized financial companies[f]	43.7	37.3	23.8	30.7	31.5	38.8	42.9	48.3	60.0	**66.2**
Public financial institutions[g]	—c	—c	—c	—c	31.5	30.5	33.6	32.9	37.2	**41.6**
Other financial intermediaries[h]	—c	—c	—c	—c	45.0	57.1	88.7	119.6	156.9	**166.8**

Others[i]	21.2	18.7	28.3	34.7	1.8	7.1	10.2	13.1	12.8	12.1
Total household loans (A + B)	303.5 (42.9)	420.9 (50.3)	493.4 (51.5)	595.4 (54.6)	734.3 (60.9)	861.4 (62.0)	960.6 (64.0)	1,138.0 (68.6)	1,369.8 (74.6)	1,504.5 (78.4)
Merchandise credits (C)	38.2	26.6	28.0	35.3	41.7	54.8	58.5	65.1	80.8	95.7
Credit-specialized financial companies	35.1	25.8	27.3	34.4	40.9	53.7	57.3	64.1	79.9	94.9
Total household credits (A + B + C)	341.7 (48.3)[1]	447.6 (53.4)	521.5 (54.5)	630.7 (57.9)	776.0 (64.4)	916.2 (66.0)	1,019.0 (67.9)	1,203.1 (72.6)	1,450.8 (79.0)	1,600.2 (83.4)

Source: Economic Statistics System of the Bank of Korea (https://ecos.bok.or.kr/EIndex_en.jsp).

Notes: The data represent outstanding volumes at year ends. The numbers in parentheses are percentages of nominal GDP.

[a] Commercial banks and specialized banks.

[b] Mutual savings banks, credit cooperatives, postal savings system, and merchant banks.

[c] Not available.

[d] Life insurance companies, non-life insurance companies, and postal insurance companies.

[e] Pension funds for government employees, members of the military, private school teachers, and so on.

[f] Credit card companies, installment financing companies, and so on.

[g] National Housing Fund, Korea Housing Finance Corporation, and so on.

[h] Includes venture capital companies and securities finance companies.

[i] Korea Student Aid Foundation and so on.

HOUSEHOLD LOAN GROWTH AND SYSTEMIC RISK

The dissipation of a runaway real estate boom called for a set of more powerful measures that included toughening the debt-to-income ratio (principal and interest payments on total loans divided by income), imposing taxes on housing transactions, and other administrative controls. These additional measures succeeded in lowering the growth of mortgage loans to 2.1 percent in 2007. But only when the global financial crisis erupted in 2008 did the liquidity crisis burst the housing bubble and stop loan growth.

As Figure 3.3 shows, the increase in housing prices had continued to decelerate since early 2000s, but the expansion of mortgage loans did not abate until 2016. Between 2001 and 2019, the volume of total household credits almost quintupled. The rapid growth of household loans raised the prospect of an increasing number of households being unable to service their debts after the housing market began showing signs of stagnation following the 2008 financial crisis. This slump, in turn, raised the question of whether it could pose systemic risk.

An April 2014 issue of the Bank of Korea's *Financial Stability Report* presented a rather optimistic outlook, claiming that the household sec-

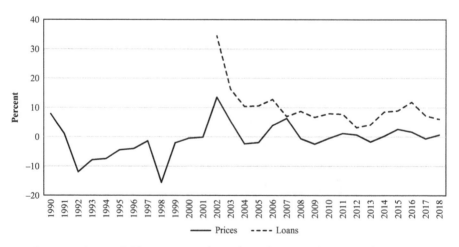

Figure 3.3. Rates of Changes in Real Residential Property Prices and Household Loans

Source: Economic Statistics System of the Bank of Korea and Bank for International Settlements.

Note: Household loan data are from total household credits in Table 3.1.

tor's debt-servicing capacity was large enough to withstand most of the adverse shocks unless they came in multiples. This view was based on the assessment that at the end of 2013, the market value of real assets was almost five times larger than—and that of financial assets was more than double—the amount of household debt.

The Bank of Korea also noted that 70 percent of household debt was held by people in the fourth and fifth quintiles of the income distribution. These wealthier households also owned relatively more real and financial assets. More importantly, the growth of debt did not outpace that of real and financial assets, suggesting that households did not use their debt to finance consumption spending and that the trend of household income growth was steady.

The 2014 report also presented the results of a stress test that chose households with negative net assets and cash flows to see how much their debt increased when subjected to various shocks. For a single shock—an interest rate hike of two percentage points—there was no visible increase in debt. Only when households were hit by a combination of three shocks (the two-percentage-point increase in the interest rate, a 20 percent decrease in income, and a 20 percent fall in the level of housing prices) did their financial soundness become significantly undermined.

In its June 2018 *Financial Stability Report*, the Bank of Korea presented a household debt profile that was as robust as the earlier one. The 2018 report saw an improvement in the debt-servicing capacity of households, while the growth of household debt was slowing. These developments led the Bank of Korea to conclude that household indebtedness did not present any threat of systemic risk.

Growth of Consumer Loan Finance Companies

In the early 2000s, after a series of financial reforms, economic analysts and policymakers thought that the diversification of financial institutions and the rapid growth of consumer lending had effectively ended the informal credit market's role in private-sector financing. However, it was still evident that a large segment of low-income households faced difficulties in accessing bank credit. This problem appears to have created room for the reemergence of a lucrative informal loan market for consumer lending.

The growth of a new informal credit market can be seen in the expansion of loosely regulated consumer loan finance companies (CLFCs), which operate outside of the organized financial system. In 2002, informal money lenders were required to register their businesses and subjected to an interest rate cap of 66 percent per annum. CLFCs were not subject to formal supervision by the financial authority because they were not considered financial institutions. Instead, they came under the supervision of local governments.

This regulatory control was a political decision in response to the reports of CLFCs' predatory debt collection practices and extremely high interest rates on their loans. The cap on the lending rate was lowered to 28 percent in 2017. The Financial Supervisory Service estimated that as of the end of June 2019, there were 8,084 CLFCs that collectively had two million borrowers and 16.5 trillion won ($16.7 billion) in loans.

Nonfinancial Corporations

CHANGES IN FUNDING STRUCTURE

In the absence of broad and deep capital markets and investment banking, large nonfinancial firms were heavily dependent on bank loans for working capital and fixed investment financing for many decades before the 1997 crisis. Since then, this dependence has declined markedly, as the firms have taken measures to reduce the risk of debt, in particular on short-term bank loans. If large firms learned one lesson from the financial crises of 1997 and 2008, it was that neither banks nor the government would provide liquidity in a financial meltdown.

In moving forward with restructuring after the 1997 crisis, regulators obliged large firms and the chaebol to reduce their ratio of debt to equity to below 200 percent. This pressure, together with the need to strengthen the resilience of balance sheets in the face of financial turbulence, has resulted in major changes in the structure of corporate financing. Specifically, nonfinancial firms have curtailed their debt financing in favor of equity and internal funding.

EQUITY FINANCING

As shown in Figure 3.4, the share of nonfinancial corporations in the total financing of the private sector has been relatively stable, fluctuating around 70 percent since the 1997 crisis. But the composition of external

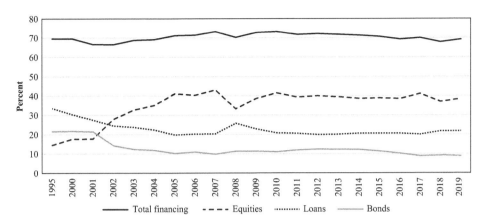

Figure 3.4. Nonfinancial Corporation Financing as a Share of Total Private-Sector Financing

Source: Bank of Korea, Financial Assets and Liabilities Outstanding table.

Note: The data exclude the "others" component of total liabilities of nonfinancial corporations to highlight the relative importance of the three major liabilities: bank loans, equities, and bonds.

financing has undergone a great deal of change, with a distinct rise in equity financing.

A breakdown of corporate financing into bank loans, corporate bonds, and equities shows a conspicuous rise in the use of equities. Their share had been less than 25 percent in the 1990s, but after the 1997 crisis, it soared to a record 59 percent of total financing in 2007, and stagnated around 55 percent thereafter until 2019 (see Figure 3.5).

INTERNAL FUNDING

There has been a marked increase in internal funds or corporate savings.[1] Internal sources include profits (net of interest and dividend payments, taxes, and other payments—collectively called retained earnings) and capital consumption allowances.[2]

Internal funds, which had amounted to less than 40 percent of total financing on average prior to the 1997 crisis, shot up to more than

---

1. The two terms are used interchangeably in comparisons with external financing.

2. In the national income account, internal funds are the sum of retained earnings and the total fixed capital formation (or gross fixed investment) of nonfinancial corporations.

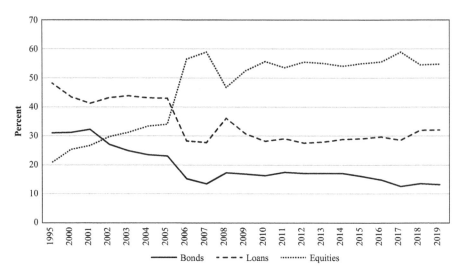

Figure 3.5. Liability Structure of Nonfinancial Corporations
Source: Bank of Korea, Financial Assets and Liabilities Outstanding table.

70 percent in 2000 as corporations reduced leverage. For the next ten years, with the growth of capital market financing, it declined continuously. But after the 2008 crisis (like during the 1997 crisis), it jumped, reaching 80 percent in 2010. However, since then (unlike during the 1997 crisis), it has remained high, at around 77 percent on average. This is due mainly to the relative decline in bond market funding (Table 3.2).

The financing gap is the balance between corporate savings and gross fixed investment. It represents the extent to which corporations need to draw on external funds. In the early 1990s, around 50 percent of corporate fixed investment was funded from external sources. The share declined gradually until 2013, when the financing gap turned positive. That is, corporate savings became larger than investment. Since then, internal funding has been consistently more than enough to finance fixed investment. In 2017, the difference, which is equal to retained earnings, amounted to 0.7 percent of internal funding sources.

The heavy reliance on internal funds has been responsible for a large increase in nondebt financing, which is the sum of internal and equity as opposed to debt financing (which consists of bank loans and corporate debentures). Since 2010, the share of nondebt financing has been more than 80 percent of total financing.

The greater reliance on the stock market and internal financing has resulted in a marked decline in the ratio of debt to equity in the business

Table 3.2. Internal and External Financing of Nonfinancial Corporations (trillion won, percent)

| | Internal (A) | External (B) | All external | | | Total financing (A+B) | Investment | Financing gap |
			Equities	Bonds	Loans			
1990	26.09 (38.8)	41.15 (61.2)	7.19	14.49	19.47	67.25	49.81	−47.6
1992	31.05 (42.2)	42.60 (57.8)	8.74	13.94	19.91	73.65	63.90	−51.4
1994	48.76 (39.9)	73.53 (60.1)	15.13	18.75	39.65	122.28	90.58	−46.2
1996	59.79 (39.4)	91.87 (60.6)	13.83	44.81	33.23	151.66	122.66	−51.3
1998	52.51 (60.6)	34.18 (39.4)	14.71	35.33	−15.86	86.69	88.85	−40.9
2000	91.95 (75.2)	30.30 (24.8)	25.48	−6.95	11.77	122.24	131.17	−29.9
2001	99.97 (70.2)	42.37 (29.8)	22.21	20.48	−0.31	142.34	135.93	−26.5
2002	125.04 (63.3)	72.37 (36.7)	32.17	−9.90	50.10	197.41	150.83	−17.1
2003	133.21 (67.1)	65.41 (32.9)	32.84	−2.31	34.88	198.62	165.33	−19.4
2004	165.86 (82.2)	35.99 (17.8)	32.64	0.07	3.28	201.86	179.77	−7.7
2005	170.34 (68.4)	78.62 (31.6)	37.65	18.46	22.51	248.96	199.44	−14.6
2006	176.44 (53.9)	150.72 (46.1)	38.89	45.82	66.01	327.16	218.54	−19.3
2007	193.44 (55.4)	155.54 (44.6)	33.64	23.28	98.62	348.97	240.25	−19.5

(continued)

Table 3.2. (Continued)

| | Internal (A) | External (B) | All external | | | Total financing (A + B) | Investment | Financing gap |
			Equities	Bonds	Loans			
2008	198.15 (51.6)	185.77 (48.4)	28.41	42.33	115.03	383.92	263.09	−24.7
2009	221.61 (62.9)	130.85 (37.1)	30.32	68.98	31.54	352.45	226.48	−2.2
2010	273.06 (80.0)	68.17 (20.0)	28.00	23.53	16.65	341.24	296.90	−8.0
2011	282.51 (74.9)	94.82 (25.1)	24.92	46.91	22.99	377.33	326.41	−13.4
2012	296.58 (75.0)	98.79 (25.0)	19.23	43.14	36.41	395.36	318.89	−7.0
2013	307.72 (79.5)	79.59 (20.5)	16.05	27.26	36.28	387.32	303.77	1.3
2014	318.94 (78.4)	87.95 (21.6)	15.59	−2.47	74.82	406.89	316.03	0.9
2015	335.61 (79.3)	87.67 (20.7)	21.33	−10.55	76.89	423.28	321.45	4.4
2016	359.06 (84.0)	68.98 (16.0)	36.13	−22.92	55.07	427.34	332.59	8.0
2017	381.40 (80.1)	94.90 (19.9)	26.24	−7.65	76.32	476.31	378.62	0.7
2018	365.58 (73.6)	130.98 (26.4)	34.89	7.33	88.76	496.56	—	—

Source: Economic Statistics System of the Bank of Korea (https://ecos.bok.or.kr/EIndex_en.jsp).

Notes: Internal financing is the gross savings of nonfinancial corporations from the national income statistics. Data on external financing exclude the "others" component (which includes financial derivatives, business-to-business trade credits, foreign direct investment, and miscellaneous items) to concentrate on the three major instruments of this financing. "Financing gap" is the percentage of corporate investment (or gross fixed investment). The figures in parentheses are the percentages of total financing.

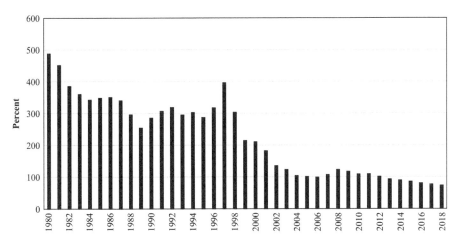

Figure 3.6. Ratio of Corporate Debt to Equity in Manufacturing
Source: Economic Statistics System of the Bank of Korea.
Note: Ratios for the manufacturing industry from the *Financial Statement Analysis*. Calculations are based on a sample survey before 2009 and a complete enumeration survey after 2009.

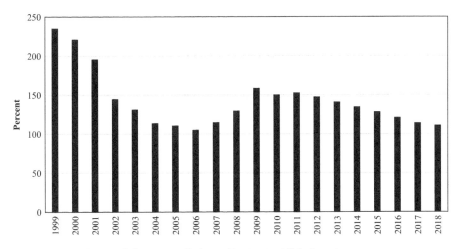

Figure 3.7. Ratio of Corporate Debt to Equity in All Industries
Source: Economic Statistics System of the Bank of Korea.

sector. Throughout the 1990s, the ratio in the manufacturing sector remained on average at around 300 percent. At the height of the crisis in 1997, it shot up to almost 400 percent. Thereafter, the ratio continued to fall, going below 100 percent in the manufacturing sector and below 110 percent in all industries by 2006. This is shown in Figures 3.6 and 3.7.

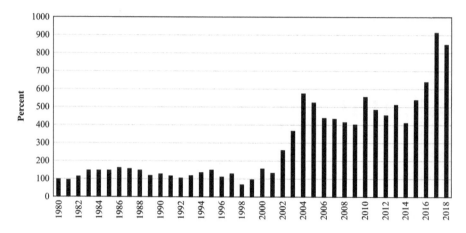

Figure 3.8. Interest Coverage Ratio in Manufacturing
Source: Economic Statistics System of the Bank of Korea.
Note: Ratios for the manufacturing industry from the *Financial Statement Analysis*. Calculations are based on a sample survey before 2009 and a complete enumeration survey after 2009.

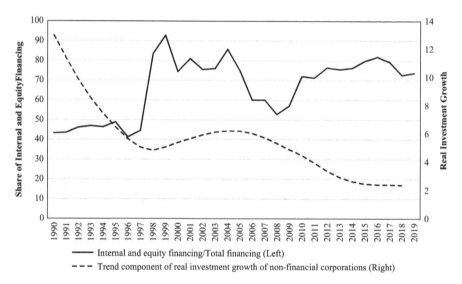

Internal and equity financing/Total financing (Left)
--- Trend component of real investment growth of non-financial corporations (Right)

Figure 3.9. Nondebt Financing and Growth of Real Investment in Nonfinancial Corporations
Source: Economic Statistics System of the Bank of Korea.
Note: The Hodrick-Prescott filter was used to extract a trend component of gross real investment growth.

The decline in the debt-equity ratio has also contributed to a massive increase in firms' interest coverage ratios, lowering their debt burden and reducing the possibility of bankruptcy or default. Throughout the 1980s and 1990s, the ratio remained on average below 130 percent, before slipping further in the run-up to the 1997 crisis. In 2000—after the corporate restructuring in 1998 and 1999—it recovered to the precrisis level before rising markedly, reaching close to 600 percent in 2004. It then fell somewhat until 2009 but rising over 800 percent in 2018 (see Figure 3.8).

The rapid growth of nondebt financing has had a significant bearing on the performance of the economy since the 1997 crisis. When the rate of growth of real investment in the nonfinancial sector is plotted against the share of nondebt financing in total financing, there is a strong negative correlation between the two sets of time-series data (see Figure 3.9). It is difficult to determine whether the sustained decrease in the growth of real investment was responsible for the rise in the relative share of nondebt financing, or vice-versa. Chapter 8 examines the causal relation between the two variables.

CHAPTER 4

Financial Liberalization and the Transformation of the Banking Industry

Control of Bank Ownership and Corporate Governance of Financial Firms

OWNERSHIP CONTROL

Since 1982, Korea has used regulatory limits on the ownership of bank stocks with voting rights by nonfinancial firms—mostly large firms and the chaebol—to ensure the separation of banking from commerce, as well as managerial independence and public accountability. But there are no limitations on the ownership of bank stocks by nonbank depository institutions, insurance firms, and a host of capital market institutions such as securities and futures companies.

Ownership control has been a controversial issue since its promulgation. People espousing free-market ideology have taken issue with it on grounds of efficiency. Specifically, they argue that in the absence of controlling interests, banks would never develop into efficient and profit-seeking business entities because bank management, however installed, would have little incentive to align its interests with those of bank shareholders. Free-market advocates invoke the agency dilemma, according to which bank managers are indifferent to earnings and profits unless such earnings and profits are closely monitored and evaluated by the major stockholders. And in the advocates' view, agency cost has been the fundamental driver of the sinking of Korea's banking industry into a dismal state of inefficiency and nontransparency, and one that lacks innovation.

In theory, small stockholders are able to join forces to form a group with enough voting stocks to control a bank, but organizing such a group is not easy. However, the government was able to act as—and exercise the voting right of—a large stock owner by combining the shares it and other public institutions held. In this way, the government found justification for appointing CEOs and other senior executives, thereby interfering with the lending operations of banks.

Progressive and liberal constituencies have consistently mounted strong opposition to lifting the limitations on equity grounds. They argue that any significant relaxation would open the door for large family-owned chaebol to acquire controlling interests in nationwide commercial banks, compelled by an eagerness to use them as a financing arm. The conglomerates would then create another type of principal-agent problem in which the interests of small stockholders and the national economy as a whole would be ignored. Ownership deregulation, they further argue, would increase the concentration of power in the hands of the industrial groups.

Progressives do not believe that introducing Western-style governance, centered on an independent board of directors, could mitigate the problems stemming from the easing of ownership control. Rather, they argue that there is no guarantee that an independent board could prevent the chaebol from controlling the banking industry, even if the supervision of banks' asset-liability management was tightened. More importantly, there is no credible process through which independent outside board members could be elected.

The government has been unable to find a solution that is satisfactory to both camps. As a result, control over bank ownership has had a history of vacillating between tight restriction and relaxation, depending on the swing of the ideological pendulum and associated changes in the government's policy for balancing efficiency with equity.

Under the Banking Act and Financial Holding Company Act, single ownership of stocks, including those owned by foreign investors, of a bank or a bank holding company is currently restricted to 10 percent of the total shares holding voting rights. The limit is 15 percent for a local bank or local bank holding company.

A series of changes in the act that have alternated between imposing more restriction and relaxation has stymied the establishment of credible and transparent bank corporate governance. Throughout the 1960s and 1970s, there were no limits on the number of bank stocks the "same person" or entity could hold.[1]

However, this changed in the early 1980s, with the privatization of certain nationwide commercial banks. Indeed, few individual investors or entities—except large family-owned industrial groups—were willing or able to acquire controlling interests in privatized banks. While the denationalization was desirable for improving bank efficiency, it also raised concerns about the possibility that the chaebol or other large family-owned firms would take controlling interests in the banks to use them as their private coffers.

Alarm over the potential takeover reinforced the opposition to privatization for fear that it would aggravate the concentration of the chaebol's economic and political power, with the potential risk of worsening distributive equity. This widespread concern led to the promulgation in 1982 of bank ownership restrictions under which a single person or entity cannot own more than 8 percent of a nationwide commercial bank's outstanding voting shares. Government-owned banks and local banks with local operational bases were exempt from this regulation.

In the 1990s, the government amended the Banking Act four times to change bank ownership control. The first change was the restriction of the ownership of local banks to 15 percent of voting stocks for the same person or entity in 1992. This was necessary because that had, in effect, become nationwide banks with the expansion of their operational boundaries.

Two years later, the general ownership limit for the same person or entity was lowered to 4 percent of voting stocks, while raising it to 12 percent at nationwide commercial banks for entities that specialized in financial business or were unrelated to the thirty largest chaebol. The rationale behind this relaxation was that it would help nurture a class of financial business entities to run the banking industry that had no ties to industrial groups.

At the same time, this change raised the limit on bank ownership for pension funds and other institutional investors to 8 percent of a bank's voting stock. It was expected that these institutions could keep a close

---

1. The term "same person" means the principal and a person having a special relationship with the principal as defined in the act.

eye on bank management, even when they did not exercise managerial control. The change was a compromise to help banks stand on their own feet while barring the entry of large industrial groups into banking.

In January 1997, before the eruption of the financial crisis, the government began deliberating a plan to amend the Banking Act to repeal the 12 percent limit, because the qualifications for specialization in financial business were too restrictive to create a new breed of bankers. A year later, in the midst of the crisis, the government revised the act to repeal the limit.

The 1998 amendment also abolished limits on foreign investors' acquisition of domestic bank stocks. For all practical purposes, foreign banks and financial holding companies were not subject to any restrictions on owning domestic bank stocks. However, they were required to report to the Financial Supervisory Commission (which changed its name in 2008 to the Financial Services Commission; FSC) if they owned more than 4 percent of the outstanding shares of a bank and to obtain approval whenever their holdings exceeded 10 percent, 25 percent, or 33 percent.

Since 2000, the government has enacted three more significant changes in the banking law for ownership relaxation. In April 2002, regulatory authorities raised the ownership limit for the same person or entity to 10 percent from 4 percent, with the proviso that holdings over 10 percent required the approval of the FSC. These changes also stipulated that a nonfinancial business operator (NFBO) could hold no more than 4 percent of the voting stock of a bank. However, NFBOs could own up to 10 percent with prior approval from the FSC, on the condition that they would not exercise any voting rights attributable to the shares that exceeded the 4 percent limit.

A 2009 amendment loosening ownership control paved the way for NFBOs to own up to 9 percent of the voting shares of a bank without any prior approval or limitations on voting rights. However, if an NFBO became the largest shareholder or engaged in the management of a bank through the acquisition of voting stocks in excess of 4 percent, prior FSC approval was required.[2]

---

2. Under the amendment, a public statutory fund that was listed in the National Finance Act would no longer be subject to the bank ownership limitations applicable to NFBOs. Prior to this amendment of the Banking Act, a private equity fund was deemed to be an NFBO if an NFBO, in its capacity as a limited partner, held more than

And in 2013 the limit on NFBO bank stock holdings with voting power was lowered from 9 percent to 4 percent—a return to the 1982 restriction. The reason was a familiar one. According to the government, the 2009 relaxation had raised the danger of concentrating the chaebol's economic power. At the same time, the government tightened the criteria for NFBOs to prevent attempts by institutions or a group of investors to control bank management.

CORPORATE GOVERNANCE OF BANKING INSTITUTIONS

Bank corporate governance refers to the processes and relations through which a bank's objectives are set and pursued in the context of the social, regulatory, and market environments.[3] It specifies the rights and responsibilities of different participants in a bank, including the board of directors, managers, shareholders, creditors, auditors, regulators, and other stakeholders. It also stipulates the mechanisms for monitoring the actions, policies, and decisions of the bank.

One of the objectives of the financial reform after the 1997 crisis was to establish a transparent and accountable corporate governance system in commercial banks that followed international best practices. To this end, the reform focused on strengthening the rights of bank minority shareholders through internal control procedures and the role of nonexecutive outside directors, audit committees, and compliance officers.[4] This was followed by a series of measures to upgrade accounting and disclosure systems. At least 50 percent of the board had to be nonexecutive di-

---

10 percent of the fund's equity interest. The amendment increased this threshold from 10 percent to 18 percent.

3. This section draws on Bank of Korea 2004, 17–22.

4. According to a survey, foreign-controlled banks have relatively more directors in absolute numbers, as well as higher shares of nonexecutive directors, on the board (Bank of Korea 2004). Note that these banks also appointed relatively more nonexecutive directors with careers in financial industries, while domestically owned banks appointed nonexecutive directors from diverse backgrounds—from academicians to nonfinancial corporate managers. On average, foreign-controlled banks also have more committee members and higher shares of nonexecutive directors on their audit committees. Domestic banks did not appoint foreign directors to their audit committees, while nine out of twelve members of the audit committees of foreign-controlled banks were foreign.

rectors, as did two-thirds of the audit committee and all of the nomination committee.

At the statutory level, therefore, the reform substantially reinforced the independence of the board and audit committee. In reality, however, this has not been the case. There has been little improvement in the corporate governance of banks or other financial firms. In the absence of controlling interests, the government has filled in, taking charge of bank management by overseeing the activities of the board (whose members were appointed by the government) and appointing through the board the bank president and other senior executives.

Essentially, government control has deprived bank boards of their independence in directing, monitoring, and supervising the conduct and operations of banks and their management. And since this control connotes implicit protection, institutional investors and other stockholders have had little incentive to monitor and scrutinize the governance and management of banks. Every bank has a succession plan, but this has been of little use because few know who the next president will be until the very last minute, when the government decides the matter.

The reorganization of financial institutions into financial holding companies (FHCs), where banks have been the dominant affiliates, has required a new governance system that delineates the authority and responsibilities of the chairs of FHCs and the presidents of banks. Commercial banks are the largest affiliates of most FHCs, accounting for more than 70 percent of the FHC's total earnings and profit, while other NBFIs are of minor significance in terms of revenue. For this reason, the typical situation is like having two bank presidents, rather than one FHC chair and one bank president. Since the government appoints both people, in reality, the line of command is often ignored—which creates internal disputes when conflicts arise over numerous management issues.

In an effort to lay the groundwork for a more efficient governance system for FHCs, the government revised the rules, standards, and organizations of corporate governance seven times during 1998–2012. Yet the problem of governance persisted.

The preceding analyses point to the restriction of bank ownership as the main cause of the governance disorder inherent in Korea's commercial banking industry. Whatever its justification, the restriction has given the government leeway to exercise a great deal of influence on the management of banks, both big and small. This influence (or control) has limited both the scope and the effectiveness of Korea's reforms for financial liberalization and opening.

Cynics would deplore the fact that ownership control has made all banks much the same in their management. In their view, the restriction has caused banks to spend more time and resources on lobbying regulators and other financial policymakers than on cultivating new potential clients and improving operational efficiencies. In short, banks have all become rent seekers, engaged in predatory competition for a larger share of the banking market within the confines of the government's rules and guidance.

Consolidation of Banks and Other Financial Firms

CREATION OF FINANCIAL HOLDING COMPANIES

The global trend toward the consolidation and conglomeration of financial industries has also taken hold in Korea, most conspicuously in banking. Following the 1997 crisis, Korea's policymakers made concerted efforts to enhance the competitiveness of the banking sector by exploiting economies of scale and scope through consolidation, asset-liability diversification, and conglomeration to create world-class banks that could vie with global financial firms offering a wide range of financial services.

The banking sector restructuring that followed the 1997 crisis created a number of large banks through mergers and acquisitions. It also loosened the regulations separating banking from securities and insurance. Banks now offer a variety of services that were previously in the domain of insurance and securities businesses, retailing a variety of investment products, beneficiary certificates, and insurance policies. Likewise, deregulation led insurance and securities firms to cross over the traditional dividing line in financial intermediation to retail some banking products.

These changes paved the way for passage of the Financial Holding Company Act (FHCA) in 2000, which facilitated financial conglomeration in which financial groups such as bank holding companies reorganized themselves to control banks and NBFIs as subsidiaries. The FHCA defines an FHC as a corporate entity whose primary business is to control firms engaged in financial business or other firms related closely to the operations of financial business.

Even before the formation of FHCs, nationwide commercial banks had reorganized into bank holding companies and set up a number of NBFIs as subsidiaries. Following the promulgation of the FHCA, however, these banks and their subsidiaries moved to reorganize into FHCs to take advantage of the new structure.

Between 2001 and 2008, the four largest banks—Woori, Shinhan, Hana, and Kookmin—reorganized themselves as FHCs by bringing their subsidiaries into the fold of a new structure. Since then, eight more FHCs have been chartered. Of the twelve such institutions, ten are bank holding companies, while the other two are nonbank FHCs. Collectively, they own 248 financial subsidiaries. (Table 4.1 shows the assets of FHCs during 2001–19.) In 2007, an amendment to the FHCA allowed foreign financial institutions to incorporate FHCs through mergers and acquisitions.

FHCs share customer information with their subsidiaries without the customers' written consent. This is for business purposes, such as cross-selling financial products and services. Subsidiaries can lower their operational costs by consolidating their back-office functions with the FHC or another subsidiary. And through their subsidiaries, FHCs can provide a large menu of financial products and services.

Although FHCs have provided a legal base for large banks to move into investment banking and the international finance business, the walls between commercial and investment banking and the demarcations among nonbank institutions remain and have limited the new structure's ability to gain economies of scale and scope. Partly for this reason, the returns on assets and on equities (ROAs and ROEs) of FHCs appear to have fallen off since the 2008 crisis (Table 4.2).

BANK ASSET AND LIABILITY MANAGEMENT

As noted above, the financial reform carried out after the 1997 crisis included a measure that expanded the scope of banking by adding a few nonintermediation activities such as securities and insurance business, to make deposit money banks more like European universal banks. In the more competitive financial setting ushered in by the reform, banks would have had to readjust their growth strategy to invest more both in improving risk management and operational efficiency and in business process innovation, while expanding the menu of financial products and services.

However, this adjustment has not been made, and banks have been unable to break out of traditional commercial banking and become

Table 4.1. Assets of Financial Holding Companies (trillion won)

	Woori	Shinhan	Hana	KB	SCB	KDB	Citibank	BNK	DGB	NH	Korea Investment	Meritz
2001	98.8	56.3	—[a]	—[a]	—[a]	—[a]	—[a]	—[a]	—[a]	—[a]	—[a]	—[a]
2002	114.8	66.8	—[a]	—[a]	—[a]	—[a]	—[a]	—[a]	—[a]	—[a]	—[a]	—[a]
2003	128.8	139.2	—[a]	—[a]	—[a]	—[a]	—[a]	—[a]	—[a]	—[a]	—[a]	—[a]
2004	136.6	146.9	—[a]	—[a]	—[a]	—[a]	—[a]	—[a]	—[a]	—[a]	3.2	—[a]
2005	164.5	160.9	95.9	—[a]	—[a]	—[a]	—[a]	—[a]	—[a]	—[a]	5.5	—[a]
2006	212.0	177.7	116.1	—[a]	—[a]	—[a]	—[a]	—[a]	—[a]	—[a]	9.4	—[a]
2007	249.6	220.9	126.2	—[a]	—[a]	—[a]	—[a]	—[a]	—[a]	—[a]	11.9	—[a]
2008	291.0	264.0	157.8	267.5	—[a]	—[a]	—[a]	—[a]	—[a]	—[a]	13.1	—[a]
2009	284.9	255.0	150.3	262.2	68.9	157.2	—[a]	—[a]	—[a]	—[a]	14.0	—[a]
2010	291.4	265.1	158.5	262.0	69.0	159.5	55.1	—[a]	—[a]	—[a]	15.3	—[a]
2011	312.8	288.0	178.2	277.6	73.7	172.0	58.5	39.4	31.3	—[a]	18.5	9.4
2012	325.7	300.8	283.7	282.0	68.3	191.9	53.3	42.9	34.2	245.9	20.8	11.1
2013	340.7	311.3	295.2	291.8	60.2	198.4	51.4	46.9	37.6	254.5	21.2	21.1
2014	—[a]	338.0	315.5	308.4	61.8	—[a]	—[a]	84.1	41.0	315.7	25.3	26.8
2015	—[a]	370.5	326.9	329.1	—[a]	—[a]	—[a]	90.3	51.1	339.8	31.5	32.0
2016	—[a]	395.7	348.2	375.7	—[a]	—[a]	—[a]	93.5	53.5	366.9	37.3	37.5
2017	—[a]	426.3	360.1	436.8	—[a]	—[a]	—[a]	94.3	56.7	388.7	48.7	42.1
2018	—[a]	459.6	385.0	479.6	—[a]	—[a]	—[a]	98.8	65.0	417.0	64.0	52.2
2019	362.0	522.4	421.5	518.5	—[a]	—[a]	—[a]	104.5	72.4	427.1	60.8	61.8

Source: Financial Statistics Information System of the Financial Supervisory Service (http://www.fss.or.kr/fss/eng/main.jsp).

Notes: The financial holding company (FHC) of Woori merged with Woori Bank in 2014. KB is Kookmin Bank. The FHC of SCB merged with SCB in 2015. The FHC of SCB merged with SCB in 2015. The FHC of the Korea Development Bank (KDB) merged with KDB in 2014. Citi FHC merged with Citibank in 2014. NH is Nonghyup Bank.

[a] Not available.

Table 4.2. Returns on Assets and Equities of Financial Holding Companies (percent)

	2001	2004	2007	2010	2013	2014	2015	2016	2017	2018	2019
ROA	0.72	0.85	0.99	0.50	0.19	0.45	0.42	0.48	0.59	0.58	0.60
ROE	14.55	13.82	13.39	6.04	2.29	5.77	6.84	8.76	7.92	8.74	9.17

Source: Financial Statistics Information System of the Financial Supervisory Service (http://www.fss.or.kr/fss/eng/main.jsp).

Table 4.3. Financial Assets and Liabilities of Depository Corporations (trillion won, percent)

	1990		1995		2000		2019	
	Assets	Liabilities	Assets	Liabilities	Assets	Liabilities	Assets	Liabilities
Currency and deposits	11.1 (8.9)	68.4 (54.6)	18.3 (6.4)	167.2 (58.8)	17.6 (2.8)	433.2 (68.6)	538.0 (12.6)	2,866.0 (67.7)
Securities other than shares	12.1 (9.7)	2.4 (1.9)	35.7 (12.6)	10.3 (3.6)	176.0 (27.9)	32.9 (5.2)	632.1 (14.8)	456.2 (10.8)
Stocks	2.7 (2.2)	5.9 (4.7)	9.1 (3.2)	8.7 (3.1)	7.6 (1.2)	15.9 (2.5)	144.5 (3.4)	206.3 (4.9)
Loans	84.2 (67.3)	13.1 (10.5)	175.0 (61.5)	14.9 (5.2)	328.4 (52.0)	19.2 (3.0)	2,462.9 (57.7)	104.9 (2.5)
Others	15.0 (12.0)	35.3 (28.2)	46.4 (16.3)	83.3 (29.3)	101.5 (16.1)	130.2 (20.6)	490.2 (11.5)	601.4 (14.2)
Total	125.1 (100.0)	125.1 (100.0)	284.5 (100.0)	284.4 (100.0)	631.1 (100.0)	631.5 (100.0)	4,267.7 (100.0)	4,234.7 (100.0)

Source: Economic Statistics System of the Bank of Korea (https://ecos.bok.or.kr/EIndex_en.jsp).

Notes: The figures in parentheses are percentages of total assets and liabilities. "Others" include financial derivatives, trade credits, other financial claims, and debts.

multifaceted financial firms. They have continued to concentrate on making household and commercial loans that are collateralized by housing and other types of real estate, with funds raised through deposits. Throughout the 1990s, the share of loans in total assets was overwhelmingly large, with small fluctuations—as was the dominance of deposits on the liability side (Table 4.3).

CHANGES IN BANK LENDING STRUCTURE

In the wake of the 1997 crisis, banks have allocated a growing share of loanable funds to housing and SME finance and investments in low-risk bonds (such as treasury and monetary stabilization bonds), at the expense of corporate loans. There were several causes for this shift. One cause was a change in nonfinancial corporations' financing strategy in favor of internal and stock market financing. This has left banks and other NBFIs with large amounts of loanable funds for which they could not find creditworthy industrial borrowers.

In an oligopolistic market structure, large banks preoccupied with market-share competition have had to find new loan clients to fill the void. They found a legion of eager borrowers in the household sector, as the search coincided with deregulation in 1998 that allowed banks and NBFIs to move into consumer and mortgage lending.

Taking advantage of the deregulation, banks plunged into courting households and the self-employed, from whom they had previously distanced themselves, as potential loan customers to make up for the loss in revenue.[5] The share of households in total loans and credit by depository corporations, which include deposit money banks and nonbank depository institutions, had remained a little over 20 percent before the 1997 crisis. After the financial reform, the share began to surge, reaching 45 percent by 2005 (Figure 4.1). Following a sharp fall in 2008, it has remained relatively stable around 41 percent.

So did mortgage loans. Banks were attracted by their relatively low credit risk and capital requirements, as well as the need for little expertise or experience in credit analysis for housing loans—since they were backed by housing collateral.

At the height of the housing market boom in 2007, almost 62 percent of household lending was classified as mortgage loans. This meant that since 2007, on average, more than 26 percent of the total loans of depository corporations have been lent to households for financing housing investment, mostly in place of loans to large corporations.

A second cause has been the change in the risk appetite of commercial banks. Having learned a bitter lesson about the perils of reckless lending to the chaebol and large firms, banks sought to tighten their credit risk man-

---

5. Unless otherwise specified, "households" and "the household sector" are used interchangeably.

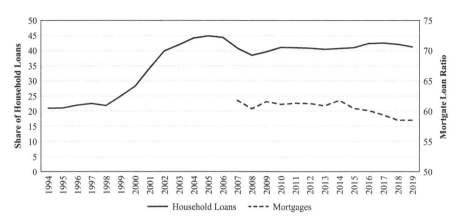

Figure 4.1. Shares of Households in Total Loans and of Mortgages in Loans to Households by Depository Corporations
Source: Bank of Korea.

agement by introducing exposure limits on corporate loans. At the same time, the regulatory authorities strengthened prudential regulations to reduce any single entity's large credit exposures.[6]

A third cause was a policy change intended to increase the access of SMEs to bank loans by obliging commercial banks to lend SMEs, on average, more than 45 percent of their lendable funds. This change has also contributed to the relative decline in bank lending to corporations.

Finally, since the 1997 crisis, regulatory authorities have phased out many of the restrictions imposed on banks' investment in bonds, equities, and other capital market instruments, clearing the way for banks to diversify their asset portfolios.[7] The relaxation has also cut into the corporate share of bank loans.[8]

---

6. In April 1999, the ceilings were lowered for credits to a single individual or juridical person and to a single large business group from 45 percent of banks' equity capital to 20 percent and 25 percent, respectively.

7. These instruments include stocks, debt securities, derivative-linked securities, beneficiary certificates, investment contract securities, depository receipts, and equities for which the redemption periods exceed three years. As for stocks issued by major shareholders, banks are required to limit their investment to less than 1 percent of equity capital.

8. However, to ensure that banks maintain sound management, the banking act prohibits excessive securities investment. It stipulates that a bank's investment in a large number of capital market instruments may not exceed 100 percent of its equity capital.

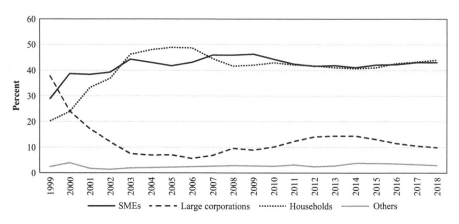

Figure 4.2. Sectoral Allocation of Loans by Deposit Money Banks
Source: Financial Statistics Information System of the Financial Supervisory Service.

As a result of these changes in the lending structure, the percentage of deposit money banks' loans that went to large corporations plunged to less than 10 percent between 2003 and 2009 from more than 21 percent in the middle of the 1990s. Only when the 2008 crisis was over did it began rising again, to recover a 10 percent level in 2018 (see Figure 4.2).

Efficiency, Competition, and the Market Structure of Financial Industries

ECONOMIES OF SCALE AND SCOPE IN THE BANKING SECTOR

Due mainly to the closing of sixteen banks in the wake of the 1997 crisis and subsequent mergers and acquisitions, the number of commercial banks had fallen to six nationwide and six regional banks by the end of 2019.

As shown in Table 4.4, over a decade after the crisis, the largest commercial banks have transformed Korea's banking system into an oligo-

---

Even within the abovementioned limits, banks are barred from investing in equity securities if the investment grants it control of another corporation. In principle, the act prohibits banks from owning more than 15 percent of shares issued by other corporations. Banks are also banned from borrowing against shares in their own possession.

Table 4.4. Shares of the Top Four Largest Commercial Banks (percent)

Year	Top 4 share	Top 4 commercial banks
1999	50.8	Kookmin, Korea Housing and Commercial Bank (KHCB), Chohung, Korea Exchange Bank
2003	62.7	Kookmin, Woori, Hana, Shinhan
2007	71.7	Kookmin, Woori, Shinhan, Hana
2011	71.1	Kookmin, Woori, Shinhan, Hana
2015	80.2	Kookmin, KEB Hana, Woori, Shinhan
2018	80.8	Kookmin, KEB Hana, Woori, Shinhan
2019	81.0	Kookmin, Shinhan, KEB Hana, Woori

Source: Financial Statistics Information System of the Financial Supervisory Service (http://www.fss.or.kr/fss/eng/main.jsp).

Notes: Shares are calculated on the basis of the total assets of banking and trust accounts of commercial banks.

polistic structure, as they continue to add to their combined market share of total commercial bank assets. The proportion jumped to 71.7 percent at the end of 2007 from 50.8 percent at the end of 1999. It surged again, reaching 81.0 percent by the end of 2019.

There were twenty-nine life insurance firms in 1999, but the top three (Samsung, Daehan, and Kyobo) had a combined market share of close to 80 percent. The top five of the seventy-eight securities firms controlled 60.7 percent of the market in the same year. At the end of 2019, there were twenty-five life insurance and fifty-five securities firms, and the shares of the top five in the two industries were 67.5 percent and 52.7 percent, respectively.

Not surprisingly, in 2019 the Herfindahl-Hirschman Index (HHI) was the lowest for the securities business: 742 compared to 1,695 for banking and 1,443 for insurance (see Figures 4.3 and 4.5). The consolidation, conglomeration, and diversification of the activities of these large financial institutions have raised two issues.

One is the question of whether these changes have produced any discernible effects on efficiency improvements and increases in the scale or scope of economies in the banking sector.[9] The other is whether the

---

9. For a brief recent survey on the efficiency of Korea's banking industry in Korean, see Seok-Young Lee (2012).

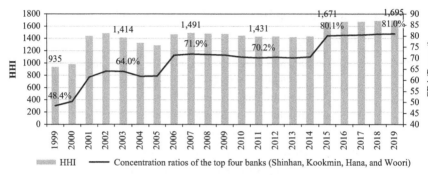

Figure 4.3. Market Concentration Ratios and Hhis of the Four Largest Commercial Banks
Source: Financial Statistics Information System of the Financial Supervisory Service.
Note: The four banks are Shinhan, Kookmin, Hana, and Woori.

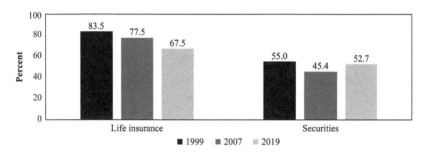

Figure 4.4. Market Concentration Ratios of the Five Largest Life Insurance and Securities Firms
Source: Financial Statistics Information System of the Financial Supervisory Service.

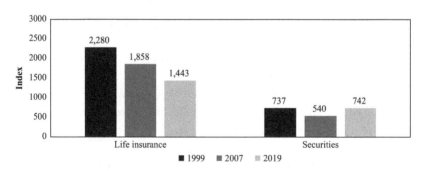

Figure 4.5. Hhis of the Five Largest Life Insurance and Securities Firms
Source: Financial Statistics Information System of the Financial Supervisory Service.

changes have concentrated market power in a few institutions and thus undermined competition in various financial industries.

In the years following the 1997 crisis, these two issues stimulated a great deal of interest in banking research, spawning a large number of empirical studies on economies of scale and scope, efficiency, and competition in the banking industry.

Because of the assortment of estimation technologies selected and the lack of reliable data sets, these studies present divergent and often conflicting results. They also cover different periods before the 2008 crisis. Since then, there has been little interest in revisiting the two issues. For these reasons, the existing studies do not shed much light on whether the reform after the 1997 crisis succeeded in achieving the proposed structural changes to revitalize the banking industry.

On the verification of the presence of economies of scale and scope, most of the studies undertaken before the 2008 crisis estimated a variety of bank cost functions for multiple products and inputs to measure changes in the average cost associated with changes in bank size. In this approach, a decrease in the average cost indicates that banks are operating with significant economies of scale. The difference between the cost of producing multiple products individually and jointly is defined as a measure of economies of scope.[10]

Empirical studies in Korean based on the cost function for the period before the 1997 crisis are more or less equally divided between those claiming significant evidence for and others reporting inconclusive findings on the existence of both scale and scope economies. Disagreement endures among the empirical studies that investigated similar issues in the early 2000s.

The existence of scale economies does not mean that bank operations are efficient in the use of inputs. The measurement of bank operational efficiency uses a nonparametric technique known as data envelopment analysis (DEA). This method is used in estimating a deterministic pro-

---

10. Practically all of the studies specified cost functions in the trans log, so that the sum of the cost elasticities of individual outputs or services that banks produce determines the presence of scale economies. If the sum is greater or less than one, this means banks are operating with decreasing or increasing returns to scale, respectively. If it is equal to one, banks are experiencing constant returns to scale. In the two-product case, the presence of scope economies is determined by comparing two cost functions.

duction frontier, which provides the benchmark for assessing the relative efficiency of a set of similar banks.

The DEA approach specifies the distance of the production functions of individual banks from the benchmark production frontier. If a bank is located beneath the frontier, then the bank's operation is inefficient. This inefficiency is then divided into technical and scale inefficiency. The distance from the frontier is a measure of technical inefficiency resulting from the inefficient use of inputs. The deviation from an optimal scale corresponding to constant returns to scale is a measure of diseconomies of scale.

Empirical studies by Kang Park and William Weber (2006), Rajiv Banker and coauthors (2010), and Dong Jin Shin and Brian Kim (2011) present evidence on the existence of both technical and scale efficiency improvements among Korean banks after the 1997 crisis. For more than a decade since the publication of these studies, however, there has been no serious attempt to examine whether their results could be replicated over the period after the 2008 global financial crisis.

CONCENTRATION IN AND THE COMPETITIVE STRUCTURE OF FINANCIAL INDUSTRIES

Market concentration in the banking industry has markedly increased since the 1997 crisis, due to the decline in the number of banks and bank mergers and consolidations that created larger banks (Figure 4.3). The concentration ratios and HHIs for the four largest banks have risen so much in the 2000s that casual observers could conclude that these two indicators present prima facie evidence for the deterioration of the competitive conditions in the banking industry.[11] But such a conclusion is not warranted, for other pieces of evidence from more rigorous studies that measured the level of competition using the H statistic of the Panzar-Rosse model prove otherwise.[12]

---

11. The HHI index for the top four banks rose to 1695 in 2019 from 935 in 1999 (Figure 4.3). The concentration index rose from 48.4 percent to 80.8 percent during the same period. According to the criteria of the U.S. Department of Justice, a financial market is underconcentrated if the HHI is lower than 1,000, moderately concentrated if it is 1,000–1,800, and highly concentrated if it is higher than 1,800.

12. In the Panzar-Rosse model, if total revenue and input prices of a firm change in the same direction, this indicates a competitive market, whereas changes in the oppo-

The concentration debate has produced a large number of studies in both English and Korean based on the Panzar-Rosse model. But depending on the period covered and the specifications of bank cost and revenue functions, the results vary significantly, rendering it difficult to judge the effects of the concentration on the competitive structure in banking. This problem also holds true for those studies that investigated data from before the 1997 crisis.[13]

Park and Weber (2006) find that the Korean banking industry was monopolistically competitive during the pre- (1992–96) and post-crisis periods (2001–4). This result is confirmed by Dong Jin Shin and Brian Kim (2013), who present evidence that the banking industry was characterized by monopolistic competition throughout the 1992–2007 period when the crisis year of 1997 is excluded.

Byung-chul Chun and Hyo-sung Kwon (2008) dispute these results by showing that the banking industry had an oligopolistic market structure over the 1999–2017 period, created by a few strategically interdependent banks. Min Hwan Lee and Mamoru Nagano (2008) also claim that the banking industry, which had been monopolistically competitive before the 1997 crisis, became perfectly competitive after that. Maximilian Hall and Richard Simper (2013) examined data from the second quarter of 2007 to the second quarter of 2011 and find that perfect competition prevailed during this period.

Many legal and structural changes that have taken place over the past decade raise questions as to whether all of these studies on efficiency, scale economies, and competition in banking are outdated. This question arises because the studies did not take into account the intensification of competition among banks, NBFIs, insurance firms, and a host of capital market institutions as a result of lowering the walls between them during the period after the 1997 crisis.

The large banks compete not only among themselves but also against NBFIs in both the funding and lending markets. Competition has become

---

site direction tend to reflect that the firm has some degree of market power (Panzar and Rosse 1987). The H statistic is the sum of elasticities of total revenue with respect to input prices. An H value equal to or less than zero indicates a monopoly; a value of one indicates competition; and a value between zero and one indicates monopolistic competition.

13. See Chun and Kwon (2008) and Shin and Kim (2013) for brief surveys on the literature in Korean.

much more intense since the wall that separated these institutions was dismantled, and especially since the opening of financial markets to foreign investors and borrowers. Given these developments, what is important and needed is information about the degree of competition throughout the financial system, rather than competition in banking or any individual financial industry alone. There have been few attempts to conceptualize and measure the overall competitive structure of the financial system in Korea.

CHAPTER 5

The Opening of Financial Intermediation Industries

Foreign Ownership of Financial Institutions

One of the most significant reforms for financial liberalization in the aftermath of the 1997 financial crisis was the deregulation of foreign entry into Korean financial industries. It was expected that the freer entry would transform Korea's financial landscape into one of the most open in the emerging world. The Foreign Investment Promotion Act of 1998, which abolished the limits on foreign ownership of an equity interest in financial institutions, set the stage for a massive increase in the foreign acquisition of the stocks of banks and other financial institutions.[1]

As part of the deregulation, Korea's policymakers sought foreign buyers for ailing banks and NBFIs. At the same time, policymakers believed that foreign equity participation would set in motion the modernization of Korea's financial system by improving not only efficiency, soundness, and corporate governance, but also the credibility and international standing of Korean financial institutions.

Two decades later, few people would argue that the financial opening has been a success story. There is little evidence that Korea has reaped many of the expected benefits of foreign entry liberalization. In short, the opening of the banking industry has been irrelevant. There remain only two foreign-owned commercial banks, each of which has just a tiny market share.

---

1. To improve the existing foreign investment system and to promote foreign investment in the service sector, the act was amended on April 5, 2010.

After the 1997 crisis, many foreign investors began investing in a large number of Korea's financial institutions in the belief that the stocks of restructured banks and NBFIs would ensure high rates of return as the Korean stock market rebounded from the 1998 crash. Two decades later, they remain speculative investors who have little interest in the managerial performance of the financial institutions in which they own quite a lot of stock. This chapter attempts to find some explanations for the lack of success in the opening of financial intermediation industries in Korea.

PRIVATE EQUITIES MOVE IN

U.S.-based private equity funds acquired three ailing Korean domestic banks for restructuring following the 1997 crisis. New Bridge Capital acquired Jaeil (First) Bank in 1999, but sold it in 2005 to Standard Chartered (SC), which renamed it SC First Bank and later SC Bank Korea (formally, Standard Chartered Bank Korea Ltd). The Carlyle Group and JP Morgan Corsair obtained a controlling interest in Hanmi Bank in 2000. Four years later, they sold it to Citigroup, which merged it with its Korea branch to create Citibank Korea.

Additionally, Lone Star Funds acquired a 51 percent stake and management control of Korea Exchange Bank (KEB) in 2003 before selling it to the Hana Financial Group Inc. in 2012. Since 2012, the shares in both the deposit and loan markets of the two remaining foreign banks, SC Bank Korea and Citibank Korea, have decreased.

FOREIGN BUYERS AS FINANCIAL INVESTORS

In contrast, foreign investors' equity investments in banks and NBFIs rose markedly following the stock market liberalization in 1999 and grew steadily thereafter. In 2019 at the four largest nationwide commercial banks—Shinhan, Woori, KB Kookmin, and Hana Banks, which had a combined market share of 80.8 percent of the assets of all deposit money banks—foreign investors held on average more than 54.5 percent of the outstanding stocks, up from 35 percent in 2000 (Figure 5.1).[2] At Woori,

---

2. In 1997 before the crisis, foreigners' average share of all commercial banks was far below 10 percent. This means that the promulgation of the Foreign Investment Promo-

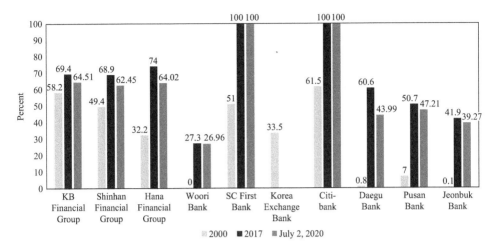

Figure 5.1. Share of Foreign Ownership in Banks
Source: Financial Statistics Information System of the Financial Supervisory Service.
Note: The numbers are as of the ends of 2000 and 2020. KB is Kookmin Bank.

the fourth-ranked bank (18.5 percent of whose outstanding stocks was government owned), the share was 27.0 percent at the end of June 2020. Between 2005 and 2007, foreign investors held almost 80 percent on average of the outstanding stocks at KB Kookmin and Hana Banks.

The shares of foreign ownership at the two largest local banks, Daegu and Busan (also spelled Pusan), were also very high—at 60 and 50 percent, respectively. In addition to the domestic banks owned or controlled by foreign investors, there were forty-three foreign bank branches at the end of 2019.[3] Overall, between 2000 and 2020, foreign ownership almost doubled, reaching 60.9 percent of the total outstanding stocks of all commercial banks.

As for the insurance industry, there has been a small increase in the number of foreign firms since 1999, though their share in the total assets of all firms grew threefold between 2000 and 2019 (Table 5.1). This suggests that the foreign firms have been successful in competing with

---

tion Act of 1998 opened the floodgates to a massive increase in foreign investments in bank stocks.

3. In the subsequent analysis, KEB is treated as a foreign-controlled bank since it was bought by Hana Financial Group only in 2012.

Table 5.1. Foreign Life Insurance Firms and Securities Companies
(billion won, percent)

	Life insurance		Securities	
	Number	*Total assets*	*Number*	*Total assets*
1999	9	5,156 (4.86)	21	1,505 (2.48)
2000	9	6,191 (5.14)	19	1,348 (2.99)
2005	11	26,024 (11.09)	15	4,898 (6.70)
2010	11	68,998 (16.89)	12	10,799 (5.40)
2015	11	99,543 (13.73)	10	6,789 (1.97)
2016	11	108,541 (13.88)	10	7,058 (1.71)
2017	11	118,117 (14.18)	11	8,503 (2.18)
2018	10	129,891 (15.15)	11	7,899 (1.80)
2019	10	140,513 (15.30)	11	8,057 (1.67)

Source: Financial Statistics Information System of the Financial Supervisory Service (http://www.fss.or.kr/fss/eng/main.jsp).
Note: The numbers in parentheses are percentages of total assets of the relevant industry.

domestic firms for market share. In contrast, foreign securities firms have not done well in the Korean market. Since 1999, there has been a decrease in the number of the firms, and their market share dwindled to 1.7 percent in 2019 from a period high of 6.7 percent in 2005.

Although as a group, foreigners own the majority of outstanding shares of KB Kookmin, Shinhan, and Hana Banks, they are mostly financial investors subject to the individual ownership limitations. They are individually too small to be represented on the board and, hence, to control the management of these banks. There is no collective mechanism enabling them to exercise their voting power or to represent their interests as a group.

Foreign investors also appear to subscribe to the notion that these banks are too big to fail. One way or another, they believe that the government will step in to bail the banks out if they are in danger of insolvency. Because of these reasons, foreign equity investors have not shown much interest in monitoring the soundness or corporate governance of Korean banks.

Complacency does not mean that the investors do not pay attention to the banks' profits and earnings prospects. As most equity investors do, they could—and in fact do—reveal their performance assessments in trading the bank stocks they hold. It is also known that foreign equity investors are more information driven, susceptible to herding, and averse to stock price volatility, relative to domestic investors.

These behavioral characteristics suggest that banks with foreign investors are likely to monitor the trading behaviors of their foreign shareholders and are under pressure to perform better than domestically owned banks do. This is because the departure of foreign equity holders could unleash a massive sellout, dealing a severe blow to a bank's market value and credit ratings and causing a rise in the cost of securing foreign funding. The pressure for better performance suggests that foreign-invested or -controlled banks are likely to be more efficient and profitable than Korean-owned banks. But there is no evidence of such a difference between the two groups.

There is also the question of whether the foreign buyers of domestic bank stocks are long-term investors or are mostly seeking short-term profit. During the 2008 global financial crisis, when Korea suffered a liquidity crisis, there was concern that foreign investors would fly to safety. However, they did not sell a substantially greater share of their bank stocks than domestic investors did.

In what follows, this section examines the relative performance of foreign- and domestically owned banks. For this purpose, KB Kookmin, Hana, and Shinhan are classified as "foreign-invested without managerial control," and the three second-tier banks (SC Korea; Citibank Korea; and KEB, before its sale in 2012 to Hana) are classified as "foreign or foreign-controlled banks." Some of the performance indicators of market share of assets and liabilities, profitability, and soundness of these banks are then compared with those of Woori Bank, which is classified as a domestic bank whose size and branch network are comparable to those of foreign-invested or -controlled banks.

An examination of the relative performance of the three groups in terms of these indicators may help assess the impact of foreign investment in bank stocks and foreign management control of domestic banks on Korea's financial intermediation industries.

Many authors have analyzed the potential benefits of foreign bank entry for the domestic economy in terms of the contribution to better resource allocation and the efficiency and stability of the financial system.[4] When foreign banks enter the domestic banking market, they are likely to intensify competition, as they have competitive advantages from access to low-cost financing and advanced financial and management technology—including advanced screening techniques. In response to the heightened competition, domestic banks have to improve the quality and diversify the menu of their financial services by developing and marketing new financial products.[5]

The entry of foreign global banks may help improve the soundness and stability of the domestic banking industry. The increasing globalization of financial markets and corporate links across economies has augmented the speed at which events in one market can affect other markets. Subsidiaries of foreign banks can be a source of stability during periods of local stress, as they are part of globally diversified entities.

For example, in times of financial turbulence such as during the 2008 liquidity crisis, when domestic banks lose their access to the short-term global funding market, subsidiaries of foreign banks may be able to obtain short-term funds from their parent banks or global financial markets directly to help ease the liquidity drought. However, this interconnectedness cuts both ways.

---

4. See, for example, Claessens et al. (2001), Lensink et al. (2004), and Claessens (2017).

5. The efforts of domestic banks to cut operating costs and reduce interest margins do not necessarily increase their profitability in the short term. Foreign global banks tend to supply credit only to top-ranked customers when handling retail and wholesale finance in the domestic market. When this cherry-picking practice becomes the norm among foreign banks, the share of domestic banks' loans to customers with relatively low credit ratings, such as SMEs, increases. In this case, total loans to the SME sector may decrease, as foreign banks have reduced loans to SMEs and domestic banks cannot make new loans to all of the SMEs whose loan applications were rejected by foreign banks. Therefore, the possibility that the financial soundness of domestic banks would deteriorate cannot be excluded.

Subsidiaries of foreign banks can be a source of instability, as they often serve as transmission mechanisms for the policies adopted by their headquarters in response to shocks in their home countries or in other places where they have large exposure. How significant have these benefits and costs been in Korea? As discussed below, Korea's experience does not provide any evidence of benefits. It also should be noted that foreign banks do not enter the local market to serve as beacons for financial modernization. They are likely to be seeking to exploit regulatory and tax loopholes. Instead of transferring new assets and liabilities, and risk management techniques, they could take advantage of the technological backwardness of their domestic counterparts.

Market Shares in Assets, Deposits, and Loans

The shares in the assets of Woori, foreign-invested, and other banks (local banks and five specialized banks) were relatively stable throughout the period. In contrast, the group of foreign-controlled banks has lost its shares of assets and in both the deposit and loan markets. Their deposit share plunged to 4.1 percent in 2018 from 15.9 percent in 2006. The decrease in the loan share was also pronounced, falling to 3.2 percent in 2018 from a high of 13.7 percent in 2006. The group has been losing out to foreign bank branches as a major supply channel for short-term foreign currency liquidity. The data are in Tables 5.2 and 5.3.

Table 5.2. Market Shares in Assets among Banks (percent)

	Woori	Foreign-invested	Foreign-controlled	Foreign branches	Others
2001	8.8	27.2	13.0	7.6	43.4
2005	9.8	30.1	13.9	7.5	38.7
2010	11.5	31.9	12.6	11.7	32.3
2015	11.5	31.7	5.5	11.6	39.8
2017	11.2	35.5	4.7	8.8	39.9
2018	11.2	36.4	4.6	8.7	39.1

Source: Financial Statistics Information System of the Financial Supervisory Service (http://www.fss.or.kr/fss/eng/main.jsp).

Notes: Assets are the sum of banking and trust accounts. "Others" include local banks and five specialized banks.

Table 5.3. Market Shares in Loans and Deposits among Banks (percent)

	Woori		Foreign-invested		Foreign-controlled		Foreign branches		Others	
	Loans	Deposits	Loans	Deposits	Loans	Deposits	Loans	Deposits	Loans	Deposits
2001	9.2	10.6	41.7	46.1	11.7	13.6	3.3	2.2	34.1	27.5
2006	11.3	12.2	38.6	40.8	13.7	15.9	2.2	1.2	34.2	29.9
2011	12.8	14.9	35.6	41.1	10.8	14.1	3.7	1.0	37.1	28.8
2016	12.7	14.8	37.2	44.9	3.6	4.5	4.2	2.7	42.2	33.0
2017	12.5	14.6	36.6	44.7	3.4	4.2	4.6	2.9	42.8	33.5
2018	12.6	14.9	39.7	46.7	3.2	4.1	1.7	2.3	44.0	33.8

Source: Financial Statistics Information System of the Financial Supervisory Service (http://www.fss.or .kr/fss/eng/main.jsp).

Notes: Loans and deposits are the sum of banking and trust accounts. "Others" include local banks and five specialized banks.

Composition of Assets, Liabilities, and Revenues

ASSET MANAGEMENT

Foreign-controlled banks appear to have maintained relatively high rates of loan-loss provision—the money a bank sets aside to cover potential losses on loans—compared to other banks. This difference explains their relatively smaller share of loans and discounts. By 2018, the share of loans and discounts at these banks had dived to 56.2 percent from a high of 66.8 a decade earlier, while similar ratios for foreign-invested banks and Woori were well over 70 percent on average throughout the period (Table 5.4).

The share of securities held by foreign-controlled banks was similar to those of other banks. However, foreign-controlled banks' assets in other categories, most of which consist of foreign-currency deposits at other banks, amounted on average to 19 percent of total assets. This share was twice as large as that of the foreign-invested bank group.

Without a retail banking network, foreign bank branches need to specialize in wholesale banking, foreign exchange, and derivatives. Like the three foreign-controlled commercial banks, they have continued to add a variety of local securities to their asset portfolios. What is so striking is that the assets classified as "others" accounted for an average 50 percent of their total assets in the 2010s, showing their heavy involvement in dealing in foreign currency.

Table 5.4. Composition of Assets (percent)

	Woori			Foreign-invested			Foreign-controlled			Foreign branches		
	A	B	C	A	B	C	A	B	C	A	B	C
2001	62.2	24.4	13.4	62.1	25.6	12.3	58.4	26.3	15.3	29.4	22.6	48.0
2005	70.0	18.6	11.4	71.4	17.3	11.3	63.5	23.7	12.8	17.8	29.8	52.4
2010	72.9	14.5	12.6	74.7	16.0	9.3	61.3	21.0	17.7	24.5	26.4	49.1
2015	77.0	12.1	10.9	75.1	14.1	10.8	55.8	19.8	24.4	27.1	16.5	56.4
2017	79.3	12.1	8.6	73.7	16.0	10.3	59.9	18.9	21.2	33.2	18.1	48.7
2018	76.0	14.5	9.5	75.1	15.6	9.3	56.2	20.9	22.9	36.4	18.1	45.5

Source: Financial Statistics Information System of the Financial Supervisory Service (http://www.fss.or.kr/fss/eng/main.jsp). Data on foreign branches are from Bank Management Statistics before 2007 and from the Financial Statistics Information System after 2008.

Notes: The table shows loans and discounts of banking accounts (A), securities (B), and other assets (C). The numbers for foreign-invested banks, foreign-controlled banks, and foreign branches are their averages.

LIABILITY MANAGEMENT

On the liability side, all three groups of banks relied heavily on deposits as a source of funding for their loans and investments. However, reflecting their limited branch network, foreign-controlled banks secured about 30 percent of their total funding from other sources in 2018 (Table 5.5).

What is surprising is that despite the relative decline in the size of the deposit market, none of the banks took advantage of the growing wholesale funding markets. Their dependence on deposits has increased.

As expected, foreign bank branches secured practically all of their funding from borrowing and other sources. The share of deposits in both local and foreign currencies was less than 10 percent before 2013. The bulk of their funding came from borrowing from wholesale funding markets abroad and their headquarters. As most of their liabilities are short-term, their assets consist mostly of short-term foreign currency loans and securities such as Bank of Korea monetary stabilization bonds.

Most foreign banks with branches in Korea are large global banks active in international finance. For this reason, their Korean branches have served as channels through which the majority of foreign capital flows in and out of Korea. During the two crisis periods (1997 and 2008), they withdrew large amounts of foreign-currency lending and unloaded their

Table 5.5. Composition of Liabilities (percent)

	Woori			Foreign-invested			Foreign-controlled			Foreign branches		
	A	B	C	A	B	C	A	B	C	A	B	C
2001	71.3	16.9	11.8	69.7	16.9	13.4	66.1	20.2	13.7	20.9	22.8	56.3
2005	64.5	20.9	14.6	64.1	21.9	14.0	63.7	21.4	15.0	8.5	29.4	62.1
2010	68.3	19.2	12.5	68.7	17.2	14.1	65.3	13.4	21.3	5.7	15.3	79.0
2017	75.6	12.0	12.4	73.9	11.7	14.4	63.2	5.9	30.9	12.0	11.2	76.8
2018	74.8	11.3	13.9	74.0	12.5	13.5	62.4	8.1	29.5	13.9	11.6	74.5

Source: Financial Statistics Information System of the Financial Supervisory Service (http://www.fss.or.kr/fss/eng/main.jsp). Data on foreign branches are from Bank Management Statistics before 2007 and from the Financial Statistics Information System after 2008.

Notes: The table shows deposits of banking accounts (A), borrowings (B), and others (C). The numbers for foreign-invested banks, foreign-controlled banks, and foreign branches are their averages.

investments in local securities, which aggravated the liquidity crisis. It is estimated that much of the $60 billion loss in foreign exchange reserves in 2008 was a result of the withdrawal of foreign currency funds by foreign bank branches. Since they account for anywhere from 30 percent to 40 percent of the volume of daily foreign currency transactions in Korea, they were singled out as having been mostly responsible for the high degree of volatility in capital flow. This assessment prompted the limiting of foreign currency forward exposure to 250 percent of their capital.

RETURNS AND PROFITABILITY

As a group, foreign-controlled banks were unable to maintain market shares in both the deposit and loan markets. This decline may have affected their profitability and soundness. Estimates of ROAs and ROEs are used to measure bank profitability. The ratios for nonperforming loans (NPLs) and liquidity, as well as the Bank of International Settlements (BIS) capital requirement, are used to assess safety and soundness.

ROAs and ROEs (Table 5.6) have been unstable and display a rather wide range of fluctuations in all three banking groups. Before the 2008 liquidity crisis, both ROAs and ROEs were lower for the foreign-controlled bank group. Thereafter, excluding the crisis years of 2008 and 2009, changes in both ROAs and ROEs among all banks and foreign bank branches did not diverge and remained within similar ranges.

Table 5.6. Profitability Indicators (percent)

	Woori		Foreign-invested		Foreign-controlled		Foreign branches	
	ROA	*ROE*	*ROA*	*ROE*	*ROA*	*ROE*	*ROA*	*ROE*
2001–5	1.32	23.84	0.6	10.9	0.6	11.3	0.54	8.84
2006–10	0.62	9.56	0.72	10.82	0.74	10.74	0.76	15.6
2011–15	0.34	4.6	0.5	6.68	0.36	4.18	0.54	7.34
2016	0.4	5.4	0.5	6.1	0.4	4.1	−0.0	4.0
2017	0.4	6.5	0.6	8.4	0.5	4.8	0.3	4.4
2018	0.6	8.8	0.6	8.7	0.5	4.7	0.3	5.1

Source: Financial Statistics Information System of the Financial Supervisory Service (http://www.fss.or.kr/fss/eng/main.jsp). Data on foreign branches are from Bank Management Statistics before 2007 and from the Financial Statistics Information System after 2008.

Notes: The numbers for foreign-invested banks, foreign-controlled banks, and foreign branches are their averages.

Table 5.7. Soundness Indicators

	Woori			Foreign-invested			Foreign-controlled			Foreign branches		
	A	*B*	*C*	*A*	*B*	*C*	*A*	*B*	*C*	*A*	*B*	*C*
2001–5	2.0	11.6	115.7	2.3	10.8	111.3	2.5	11.6	112.6	0.8	18.6	—[a]
2006–10	1.5	12.8	117.3	1.1	13.5	112.9	1.0	13.3	119.2	0.7	14.5	—[a]
2011–15	2.0	14.4	119.7	1.2	14.9	116.9	1.2	15.7	121.7	0.5	19.6	—[a]
2016	1.0	15.3	109.6	0.7	16.0	101.0	0.7	16.9	114.2	1.0	20.2	—[a]
2017	0.8	15.4	101.2	0.6	15.9	97.8	0.6	17.4	109.5	1.2	—[a]	—[a]

Source: Financial Statistics Information System of the Financial Supervisory Service (http://www.fss.or.kr/fss/eng/main.jsp). Data on foreign branches are from Bank Management Statistics before 2007 and from the Financial Statistics Information System after 2008.

Notes: The table shows NPL ratio (A), BIS ratio (B), and liquidity ratio (C). The numbers for foreign-invested banks, foreign-controlled banks, and foreign branches are their averages.

[a] Not available.

As far as soundness (Table 5.7) and stability indicators are concerned, there was virtually no difference among the three groups. Finally, there was no evidence that foreign entry has had any positive impact on improving corporate governance in the banking industry. At the foreign-controlled banks, outside board directors do not have an independent voice, and the boards of directors are completely controlled by the major stockholders. It should be noted that foreign financial investors came to Korea in search of higher returns and foreign financial institutions, not as crusaders for financial reform and development.

Most of the performance indicators show that the three foreign-controlled banks have not done well since their inception in terms of returns and profitability. Citibank Korea and SC Korea have posted losses or seen a sharp decrease in earnings, prompting them to downsize their operations. Before being acquired by foreign investors, all three local banks—Jaeil, KEB, and Hanmi—had suffered heavy losses and piled up large amounts of NPLs during the 1997 crisis that caused many of their corporate customers to fold. Since they were too big to fail, the Korean government decided to remove a substantial portion of the bad loans from their balance sheets, terminate their management, and put them on the market. Given the ownership imitations, however, the government was unable to find qualified domestic buyers capable of restoring the banks' soundness. It had to search for foreign buyers in the expectation that they would be able to turn the banks around.

Absence of a Long-Term Development Strategy

When foreigners bought the ailing domestic banks, it was unclear whether they had a long-term strategy for establishing a foothold in Korea's banking market. For the three foreign-controlled banks, rebuilding the corporate customer base, much of which had been damaged during the 1997 crisis, was costly and time-consuming. This was especially true in a market characterized by relationship banking. In view of this limitation, it is not surprising that they chose an asset management strategy of drawing the bulk of their income and profits from consumer lending and investments in bonds, equities, and derivative instruments rather than corporate lending. This has been even more the case since the 2008 liquidity crisis.

Lone Star's main objective for acquiring KEB in 2003 was to improve the bank's income statement and balance sheet as soon as possible to sell it for a profit rather than to nurture it into a competitive bank. Two years after the acquisition, Lone Star put the bank on the market. In 2006, it reached a deal to sell its stake to KB Kookmin Bank for more than $7 billion. However, a probe into the circumstances under which Lone Star bought KEB derailed the transaction. Lone Star had to wait until 2012 to find another buyer, and then it received substantially less money. During this period of uncertainty, the bank had to maintain its status quo, losing shares in both the deposit and loan markets.

Concentration in Retail Banking

It was expected that the foreign banks would engage in both domestic and international corporate banking, as they are presumed to have an advantage vis-à-vis their domestic rivals. But most large Korean firms use a domestic bank as their main bank, and there has been little room in this crowded market for foreign banks. Contrary to initial expectations, therefore, foreign banks shifted to retail banking. This strategy also has not been successful.

Foreign-controlled banks have had little interest in lending to SMEs because of the SMEs' relatively low credit ratings. Although all three banks were domestic banks, since they were acquired by foreign buyers they have not been able to expand their retail banking market base for two related reasons.

One is home bias. Local deposit customers appear to have a bias against foreign banks. All other things being equal, they prefer domestic banks. The other reason has been the downsizing of the foreign banks' branch networks to concentrate on expanding the customer base of high-income households in large cities. This strategy has not necessarily succeeded in attracting high-income customers, while losses have been seen elsewhere.

Regulations

There have been widespread complaints among foreign-controlled banks that regulatory controls have limited the scope of their operations. They claim that regulations on asset and liability management, which do not exist in their home markets, have prevented them from introducing many sophisticated financial products such as derivatives, other structured products, and services in which they have a competitive advantage over domestic banks.

The pressure from regulators to keep fees and interest rate margins at levels below what the banks consider appropriate has also been a source of grievances. So has regulatory intervention, including the pressure to restrict dividend payments, requests for the reduction of fees and interest rates, and requirements that the banks process data in Korea instead of at their regional headquarters. The banks claim that these excessively stringent regulations and supervision have deterred the expansion of foreign-controlled banks and undermined their financial development.[6]

6. "Korea remains our most difficult market," a UK-based bank told investors in August as it announced a $1 billion writedown on its subsidiary in the country, complaining of "multiple policy and regulatory interventions" that had exacerbated the effect of a slowing economy. Lone Star, the U.S. private equity group that bought KEB in 2003, wrote a scathing letter to former president Lee Myung-bak in 2012, alleging "arbitrary and discriminatory conduct" by regulators who repeatedly blocked its efforts to sell KEB—which it finally offloaded to Hana Financial Group in February 2012 (Mundy 2013).

CHAPTER 6

Effects of Financial Liberalization on the Growth and Efficiency of the Financial Sector

Growth of the Financial System

During Korea's liberal reform of its financial system in the aftermath of the 1997 crisis, advocates argued that liberalization would spur growth and improve the system's efficiency and stability. This was because reform would intensify competition, expand the menu of financial assets, and diversify institutions. In turn, these changes would improve both the productivity of the real economy and the ability of firms and households to manage the risks in their asset portfolios. The objective of this chapter is to examine empirically the extent to which the reform has contributed to promoting growth and improving the efficiency of the financial sector.

An in-depth analysis of the causal nexus between financial reform and the growth of the financial sector needs to construct a quantitative measure of the degree of reform for financial liberalization. The reform is a complex process that involves many facets of privatization; the decontrol of entry, financial prices, and asset and liability management; and the opening of financial markets and intermediation industries. Given this complexity, it is not surprising that there are few comprehensive measures or indicators for gauging the degree of overall financial liberalization.

As a proxy variable, this study uses the capital account liberalization indexes developed by Menzie Chinn and Hiro Ito (2006) and Soyoung

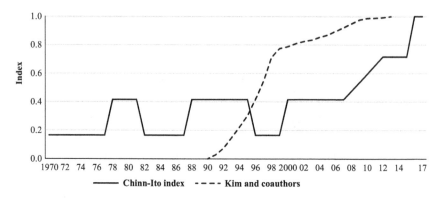

Figure 6.1. Capital Account Liberalization Indexes of Chinn and Ito and Kim and coauthors
Sources: Chinn and Ito (2006) and Soyoung Kim et al. (2014).

Kim and coauthors (2014), as shown in Figure 6.1. Korea did not pursue a "big bang" approach, which would have required the government to implement all reform measures immediately and simultaneously. Instead, the reform was selective and spaced out over time. The indexes of Chinn and Ito (CI) and Soyoung Kim and coauthors fit the gradual pattern of liberalization.

Although they do not cover the degree of domestic financial market deregulation, the indexes probably reflect the overall degree of financial liberalization. This is because throughout the period under consideration, Korea's policy makers have carried out reform in a sequential manner. Specifically, the deregulation of domestic financial industries and markets has always preceded the liberalization of capital account transactions.

To provide an empirical examination of the effects of financial liberalization on the growth of the financial sector, this chapter postulates that financial growth is positively related to the CI index and foreign investments in the Korean stock market.

The model specified below in equation 6.1 also introduces several interaction terms between the CI index, foreign equity investment, and a dummy variable D (equal to 1 for the years after 1997), as well as a set of control variables. It is estimated with time-series data for 1969–2015 in terms of the fully modified ordinary least square (FMOLS) method to address both the problems of nonstationary regressors and simultaneity bias.

For the measures of financial growth (the dependent variable), three ratios are used: of total finance to GDP (FAY), indirect finance to GDP (IDFY), and direct finance to GDP (DFY). These three alternative specifications of the dependent variable may help determine whether financial liberalization has expanded the market share of the money and capital markets at the expense of the bank intermediation.

In our estimation of equation 6.1, the dependent variables are the trend components of the three financial growth indicators from which cyclical components of credit and asset price movements are removed by the Hodrick-Prescott filter.

$$lnFAY_t = \beta_0 + \beta_1 CI_{t-1} + \beta_2 Fstock_{t-1} + \beta_3 CI_{t-1}{}^*Fstock_{t-1} + \beta_4 CI_{t-1}{}^*D_t$$
$$+ \beta_5 Fstock_{t-1}{}^*D_t + \beta_6 CI_{t-1}{}^*Fstock_{t-1}{}^*D_t + \beta_c Control_{t-1} + e_t \qquad 6.1$$

Where lnFAY: log of FAY,
  CI: Chinn-Ito index (minimum: 0, maximum: 1),
  Fstock: Foreign share of stock market capitalization, and
  D: Dummy variable for the period after the 1997 financial crisis.
Control variables include:
  lnexport (log of the ratio of global exports to GDP),
  lnsave (log of the ratio of savings to GDP),
  Infl (inflation rate), and
  lngov (log of the ratio of government spending to GDP)

The interaction term (CI*Fstock) captures the effect of change in the CI index on foreigners' investment in the domestic stock market. The slope dummy (CI*D) is introduced to gauge the extent to which the 1997 crisis and subsequent financial reform have changed the behavior of financial institutions and markets in adjusting to the emergence of a liberal financial regime. To capture similar developments related to financial liberalization, Fstock*D and CI*Fstock*D are also included in the equation.

The estimation results reported in Table 6.1 are consistent with the theory and provide some evidence of a positive causal relationship between financial growth (FAY) and a proxy for financial liberalization (CI), because the combined coefficient of CI and CI*D is positive. The positive sign of the combined coefficient for DFY also shows that the liberalization of capital account transactions has been the main driving force behind total and direct financial growth but has had hardly any effect on indirect financial growth.

Table 6.1. Estimation Results of Equation 6.1

Y	FMOLS (Y)			FMOLS (lnY)		
	FAY	IDFY	DFY	FAY	IDFY	DFY
C	3.223***	1.952***	1.271**	1.533**	1.450***	−0.343
	(2.916)	(6.284)	(1.552)	(2.176)	(4.122)	(0.227)
CI	0.549	0.076	0.473	0.187	0.073	−0.025
	(0.913)	(0.450)	(1.062)	(0.488)	(0.379)	(0.030)
Fstock	3.727	0.636	3.091	1.650	0.518	1.491
	(1.062)	(0.646)	(1.189)	(0.738)	(0.464)	(0.311)
CI*Fstock	2.714	2.578	0.136	0.665	1.300	3.392
	(0.263)	(0.888)	(0.018)	(0.101)	(0.395)	(0.240)
CI*D	3.420***	0.931***	2.489***	1.369**	0.532*	2.201
	(3.388)	(3.283)	(3.327)	(2.128)	(1.656)	(1.593)
Fstock*D	−1.847	−0.689	−1.157	−0.637	−0.617	0.202
	(0.612)	(0.813)	(0.518)	(0.332)	(0.643)	(0.049)
CI*Fstock*D	−10.757	−4.321	−6.436	−4.025	−2.387	−7.628
	(1.148)	(1.641)	(0.926)	(0.673)	(0.800)	(0.595)
Lnexport	−0.618	−0.246*	−0.371	−0.689**	−0.346**	−1.132*
	(1.333)	(1.893)	(1.081)	(2.335)	(2.350)	(1.787)
Infla	−1.737**	−0.588**	−1.149*	−0.938*	−0.677**	1.196
	(2.008)	(2.419)	(1.792)	(1.702)	(2.460)	(1.010)
Lngov	1.025*	0.525***	0.500	0.597*	0.689***	0.097
	(1.922)	(3.052)	(1.265)	(1.756)	(4.060)	(0.133)
Lnsave	0.276***	0.151***	0.125*	0.419***	0.283***	0.787***
	(2.916)	(5.869)	(1.843)	(7.186)	(9.707)	(6.280)
Johansen test	Trace: 10	Trace: 10	Trace: 10	Trace: 10	Trace: 10	Trace: 9
	Max-Eig: 6	Max-Eig: 5	Max-Eig: 5	Max-Eig: 6	Max-Eig: 6	Max-Eig: 6

Notes: There were forty-four observations in the sample period (1972–2015). The numbers in parentheses are *t*-values. The result of the Johansen test is the selected number of cointegrating relations. Max-Eig is a maximum eigen value. The acronyms are explained in the text. *$p < 0.10$ **$p < 0.05$ ***$p < 0.01$.

To be more specific, the evidence supports the view that financial market opening has been a primary factor in the creation of profitable opportunities for foreign investors to increase their holdings of Korean securities, which has resulted in large capital inflows that have propelled the rapid growth of the capital market and overall financial sector.

Efficiency of the Financial System

One of the most widely expected benefits of financial liberalization was that it would heighten competition, and that in turn would drive financial markets and institutions to upgrade their operational efficiency. To verify the realization of these benefits, this section of the chapter examines the trends of some of the efficiency indicators before testing empirically whether the available data show that initial expectations were realized.

In contrast to the large increase in FAY (the ratio of total finance to GDP), the value-added share of the financial sector, including insurance, in the nominal GDP grew steadily from about 4.5 percent in the early 1990s to reach a period high of 6.4 percent in 2002. Since then, it has tapered off to below 5.5 percent (Figure 6.2).

The share of 5.5 percent in 2019 in Korea, which was below the average of 5.9 percent in countries in the Organization for Economic Cooperation and Development (OECD), was much higher than that in Germany (4.0 percent) or France (4.0 percent) and similar to that of Italy (5.3 percent), but it was still lower than shares in the United Kingdom and United States (both 7.0 percent (see the 2017 OECD database).[1]

The financial sector's share in total employment was over 5 percent in the early 1990s. In the wake of the 1997 crisis, its share declined, dropping to 3.2 percent in 2018.

Due mostly to the contraction of the employment share, labor productivity in the financial sector (measured in terms of nominal value added per person) has grown rapidly. By 2018, productivity had risen to nearly 146 million won ($134,958 at the 2018 exchange rate) per person,

---

1. Stephen Cecchetti and Enisse Kharroubi (2012) find that when the financial sector represents more than 3.5 percent of total employment or 8.4 percent of total value added, further increases in financial-sector size tend to be detrimental to economic growth. Judging by cost and labor productivity, it appears that Korea's financial sector has become more efficient, with more room to develop and support Korea's potential growth by providing adequate financial services.

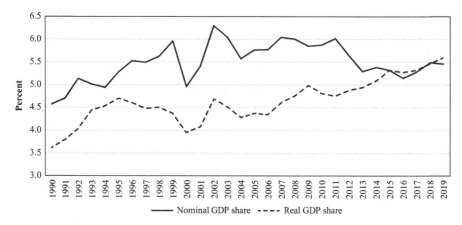

Figure 6.2. Shares of the Financial Sector in Nominal and Real GDP
Source: Economic Statistics System of the Bank of Korea.

which was more than six times that in the early 1990s, but about half of the Japanese and a quarter of the U.S. levels (Figure 6.3).

Ratna Sahay and coauthors (2015) report the estimates of efficiency indexes for Korea's financial institutions and markets in 1980–2013. As shown in Figure 6.4, Korea's financial markets did not achieve any efficiency improvements after the 1997 crisis. During the whole sample period, financial institutions did realize some degree of efficiency enhancement, but the increase was insufficient to support or disregard the efficiency hypothesis.

Thomas Philippon (2015) measures the unit cost of financial intermediation as the ratio of the income (value added) of the financial sector to the quantity of intermediated assets. Changes in the unit cost in terms of stocks of intermediated assets from 1982 to 2019 are shown in Figure 6.5. The cost had been rising until 1989. Since then, it has been declining, dropping to 1.3 percent in 2019. Compared to other countries, it appears that the cost of financial intermediation has not been excessive in Korea.[2]

Measures of the efficiency of the financial sector portrayed in Figures 6.2 through 6.5 do not provide any indication as to whether financial reform has created incentives for improving the operational efficiency of financial institutions and markets. A more rigorous investigation

---

2. For example, when measured as a share of the stock of intermediated assets, the unit cost of financial intermediation has been fluctuating between 1.3 percent and 2.3 percent since 1880 in the United States.

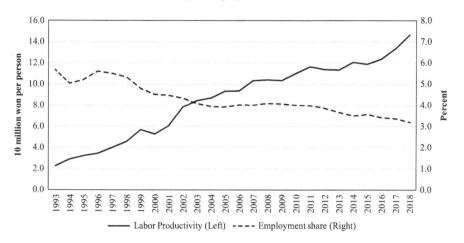

Figure 6.3. Share in Total Employment and Labor Productivity of the Financial Sector
Source: Economic Statistics System of the Bank of Korea.
Note: Labor productivity is the value-added per worker (10 million won per person).

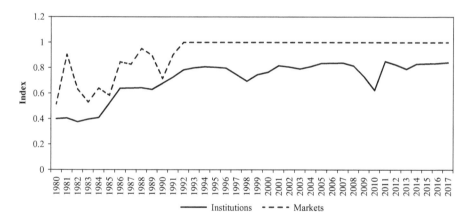

Figure 6.4. Efficiency Indexes of Financial Institutions and Markets
Source: Sahay et al. (2015).
Notes: Each indicator is normalized between 0 and 1, using a procedure that involves a global minimum (5 percent) and maximum (95 percent). The index for banking institutions is the weighted average of a normalizing score of six indicators: net interest margin, the spread between lending and deposits, ratio of noninterest income to total income, ratio of overhead costs to total assets, return on assets, and return on equity. The index for financial institutions is a normalizing score of the stock market turnover ratio.

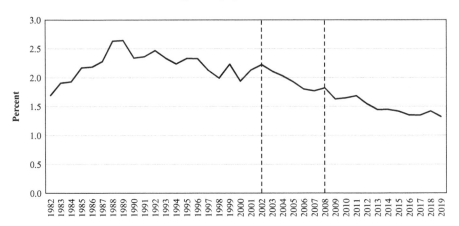

Figure 6.5. Unit Cost of Intermediation

Source: Economic Statistics System of the Bank of Korea.

Note: The unit cost of intermediation is defined as the ratio of GDP of the financial sector to intermediated assets (see Philippon 2015). Intermediated assets include (1) M2 (broad money) for liquidity services; (2) lending to nonfinancial corporations and households by financial corporation's net of their intra-lending; (3) securities other than shares (that is, mostly bonds) net of holdings by nonfinancial corporations; and (4) shares and other equities net of holdings by nonfinancial corporations. There have been a series of changes in the System of National Accounts (SNA): 1968 SNA (1982–2001), 1993 SNA (2002–2007), and 2008 SNA (2008–2019).

requires an empirical test of the causal effects of financial reform on efficiency.

To this end, we estimated equation 6.2. It replaces the dependent variable in equation 6.1 with a three-year moving average of annual total factor productivity (TFP) for the financial sector and introduces a different set of control variables. Because it has a unit root, the FMOLS method was used for the estimation.

$$lnFinTFP_t = \beta_0 + \beta_1 CI_{t-1} + \beta_2 Fstock_{t-1} + \beta_3 CI_{t-1}{}^*Fstock_{t-1}$$
$$+ \beta_4 CI_{t-1}{}^*D_t + \beta_5 Fstock_{t-1}{}^*D_t + \beta_6 CI_{t-1}{}^*Fstock_{t-1}{}^*D_t$$
$$+ \beta_c Control_{t-1} + e_t \qquad\qquad 6.2$$

Where lnFinTFP: A log of financial sector TFP Index (2010 = 100), which is calculated by the growth rate of financial sector TFP, using data from the Korea Productivity Center,

    CI: Chinn-Ito index (minimum: 0, maximum: 1),

    Fstock: Foreigner's share in the Korean stock market, and

    D: Dummy variable for the period after the 1997 financial crisis.

Control variables include:

lntrade (log of the ratio of global exports and imports to GDP),

lndrf (log of the ratio of direct to total finance),

lnatm (log of the number of ATM machines),

lnbanker5 (log of CR5 of the banking industry),

lnfininy (log of the ratio of invest to GDP for the financial and real estate industries), and

lnucost (log of the unit cost of financial services)

The estimation results presented in Table 6.2 do not provide any evidence on whether financial liberalization had positive effects.

The sum of the coefficients of the CI index and its interaction term with the period dummy D (1 for the years after 1997) is not statistically significant: there is no reliable evidence that financial reform improved the efficiency of the financial system. This result is consistent with the changes in the indexes of efficiency of financial institutions and markets based on Sahay and coauthors (2015) in Figure 6.4.

Given the limitations of a time series analysis with only forty-two observations, the results of the empirical examinations brought together in Tables 6.1 and 6.2 are by no means conclusive. However, they are indicative of the development in which the market-oriented reform launched in the wake of the 1997 financial crisis succeeded in nurturing rapid growth in the financial sector but failed to improve its efficiency.

Table 6.2. Estimation Results of Equation 6.2

Variables	FMOLS			
	A	B	C	D
C	4.938***	4.943***	4.926***	4.912***
	(30.120)	(31.726)	(30.492)	(30.500)
CI	0.174	0.175	0.158	0.240
	(1.334)	(1.474)	(1.262)	(1.555)
Fstock	−0.978***	−0.978***	−0.979***	−0.278
	(3.376)	(4.114)	(3.991)	(0.334)
CI*Fstock	0.978	0.760	1.011	−0.978
	(1.434)	(1.015)	(0.797)	(0.130)
CI*D		0.072	0.132	0.130
		(0.445)	(0.504)	(0.502)
Fstock*D			−0.358	−0.618
			(0.235)	(0.884)
CI*Fstock*D				1.428
				(0.577)
Lntrade	0.425***	0.430***	0.425***	0.413***
	(5.662)	(5.871)	(5.430)	(5.211)
Lndrf	0.444***	0.444***	0.447***	0.442***
	(10.302)	(11.165)	(10.519)	(10.406)
Lnatm	0.008	0.008	0.007	0.006
	(1.584)	(1.740)	(1.660)	(1.371)
Lnbankcr5	0.088	0.074	0.084	0.066
	(1.177)	(1.085)	(1.028)	(0.794)
Lnfininv	0.006	0.008	0.007	0.003
	(0.372)	(0.491)	(0.478)	(0.176)
Lnucost	0.124**	0.124**	0.132**	0.117*
	(2.080)	(2.247)	(2.296)	(1.982)
Johansen test	Trace: 7	Trace: 8	Trace: 9	Trace: 10
	Max-Eig: 6	Max-Eig: 6	Max-Eig: 8	Max-Eig: 8

Notes: There were forty-two observations in the sample period (1972–2013). The numbers in parentheses are *t*-values. The result of the Johansen test is the selected number of cointegrating relations. Max-Eig is a maximum eigen value. The acronyms are explained in the text. *$p<0.10$ **$p<0.05$ ***$p<0.01$.

CHAPTER 7

Financial Development and the Growth and Stability of the Industrial Sector

Review of Recent Literature

The pace of financial deepening since the mid-1970s has been remarkable in a way that has exceeded expectations (chapter 1). Yet the trends in the growth rates of both per capita real GDP and productivity have continued to decline (Figure 7.1). These contrasting developments (analyzed more extensively in chapter 8) cast doubt on whether the causal connection goes from financial deepening to economic growth in the context of the Korean economy. So do the different movements indicate that financial development has no significant bearing on economic growth? Or could any deepening after an optimal level is reached hold back growth and productivity improvements? The rest of this chapter is devoted to analyzing issues related to the role of finance in economic development.

This chapter attempts to determine how significant the positive effects of the rapid expansion of the financial system on growth and stability have been and whether they have come from the quantitative deepening itself or the enhanced qualitative efficiency of the system. Our conclusions are broadly negative. It appears that financial growth and diversification have delivered less than promised.

Many recent studies, both theoretical and empirical, have established that a causal link runs from finance to growth. The link is built on the functions of the financial system, including reducing the cost of acquiring

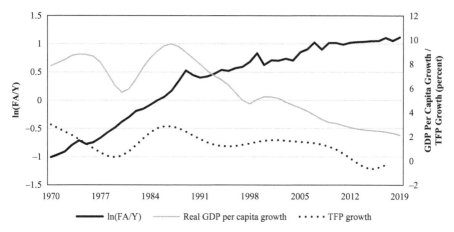

Figure 7.1. Financial and GDP Growth
Sources: Economic Statistics System of the Bank of Korea and Penn World Table.
Notes:. The Hodrick-Prescott filter is used to extract the trend components of per capita income and TFP growth.

information, monitoring corporate investments and governance, managing risk, converting pooled savings into long-term funds, and enforcing contracts and easing the exchange of goods and services (Levine 2005). By providing these services, the financial system can influence saving rates, investment decisions, technological innovation, and hence the allocation of resources across space and time as well as long-run growth. A sequel to this argument is that by enhancing the effectiveness of these functions, financial deepening could exert positive effects on growth and allocative efficiency. Finance is not merely a by-product of economic development, as it can be an engine of economic growth.

However, economic expansion also increases the demand for a greater variety of financial instruments and intermediation services. This interface means that the causal nexus between finance and economic growth is likely to be bidirectional, with each reinforcing the other to increase the size of the financial system. In theory, therefore, financial development could follow rather passively, to meet the increase in the demand for financial intermediation. It could also be driven by supplying financial services and constructing a financial infrastructure ahead of the growth in demand. In reality, these two forces are likely to evolve at the same time and interact with each other.

Robert King and Ross Levine (1993) were the first to show the positive effects of financial deepening—measured by various financial indicators, including the ratio of private credit to GDP—on economic growth. Ross Levine and Sara Zervos (1998) also found evidence that stock market liquidity is a predictor of GDP growth, but the size of the stock market is not. More evidence on the existence of a causal relationship between finance and growth was presented by Ross Levine, Norman Loayza, and Thorsten Beck (2000) and Beck, Levine, and Loayza (2000). Raghuram Rajan and Luigi Zingales (1998) found evidence that industrial sectors that rely more on external finance for technological reasons grow relatively faster in countries with a larger financial sector.

Notwithstanding the strong evidence of the role of finance in fostering growth, a series of financial crises in Asia, Latin America, and Russia in the 1990s and the global financial crisis in 2008 have raised doubts about and subsequently provoked a reexamination of the robustness of the finance-growth nexus.

In fact, some of the more recent studies argue that as per capita incomes grow and financial systems mature, advanced and even some emerging economies may find that the favorable effects of financial growth can diminish and vanish over time. That is, beyond a certain stage of financial development, financial growth could undermine the efficiency and stability of the economy, yielding an inverse U shape. In short, there can be too much finance as the relationship between that and economic growth becomes nonlinear.

In a series of papers, Stephen Cecchetti and Enisse Kharroubi (2012), Jean Louis Arcand and coauthors (2015), and Ratna Sahay and coauthors (2015) report on the results of country panel studies that examined incidences of too much financial growth. They all present evidence that once financial depth exceeds an optimal level, additional deepening slows growth.

For example, the beneficial effect of financial deepening on economic growth begins to vanish when the ratio of private credit to GDP rises above 100 percent (Cecchetti and Kharroubi 2012) or 120 percent (Arcand et al. 2015). Cecchetti and Kharroubi also find that when the financial sector accounts for more than 3.5 percent of total employment or 8.4 percent of total value added, further increases in the size of the sector tend to be detrimental to growth.

What, then, are the potential causes of the nonlinearity? The empirical studies quoted above suggest that:

- In the early stages of economic development, financial deepening helps economies catch up to the productivity frontier, but in countries close to or at the frontier, it generates limited or no growth.
- Much of the growth effect of financial deepening comes through enterprise rather than household credit. In advanced economies, where a large share of credit is allocated to households, the consequential inefficiency of credit allocation is likely to slow growth.
- The financial system may extract excessively high informational rents and thus attract too much young talent to finance and away from more productive industries (Bolton et al. 2016; Philippon 2010). During periods of rapid financial growth (in part propelled by market liberalization) where labor productivity is relatively low, financial institutions are likely to hire skilled workers away from more productive sectors, thereby lowering the overall productivity of the economy.
- The transfer of skilled workers also brings down the cost of recovering loans and other claims in default. This cost reduction may allow banks and NBFIs to lend proportionally more than before to those less productive industries, thereby changing the composition of loans to cause a growth slowdown.
- Financial development, which has its sources in the rapid growth of trading in securities for institutions' own and customers' accounts and advisory services at banks and NBFIs, has no long-run effect on real sector outcomes.[1]
- Banks and NBFIs favor borrowers who can pledge physical collateral for their loans. Most of these borrowers are from industries such as construction, textiles, and iron and steel, which usually own assets that are relatively easy to pledge as collateral but have low research and development (R&D) and skill intensity. In contrast, many firms from R&D-intensive industries such as aircraft manufacturing and computing are also skill intensive and may often find that their access to credit is limited by the lack of collateral assets (Cecchetti and Kharroubi 2015).

Most of the empirical studies on the finance-growth nexus have been criticized for their use of crude indicators such as the ratio of private credit to GDP to measure for financial depth and intermediation, since these

---

1. A study based on a sample of seventy-seven countries in 1980–2007 found that intermediation activities increase growth and reduce volatility in the long run, whereas an expansion of the financial sector along other dimensions has no long-run effect on real-sector outcomes (Beck, Degryse, and Kneer 2014).

indicators may not capture the quality of financial arrangements. In fact, the ratio of private credit to GDP says nothing about financial-sector components beyond banks, the quality of financial services, the efficiency of the financial sector, or its stability.

Short-term variations in the ratio of private credit to GDP for a given country are thus unlikely to reflect changes in the efficiency and development of financial markets and institutions. More importantly, credit cycles are often related to asset price cycles, so rapid increases in the ratio might reflect credit bubbles rather than rapid improvements in the efficiency and development of financial systems (Beck, Carletti, and Goldstein, 2015).

Sahay and coauthors (2015) developed a more comprehensive index (known as the financial development index) by taking into account the World Bank's multidimensional indicators that cover (1) the size and liquidity of financial institutions and markets, (2) accessibility to financial services, (3) efficiency of financial institutions, and (4) the level of capital market activity.

In a panel study covering 170 countries over the 1980–2013 period, the authors found that the positive effect on economic growth begins to decline, while costs in terms of economic and financial volatility begin to rise, for those countries in a 95 percent confidence interval band around the turning point of the development index from 0.4 to 0.7. The authors also showed that high levels of financial development do not impede capital accumulation but do lead to a loss of efficiency of investment.

All of the studies on "too much finance" obtain their results of non-linearity between financial deepening and growth from panel studies that covered a large number of countries over periods from the early 1970s to the early 2000s. For their panel studies, they estimate variations of the equation below:

$$y_t = \beta_0 + x_{1,t}\,\beta_1 + x_{2,t}\,\beta_2 + x_{c,t}\,\beta_c + e_t \qquad\qquad 7.1$$

Where y : growth or real GDP per capita,

x_1: a measure of financial deepening such as the volume of private credit as a proportion of GDP,

x_2: x_1^2, a quadratic term of x_1, and

x_c: a set of control variables.

In this specification, initial per capita income is included to capture the effect of the convergence process, where economic growth is expected to slow with increases in per capita income. The negative sign of the quadratic term means that there is too much financial growth, which supports the argument that once financial depth exceeds an optimal level, additional financial deepening reduces rather than increases growth.

William Cline (2015) claims that the panel studies cited above are subject to an endogeneity problem that negates the validity of the "too much finance" argument. If there is a positive relationship between per capita income and financial depth, he argues that the specification of the per capita income term is inadequate to capture convergence fully and in part falsely attributes convergence to financial depth—thereby forcing a negative coefficient on the quadratic term. In their rebuttal, Arcand and coauthors (2016) argue that they had been careful about endogeneity between per capita income and financial growth and maintain that their results hold across a broad cross section of countries. The controversy has yet to be settled.

Effects of Financial Deepening on the Growth of Industrial Value Added: Industry-Level Panel Estimation for Five-Year Nonoverlapping Periods, 1991–2015

All of the panel studies on "too much finance" surveyed in the preceding section of this chapter show that by the middle of the 1990s, Korea had developed a mature financial sector.[2] Furthermore, the sector's depth surpassed the optimal level defined by a number of authors. This raises the question of whether the Korean data on financial depth measured by our study (the sum of indirect and direct finance as a proportion of GDP) would produce similar results.

More specifically, this section of the chapter investigates whether there was a threshold below which the positive effects of financial development on economic growth started to diminish. If such a threshold emerged in the 1990s, does that mean that Korea belongs to the group of advanced economies characterized by "too much finance"?

This chapter develops an empirical model based on the work of Arcand and coauthors (2015) and Cecchetti and Kharroubi (2012 and 2015) and uses the model to develop estimates with industry-level data. The model is then modified to account for the evidence presented by Rajan

---

2. This section draws on Jungsoo Park et al. 2018.

and Zingales (1998), which shows that industrial sectors that for technological reasons need more financial resources do better in countries with large domestic financial markets.

The specification of the model addresses the problem of bidirectional causality between finance and economic growth, because the growth of a specific industry will not affect financial depth as measured by the ratio of total finance to GDP.

This study estimates the model of panel regression specified in equation 7.2 below with a fixed-effects method using data on twenty-seven industrial sectors for the 1991–2015 period divided into nonoverlapping five-year subperiods (1991–95, 1996–2000, 2001–5, 2006–10, and 2011–15).

$$VAGR_{it} = \beta_0 + \beta_1 EF_i * FAY_{t-1} + \beta_2 EF_i * FAY_{t-1}^2 + \beta_3 FAY_{t-1}$$
$$+ \beta_4 ln(VAPCini)_{it} + \beta_c control_{it} + \mu_i + \delta_t + e_{it} \qquad 7.2$$

Where VAGR: real value-added growth in industry i,
   EF: Rajan-Zingales index for external finance dependence for industry i,
   FAY: ratio of total finance to GDP,
   $Ln(VAPCini)_{it}$: log of initial per capita real value added (which is included to capture growth convergence),
   μ_i : industry fixed effect,
   δ_t: a five-year time-dummy variable, and
   e_{it}: an error term.
Control variables for industry i include:
   PPI (Producer Price Index) for $Infla_{it}$ (a rate of inflation),
   $Ln(R\&D)_{it}$ (log of the ratio of R&D expenditure to total revenue),
   $LnEdu_{it}$ (log of an average training period of employees), and
   $FDIY_{it}$ (the ratio of FDI to value added).
External finance dependence (EF_i) is measured by the ratio of total borrowing and bonds issued to assets from the Bank of Korea's *Financial Statements Analysis*. Although endogeneity between VAGR and FAY is not an issue, FAY is lagged in the estimation to remove any unaccounted factors that might cause a reverse causality between the two variables.

This study uses the 1991–96 data for the estimation of a benchmark EF in equation 7.2. But since the 1997 financial crisis, there has been a substantial decline in the index. This change required us to divide the sample period into two subperiods (1991–96 and 2000–15) and the averages of the indexes for the two periods are used for a robustness check. The findings for the entire sample period in Table 7.1 show that the coefficients of Ln (VAPCini) are negative and statistically significant, which confirms the validity of the growth convergence hypothesis.

The hypothesis of nonlinearity between financial depth and industry growth implies that the coefficients of the interaction terms between EF and FAY (β_1) and EF and the square of FAY (β_2) are positive and negative, respectively.

Table 7.1 shows that the coefficient of EF*FAY in specification 1 is positive and statistically significant. In specifications 2–4 with different sets of independent and control variables for the 1991–2015 period and specifications 7–10 for the 2001–15 period, both β_1 and β_2 have correct signs but are statistically insignificant.

Table 7.2 reports the results of the estimation of the same equations in Table 7.1 with the 2000–2015 EF average for a robustness check. The results for the whole sample period are similar to those presented in Table 7.1. But β_1 and β_2 in estimations 7–10 for the 2001–15 subperiod have the wrong signs and are statistically insignificant. Overall, the results do not support the nonlinearity argument, as they do not provide any evidence on whether financial deepening measured by FAY contributed to the growth of the twenty-seven industries or whether the results imply that the financial system has become overgrown in Korea (too much finance).

Contrary to the findings of several other studies, our estimations provide little evidence of any causal relation going from financial deepening to growth at the industry level. What could be the causes of the insignificance? One possible cause is that two of the main channels—efficiency and investment growth—through which financial deepening could spur economic growth might not have been as powerful as they are often claimed to be.

To explore the avenue of efficiency improvement, which is expected to foster an increase in productivity at the industry level, we conducted a panel regression of equation 7.3, where the dependent variable of equation 7.2 is replaced by $TFPGR_{it}$, the rate of growth of TFP estimated by Korea Productivity Center. Equation 7.3 has the same independent and control variables and is estimated with a fixed-effects method.

$$TFPGR_{it} = \beta_0 + \beta_1 EF_i * FAY_{t-1} + \beta_2 EF_i * FAY_{t-1}^2 + \beta_3 \ln(VAPCini)_{it}$$
$$+ \beta_c control_{it} + \mu_i + \delta_t + e_{it} \qquad\qquad 7.3$$

Table 7.1. Financial Deepening and Industrial Growth: 1991–2015 with the 1991–96 Average of External Finance Dependence (EF)

	1991–2015					2001–15				
	1	2	3	4	5	6	7	8	9	10
EF*FAY	0.135***	0.219	0.216	0.264	0.011	0.082	1.734	1.228	1.354	1.451
	(3.246)	(0.376)	(0.333)	(0.414)	(0.017)	(1.429)	(0.841)	(0.489)	(0.545)	(0.571)
EF*FAY²		-0.017	-0.016	-0.027	0.029		-0.335	-0.228	-0.253	-0.272
		(-0.137)	(-0.113)	(-0.193)	(0.206)		(-0.819)	(-0.450)	(-0.505)	(-0.530)
Ln (VAPCini)	-0.046**	-0.046***	-0.046**	-0.046**	-0.049**	-0.041*	-0.042**	-0.038*	-0.034	-0.035
	(-2.680)	(-3.101)	(-2.732)	(-2.701)	(-2.721)	(-1.799)	(-2.163)	(-1.869)	(-1.585)	(-1.583)
Ln (R&D)		0.010*	0.010	0.010	0.011		0.005	0.006	0.007*	0.007*
		(1.778)	(1.646)	(1.593)	(1.593)		(1.507)	(1.700)	(1.932)	(1.971)
Ln (Edu)			-0.003	-0.006	-0.021			-0.093	-0.120	-0.105
			(-0.021)	(-0.033)	(-0.126)			(-0.591)	(-0.712)	(-0.601)
Infla				-0.077	-0.057				-0.091	-0.082
				(-0.766)	(-0.556)				(-0.959)	(-0.822)
FDIY					0.105*					0.046
					(1.812)					(1.067)
Constant	-0.122**	-0.117	-0.107	-0.124	0.063	-0.130	-1.194	-0.653	-0.668	-0.771
	(-2.650)	(-0.326)	(-0.161)	(-0.185)	(0.095)	(-1.466)	(-0.856)	(-0.343)	(-0.348)	(-0.391)
R squared	0.755	0.763	0.763	0.764	0.770	0.751	0.764	0.765	0.768	0.769

Notes: Columns 1–5 present the results of the estimation of equation 7.2 with an average EF for the full sample period and columns 6–10 for the 2001–15 subperiod. There were twenty-seven industries. There were 135 observations in the full sample period and 81 in the 2001–15 subperiod. The data are averages for each of the five-year subperiods. The numbers in parentheses are t-values. The 1991–96 EF average is used for the fixed-effects model estimation. Acronyms are explained in the text. *p < 0.10 **p < 0.05 ***p < 0.01.

Table 7.2. Financial Deepening and Industrial Growth: 1991–2015 with the 2000–15 Average of External Finance Dependence (EF)

	1991–2015					2001–15				
	1	*2*	*3*	*4*	*5*	*6*	*7*	*8*	*9*	*10*
EF*FAY	0.152	0.175	0.137	0.242	−0.050	0.103	−4.101	−4.102	−4.114	−4.180
	(1.544)	(0.231)	(0.174)	(0.325)	(−0.063)	(1.387)	(−1.252)	(−1.241)	(−1.230)	(−1.230)
EF*FAY²		−0.007	−0.005	−0.028	0.036		0.850	0.850	0.853	0.867
		(−0.045)	(−0.031)	(−0.180)	(0.217)		(1.297)	(1.286)	(1.272)	(1.271)
Ln (VAPCini)	−0.044**	−0.044***	−0.050***	−0.050***	−0.054***	−0.042	−0.044*	−0.044	−0.044	−0.044
	(−2.548)	(−2.795)	(−3.029)	(−2.995)	(−3.051)	(−1.648)	(−1.718)	(−1.665)	(−1.470)	(−1.485)
Ln (R&D)		0.007	0.005	0.006	0.006		0.004	0.004	0.004	0.004
		(1.121)	(0.777)	(0.782)	(0.766)		(1.161)	(1.108)	(1.048)	(1.028)
Ln (Edu)			0.218*	0.209*	0.217*			0.003	0.003	0.012
			(1.844)	(1.778)	(1.906)			(0.033)	(0.035)	(0.116)
Infla				−0.083	−0.065				0.003	0.009
				(−0.823)	(−0.645)				(0.024)	(0.080)
FDIY					0.106*					0.020
					(1.901)					(0.348)
Constant	−0.080	−0.043	−0.526	−0.540	−0.442	−0.110	1.752	1.746	1.749	1.755
	(−1.328)	(−0.141)	(−1.276)	(−1.312)	(−1.117)	(−1.437)	(1.207)	(1.132)	(1.129)	(1.121)
R squared	0.737	0.742	0.748	0.749	0.756	0.742	0.758	0.758	0.758	0.758

Notes: Columns 1–5 present the results of the estimation of equation 7.2 with an average EF for the full sample period and columns 6–10 for the 2001–15 subperiod. There were twenty-seven industries. There were 135 observations in the full sample period and 81 in the 2001–15 subperiod. The data are averages for each of the five-year subperiods. The numbers in parentheses are *t*-values. The 2000–15 EF average is used for the fixed-effects model estimation. Acronyms are explained in the text. *$p<$0.10 **$p<$0.05 ***$p<$0.01.

The estimation results of equation 7.3 with different sets of independent and control variables are presented in Table 7.3. In all specifications of the equation, both EF*FAY and EF*FAY^2 have the wrong signs or are statistically insignificant. Financial growth has done little to improve the productivity of the twenty-seven industries during either the entire period or the 2001–15 subperiod.

To gauge the effects of financial deepening on investment growth, equation 7.4 was estimated with real investment growth in the twenty-seven industries as the dependent variable, with the same independent and control variables as in equation 7.3.

$$INVGR_{it} = \beta_0 + \beta_1 EF_i * FAY_{t-1} + \beta_2 EF_i * FAY_{t-1}^2 + \beta_3 ln(VAPCini)_{it}$$
$$+ \beta_c control_{it} + \mu_i + \delta_t + e_{it} \qquad\qquad 7.4$$

The results of the estimation of equation 7.4 are reported in Table 7.4. In all specifications except the first, the signs of the coefficients of both EF*FAY and EF*FAY^2 (β_1 and β_2) were correct but statistically insignificant for the entire sample period. But in specifications 7 and 8 for the 2001–15 period, $\beta_1 > 0$, $\beta_2 < 0$, and both were statistically significant, which provides evidence to support the "too much finance" hypothesis. In view of the conflicting results, however, it would be reasonable to conclude that the estimation of equation 7.4 does not provide any credible evidence on whether financial growth has been instrumental in fostering the growth of investment in the twenty-seven industries.

In the short run, one possible cause of this insignificance may lie in a misalignment between the business and financial cycles. Jungyeoun Lee and Yang Su Park (2015) show that, in general from the first quarter of 1986 to the third quarter of 2014, the financial cycle did not align with the GDP cycle across different frequencies. This misalignment is a rather unusual phenomenon. The correlation between the two cycles was very low, at -0.0049. But during the period between the 1997 and 2008 financial crises, the financial cycle was highly correlated (0.3091) with the standard business cycle, though this correlation has waned since then.

These episodes suggest that except for the periods of severe financial distress, the two cycles evolve along different trajectories over time. This heterogeneity therefore presents another piece of evidence for the weaker role of financial growth in bolstering investment in the long run in Korea.

Table 7.3. Effects of Financial Growth on TFP: 1991–2015 with the 1991–2015 Average of External Finance Dependence (EF)

	1991–2015				2001–15			
	1	2	3	4	5	6	7	8
EF*FAY	0.613	0.566	0.645	0.748	-1.997	-2.111	-2.576	-2.578
	(0.566)	(0.502)	(0.583)	(0.671)	(-0.915)	(-0.980)	(-1.165)	(-1.155)
EF*FAY^2	-0.133	-0.123	-0.140	-0.163	0.400	0.425	0.522	0.523
	(-0.588)	(-0.520)	(-0.603)	(-0.694)	(0.908)	(0.974)	(1.164)	(1.155)
Ln (VAPC_ini)	-0.022***	-0.021***	-0.021***	-0.021***	-0.033**	-0.031**	-0.034**	-0.034**
	(-3.346)	(-3.231)	(-3.272)	(-3.397)	(-2.270)	(-2.080)	(-2.357)	(-2.329)
Ln (R&D)		-0.002	-0.002	-0.002		-0.003	-0.003*	-0.003*
		(-0.812)	(-0.687)	(-0.683)		(-1.287)	(-1.827)	(-1.783)
Infla			-0.054	-0.059			0.075	0.075
			(-0.879)	(-0.920)			(1.073)	(1.095)
FDIY				-0.024				0.002
				(-0.537)				(0.051)
Constant	-0.281	-0.273	-0.305	-0.352	1.063	1.099	1.324	1.325
	(-0.552)	(-0.523)	(-0.594)	(-0.679)	(0.938)	(0.994)	(1.168)	(1.158)
R squared	0.469	0.472	0.475	0.477	0.628	0.638	0.647	0.647

Notes: The numbers in parentheses are t-values. Acronyms are explained in the text. *p < 0.10 **p < 0.05 ***p < 0.01.

Table 7.4. Effects of Financial Growth on Investment Growth: 1991–2015 with the 1991–2015 Average of External Finance Dependence (EF)

	1991–2015				2001–15			
	1	2	3	4	5	6	7	8
EF*FAY	−0.471	4.738	6.359	6.782	6.667	6.653	11.928**	12.309**
	(−0.270)	(0.906)	(1.031)	(1.049)	(1.540)	(1.529)	(2.269)	(2.231)
EF*FAY^2	0.214	−0.928	−1.287	−1.381	−1.224	−1.217	−2.322**	−2.403**
	(0.578)	(−0.824)	(−0.969)	(−0.989)	(−1.452)	(−1.434)	(−2.234)	(−2.202)
Ln (VAPC_ini)	−0.039	0.007	0.010	0.010	0.000	0.000	0.031	0.030
	(−1.349)	(0.192)	(0.273)	(0.245)	(0.001)	(0.001)	(1.052)	(1.040)
FDIY		−1.294	−1.354	−1.356		0.071	−0.022	−0.016
		(−1.196)	(−1.216)	(−1.124)		(0.669)	(−0.251)	(−0.183)
Infla			−1.021	−1.074			−0.897***	−0.926***
			(−1.519)	(−1.537)			(−5.116)	(−4.685)
Ln (R&D)				0.016				0.005
				(0.739)				(0.387)
Constant	0.102	−2.299	−2.987	−3.082	−3.905	−3.913	−6.491**	−6.643**
	(0.125)	(−0.943)	(−1.047)	(−1.053)	(−1.635)	(−1.651)	(−2.310)	(−2.274)
R squared	0.429	0.518	0.532	0.535	0.637	0.638	0.716	0.718

Notes: The numbers in parentheses are t-values. Acronyms are explained in the text. *p < 0.10 **p < 0.05 ***p < 0.01.

Has the Transition from a Bank-Based to Market-Based Financial System Spurred Economic Growth?

Despite a long history of debates about the relative merits of bank- versus market-based financial systems in improving allocative efficiency and fostering growth, a consensus has yet to emerge. Many economists argue that a market-based system is more efficient in allocating capital than a bank-based system because as debt issuers, banks have an inherent bias toward nominally low-risk borrowers.

In particular, larger banks prefer to make loans to established firms rather than start-ups. They are also able to acquire inside information about the firms they lend to, which allows them to extract a large share of the firms' profits and thereby reduces firms' incentives to undertake profitable projects. For these reasons, the bank-based system hinders innovation and growth.

However, an equally large number of authors stress the advantages that banks have over markets.[3] Banks have a comparative advantage in reducing the market frictions associated with financing standardized, shorter-term, lower-risk, well-collateralized investment projects. Capital markets are relatively more effective in offering financing for more customer-specific, longer-run, higher-risk projects relying more on intangible inputs (Allen and Gale 1997, 1999). These contrasting views imply that the services provided by capital markets have an increasingly significant impact on economic activity as an economy grows and banking services become less important.

The issue of the relative efficiency of the two systems is essentially an empirical one. Asli Demirgüç-Kunt and coauthors (2013) find that as

---

3. A third group of authors argue that the bank- versus market-based debate is of only second-order importance. According to this view, the first-order issue is the ability of the financial system to reduce the costs of exchanging information and performing transactions, not whether banks or markets provide these services (Levine 1997). Furthermore, banks and markets might act as complements in providing financial services (Boyd and Smith, 1998; Huybens and Smith, 1999). In contrast, the law and finance view (La Porta et al., 2000) emphasizes the role of the legal system in determining the level of financial development. This view holds that distinguishing countries by the efficiency of the legal system in supporting financial transactions is more useful than distinguishing countries by financial structure. It argues that legal systems that protect outside investors by enforcing contracts effectively boost financial development and thereby facilitate external financing, new firm formation, and efficient capital allocation.

economies develop, the marginal increase in economic activity associated with an increase in the development of banks is reduced, while the marginal increase in economic activity related to an increase in the development of the securities market grows. In a cross-country examination, Levine (2002) shows that although the link between overall financial development and economic growth is robust, there is no clear evidence on the relative efficiency of bank-based or market-based systems. Additionally, Beck and Levine (2002) find no evidence for the validity of either the market-based or the bank-based hypothesis.

Beck and Levine (2002) suggest that although having an efficient legal system and overall financial development boost industry growth, for the creation of new firms and efficient capital allocation, having a bank- or market-based system does not matter much. In an endogenous growth model, neither system is unequivocally better for growth. Instead, the authors argue, growth depends more on the efficiency of financial and legal institutions.

From the early 1960s until the late 1990s, banks dominated Korea's financial system as the major source of external financing for both firms and households. The restructuring of the banking sector after the 1997 crisis set the stage for a marked decline in the share of indirect finance. By 2000, the share of money and capital markets in total finance had risen to 54.3 percent. Judging from raw data, Korea was no longer a bank-based or financial intermediary–based economy (see Table 1.1).

An interesting question is whether this transformation made any difference in the growth and efficiency of the economy—or, more specifically, whether the growth of money and capital markets has been more efficient in promoting the expansion of industries that depend heavily on direct finance.

To shed light on this question, this study investigates whether a relative increase in direct finance, measured by the share of money and capital markets in total finance, has been more efficient in boosting the growth of industries relying heavily on financial market financing in Korea. For this purpose, using annual data for twenty-three manufacturing industries over the 2008–17 period, we conducted a generalized least squares estimation of a panel model. (Because of changes in industrial classification, comparable data from before 2008 are unavailable.)

The period averages of the ratio of direct to total finance vary significantly across the twenty-three industries. The averages ranged from

73.4 percent for the sector for coke, refined petroleum, and nuclear fuel to 30.4 percent for the manufacture of fabricated metal products. This wide range is likely to help determine the existence of any causal relationship between growth and dependence on direct finance in the selected industries.

A reduced-form equation for the determination of the growth rate of the real value added of industry i ($vagr_{i,t}$) is specified as:

$$vagr_{i,t} = \beta_0 + \beta_1 \, direct_{r_{i,t}} + \beta_2 go_t + \beta_3 \, pop_t + \beta_4 \, cpi_t + \beta_5 \, dlogy_t + \beta_6 \, rnd_{i,t}$$
$$+ \beta_7 \, capital_{i,t} + f_t + \varepsilon_{i,t} \qquad\qquad 7.5$$

Where $\varepsilon_{i,t}$ is an error term.

The independent variables are:

direct_r (the share of direct finance),

rnd (research and development expenditure as a percent of sales revenue),

capital (tangible constructed assets as a percent of sales revenue),

go (global real GDP growth rate),

cpi (Consumer Price Index growth rate),

dlogy (per capita real GDP growth rate),

pop (population growth rate), and

f_t (year dummy variables).

Definitions of the variables are:

$$vagr_{i,t} = \frac{(Real\ value\ added_{i,t} - Real\ value\ added_{i,t-1})}{Real\ value\ added_{i,t-1}} * 100$$

$$direct\_r_{i,t} = \frac{Direct\ financing_{i,t}}{(Direct\ financing_{i,t} + Indirect\ financing_{i,t})} * 100$$

$$rnd_{i,t} = \frac{RD\ spending_{i,t}}{Sales\ revenues_{i,t}} * 100$$

$$capital_{i,t} = \frac{(Tangible\ assets_{i,t} - Tangible\ assets\ in\ construction_{i,t})}{Sales\ revenues_{i,t}} * 100$$

$$go_t = global\ real\ GDP\ growth\ rate_t$$

$$dlogy_t = \left(log(per\ capita\ real\ GDP_t) - log(per\ capita\ real\ GDP_{t-1})\right) * 100$$

$$cpi_t = \frac{(CPI_t - CPI_{t-1})}{CPI_{t-1}} * 100$$

Table 7.5. Results of a Generalized Least Squares Estimation

	(1)	(2)	(3)	(4)	(5)	(6)
direct_r	0.038	0.038	−0.097	0.016	0.027	−0.097
	(0.075)	(0.075)	(0.069)	(0.074)	(0.074)	(0.065)
go	4.332**	0.444	4.511	1.856***	1.629***	2.423
	(2.038)	(1.585)	(5.284)	(0.539)	(0.545)	(2.813)
pop	22.852*	6.787	2.158	2.250	3.106	9.583***
	(12.786)	(22.292)	(14.495)	(4.039)	(4.030)	(3.665)
cpi		−4.861	−7.037**		−1.527*	−4.268**
		(4.272)	(3.429)		(0.811)	(1.665)
dlogy	−0.588	0.190		0.048	0.066	
	(0.958)	(0.337)		(0.071)	(0.071)	
rnd	0.509	0.509		0.605	0.538	
	(0.672)	(0.672)		(0.675)	(0.677)	
capital	0.000	0.000		0.000	0.000	
	(0.000)	(0.000)		(0.000)	(0.000)	
dlogy(−1)			0.118			0.136**
			(0.184)			(0.064)
rnd(−1)			1.045			1.031
			(0.686)			(0.683)
capital(−1)			0.000			0.000
			(0.000)			(0.000)
constant	16.180	−6.214	−3.224	−7.245*	−5.379	−4.639
	(52.185)	(34.074)	(22.253)	(3.813)	(3.921)	(7.095)
year dummy	Yes	Yes	Yes	No	No	No
observations	203	203	178	203	203	178

Notes: Columns 1–6 present the results of the estimation of equation 7.5. The numbers in parentheses are standard errors. Acronyms are explained in the text. $*p<0.10$ $**p<0.05$ $***p<0.01$.

$$pop_t = \frac{\left(Population_t - Population_{t-1}\right)}{Population_{t-1}} * 100$$

Table 7.5 presents the results of the estimation. There is no evidence that the sustained increase in the share of direct finance improved the growth performance of the twenty-three manufacturing industries during the period under consideration. This finding is consistent with the findings of a number of the empirical studies cited above that there is no evidence of improved performance for either the market- or bank-based hypothesis. The results are broadly consistent with the view that it is more useful to distinguish economies by their overall financial development and efficiency of their legal system than by whether they are relatively bank- or market-based.

Financial Growth and Financial Stability

Financial stability defies a precise definition or measurement, given the complexity and interdependence of a large number of financial and real economic variables. Nonetheless, it is a commonly used term. The European Central Bank defines financial stability as a "condition whereby the financial system is able to withstand shocks and the unraveling of financial imbalances, thereby mitigating the likelihood of disruptions in the financial intermediation process which are severe enough to significantly impair the allocation of savings to profitable investment opportunities" (2007, 12).

Garry Schinasi defines it "in terms of its ability to facilitate and enhance economic processes, manage risks, and absorb shocks," adding that "financial stability is considered a continuum: changeable over time and consistent with multiple combinations of the constituent elements of finance" (2004, 1).

A problem with these qualitative definitions is the difficulty of defining and estimating their quantitative counterparts. This is so even though numerous measures have been proposed and estimated (World Bank 2018).

The most comprehensive measure is represented by a set of financial soundness indicators (FSIs), first developed in 2006 and subsequently adjusted by the International Monetary Fund—most recently in 2018. There are twelve indicators. Data for Korea have been available since 2016 (for details, see International Monetary Fund 2019).

Many central banks have attempted to estimate single overarching aggregate measures of financial stability by adding up the weighted and normalized values of individual component indicators. At this stage, it is unclear how reliable these estimates are for empirical studies like those that analyze the effects of financial deepening on financial stability, because results depend on which component indicators are chosen and how they are weighted. The Bank of Korea has been developing a financial stability index based on the standardization of twenty monthly real and financial indicators. A prototype is shown in Figure 7.2.

Since 1996, the index shows that various events of financial turbulence have undermined the stability of Korea's financial system. Except

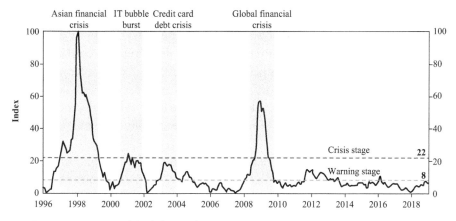

Figure 7.2. Financial Stability Index
Source: Bank of Korea.
Notes: A composite index calculated by standardizing twenty monthly real- and financial-sector indicators related to financial stability. The warning and crisis stage thresholds are set at 8 and 22, respectively, using the "noise-to-signal ratio" method. IT is information technology.

for the two years before the 2008 crisis and after 2014, Korea has been in a crisis or struggling in a warning stage. Those are the periods that witnessed rapid financial growth powered by the progress in financial liberalization.

A visual inspection of both the index and FAY suggests that the pace of financial deepening has failed to make it easier for financial markets and institutions to adjust to the impact of home-grown financial crises and the boom-and-bust cycle in the housing market. Financial growth may have triggered and aggravated these events of turbulence.

Partly because of the difficulty of constructing measures of financial stability, few studies have analyzed the underlying relationship between financial deepening and financial stability. At the level of individual financial institutions, financial stability is measured by the z-score, which compares capitalization and return on assets as buffers with the volatility of returns as a risk to evaluate a bank's solvency risk.[4]

Sahay and coauthors (2015) approximate the financial stability of banking institutions by the z-score. A lower z-score means a greater risk of

---

4. The z-score is calculated as $(k+\mu)/\sigma$, where k is equity capital as a percentage of total assets, μ is the return as a percentage of assets, and σ is the standard deviation of the return on assets.

financial stability.[5] The z-scores they compile for Korea and the other countries in their sample show that initially, financial instability degenerates with an increase in the depth of financial institutions (banks). The authors argue that this takes place because banks tend to take more risks and increase their leverage, particularly when the financial system is poorly regulated. However, at a level above 0.7 on the financial development index the authors developed, they find that the stability of banks returns and begins to improve.[6]

For the stability of the real sector, the authors find contradicting results. At the early stage of financial development, the volatility of GDP growth falls. However, with an increase in the pace of financial deepening in institutions, it begins to deteriorate—which is precisely when financial institutions recover greater stability.[7] These contradictory results mean that the pace of financial deepening in institutions has a divergent effect on the stability of financial institutions and GDP growth. The authors do not provide any explanation for the divergence.

Macroeconomic Stability

In contrast to the dearth of studies on the relationship between financial depth and financial stability, a large and growing empirical literature analyzes the effects of financial development on macroeconomic stability. Most studies that cover the period before the 2008 crisis find that financial deepening serves to dampen the volatility of output, consumption, and investment growth, which contradicts the evidence of Sahay and coauthors (2015).

On the relationship between finance and economic stability, there are two opposing views. One view stresses that financial development reduces volatility by mitigating informational asymmetries. Furthermore, it lowers the sensitivity of financing conditions to changes in the net

---

5. One of the most serious limitations of the z-score is that it is based entirely on accounting data, which suggests that it is only as good as the underlying accounting and auditing framework. Since it examines individual institutions separately, it cannot capture the effects of contagion, when stress at one institution leads to stress at other institutions (World Bank 2018).

6. That is, the quadratic term for financial institutions in their estimated equation becomes positive.

7. There is a significant and positive nonlinear relationship between the two variables. There are no data for the z-score in Korea for a long period that began in the early 1980s.

worth of borrowers, thereby reducing the amplification of cycles that occurs through the financial accelerator mechanism—which expands the capacity of banks to absorb adverse shocks (Bernanke, Gertler, and Gilchrist 1999).

Financial development could also promote risk sharing, reduce financial constraints, enhance the ability of firms and households to absorb shocks, and allow greater consumption smoothing. Through these channels of positive effects, financial deepening is likely to dampen the volatility of output, consumption, and investment (Aghion, et al. 2010; Dabla-Norris and Srivisal 2013). Deeper financial systems also stabilize intrasectoral output, as they induce an intersectoral reallocation of output away from sectors with a high degree of susceptibility to market volatility.

In spite of these favorable effects, many studies find that financial growth is positively correlated with output volatility. According to Andrei Shleifer and Robert Vishny (2010), financial development can lead to more risk taking by firms and banks or excessive leverage, either of which can increase volatility within the financial sector. Vincenzo Quadrini (2011) and Markus Brunnermeier and coauthors (2012) show that financial instability, characterized by the procyclicality of the financial system, amplifies shocks and leads to higher economic volatility.

In both advanced and emerging economies, financial liberalization and innovation have produced a large array of derivatives and other structured products as hedging instruments intended to better allocate risk. But they have also induced excessive risk taking. Together with the asset transformation function at banks, this has rendered the financial system vulnerable to adverse shocks, increasing the possibilities of bank and liquidity runs (Rajan 2006; United Nations Conference on Trade and Development 2008).[8]

---

8. Bernanke and Gertler (1989) show that the credit cycle is highly correlated with the business cycle. In a booming economy, therefore, credit cycles often feed and are fed by asset price cycles, which leads to financial crises. Under these circumstances, the opacity of bank financial statements and the large number of creditors (compared to a real-sector company) undermine market discipline. This encourages banks to take on too much risk, ultimately resulting in increasing macroeconomic volatility and incidences of financial crisis (Rajan 2006, Carletti 2008, and United Nations Conference on Trade and Development 2008).

Therefore, rapid increases in the ratio of private credit to GDP might reflect credit bubbles that are bound to bust and inflict damage on the real sector of the economy (Arcand et al. 2015).

In a cross-country panel estimation for the 1974–2008 period, Era Dabla-Norris and Narapong Srivisal (2013) find that a deeper financial system, measured by the ratio of private credit to GDP, is more effective in dampening the volatility of output, consumption, and investment across countries. But when the ratio exceeds 100 percent, financial depth magnifies consumption and investment volatility. This suggests that the causal relationship between financial development and macroeconomic volatility weakens and eventually vanishes, becoming nonlinear and U-shaped.[9]

The Korean Case

In this section of the chapter, we examine Korean data to see if there is any evidence of a nonlinear relationship between financial development and macroeconomic volatility. This was done by conducting a cross-industry panel estimation of equation 7.6, covering twenty-seven industrial sectors in the 1991–2015 period. To address the endogeneity issue that may arise in a model with unobserved industry-specific fixed effects, equation 7.6 is estimated by the system Generalized Method of Moments (GMM) dynamic panel model used by Dabla-Norris and Srivisal (2013).

$$V_{it} = \alpha V_{it-1} + \beta_1 FAY_t + \beta_2 FAY_t^2 + \beta_c Control_{it} + \mu_i + e_{it} \qquad 7.6$$

Where V_{it}: macroeconomic volatility (standard deviation of the mean of the five- and three-year moving averages of real value added or investment growth) at time t for industry i, and
  FAY: the ratio of total financial to nominal GDP.
Control variables include:
  $vapcgr_t$: per capita growth rate,
  Inflait: Producer Price Index inflation rate in industry i at time t,
  FDIY: the ratio of FDI to value added $FDIY_{it}$,
  $exratio_{it}$: the ratio of export to output,

---

9. Another cross-country study obtained a similar result (Ma and Song 2018).

ln (FXstdev$_t$): standard deviation of change in the daily foreign
exchange rate, and

μ_i: unobserved industry-specific fixed effect.

The panel data for 1991–2015 are divided into five-year subperiods
(1991–95, 1996–2000, 2001–5, 2006–10, and 2011–15) for the twenty-seven
industries. Table 7.6 shows the financial dependence of twenty-seven
industries.

Although the signs of FAY in specifications 1, 3, 4, and 5 are significantly negative, the coefficients of FAY^2 in specifications 2, 4, and 6 are
statistically insignificant (Table 7.7). The effects of financial deepening on
the volatility of value-added growth are inconclusive: they do not strongly
support either the linear or the nonlinear hypothesis.

Similar results for investment growth in Table 7.8 are equally inconclusive. In all specifications, the volatility of investment growth falls as
the financial sector becomes deeper over time. If anything, the relationship between financial deepening and the volatility of investment growth
appears to be an inverse U-shape. However, except for the nonlinear specification all other coefficients of FAY^2 are statistically insignificant. In
view of these conflicting results, it is reasonable to conclude that there
has been no credible evidence on the nonlinear hypothesis of Dabla-Norris
and Srivisal (2013) in Korea.[10]

---

10. Dabla-Norris and Srivisal (2013) suggest that when the FAY is 186–230 percent,
financial deepening tends to lower the volatility of GDP growth.

Table 7.6. Industry Classifications and External Financial Dependence

	1991–95	1996–2000	2001–5	2006–10	2011–15
Agriculture, forestry, and fishing	0.558	0.493	0.392	0.346	0.365
Mining and quarrying	0.435	0.570	0.533	0.360	0.489
Manufacture					
Food, beverages, and tobacco products	0.470	0.500	0.348	0.273	0.272
Textiles and leather products	0.463	0.462	0.352	0.316	0.311
Wood, paper, printing, and reproduction products	0.430	0.452	0.348	0.366	0.346
Coal and petroleum products	0.518	0.517	0.344	0.328	0.308
Chemical products	0.473	0.455	0.302	0.268	0.262
Nonmetallic mineral products	0.427	0.464	0.300	0.262	0.271
Basic metal products	0.431	0.413	0.294	0.268	0.296
Fabricated metal products	0.426	0.395	0.337	0.367	0.381
Machinery and furniture	0.398	0.410	0.278	0.300	0.324
Electrical and electronic equipment	0.466	0.405	0.288	0.250	0.213
Precision equipment	0.514	0.387	0.292	0.243	0.261
Transport equipment	0.434	0.536	0.266	0.174	0.255
Other	0.443	0.435	0.272	0.293	0.268
Electricity, gas, steam, and water supply	0.328	0.407	0.285	0.300	0.365
Construction	0.435	0.486	0.263	0.278	0.265
Wholesale and retail trade	0.359	0.428	0.290	0.274	0.309
Transportation	0.335	0.422	0.467	0.393	0.435
Accommodation and food service activities	0.356	0.336	0.231	0.240	0.278
Publishing, broadcasting, film, and information services	0.095	0.108	0.190	0.222	0.223
Communication	0.065	0.221	0.369	0.266	0.286
Financial and insurance activities	0.306	0.306	0.298	0.325	0.388
Real estate	0.120	0.146	0.191	0.436	0.528
Professional, scientific, and technical activities	0.237	0.184	0.114	0.217	0.244
Business support services	0.356	0.196	0.140	0.205	0.302
Cultural and other services	0.195	0.226	0.188	0.239	0.299

Sources: Economic Statistics System of the Bank of Korea (https://ecos.bok.or.kr/EIndex_en.jsp) and authors' estimates.

Note: The numbers are the external financial dependence of the industries.

Table 7.7. Estimation Results: Five-Year Non-Overlapping Panel with Standard Deviation of the Value-Added Growth in Industry as the Dependent Variable V

Variables	(1)	(2)	(3)	(4)	(5)	(6)
V(t–1)	0.189*	0.167	0.098	0.168	0.173	0.162
	(1.671)	(1.014)	(0.659)	(1.014)	(1.424)	(0.965)
FAY	-0.035***	-0.048	-0.129***	-0.314**	-0.037***	-0.047
	(-3.774)	(-0.898)	(-2.622)	(-2.001)	(-3.798)	(-0.886)
FAY^2		0.003		0.020		0.003
		(0.267)		(1.038)		(0.251)
vapcgr	0.047	-0.004	-0033	-0.053	-0.011	-0.004
	(0.397)	(-0.026)	(-0.270)	(-0.294)	(-0.076)	(-0.027)
Infla	0.041	0.176	0.256**	0.216	0.156	0.182
	(0.190)	(0.951)	(1.983)	(0.963)	(0.719)	(1.000)
FDIY	0.027		0.007	0.005	-0.004	-0.003
	(0.512)		(0.170)	(0.167)	(-0.102)	(-0.089)
exratio		0.089***	0.096***	0.090***	0.095***	0.089***
		(3.002)	(3.380)	(3.354)	(3.125)	(2.923)
CI			0.239*	0.515**		
			(1.866)	(2.569)		
ln(FXstdev)	0.032***	0.032**	0.062***	0.115**	0.031***	0.032**
	(4.106)	(2.288)	(3.276)	(2.442)	(4.045)	(2.281)
Observations	108	108	108	108	108	108
No. of ID	27	27	27	27	27	27
Hansen test p-value	0.080	0.108	0.275	0.280	0.061	0.112
AR(2) test p-value	0.405	0.337	0.223	0.177	0.337	0.343

Notes: Columns 1–6 present the results of the estimation of equation 7.6. The numbers in parentheses are *t*-values. There are 108 observations and twenty-seven industries. Acronyms are explained in the text. $*p < 0.10$ $**p < 0.05$ $***p < 0.01$.

Table 7.8. Estimation Results of Equation 7.6 with Standard Deviation of the Investment Growth in Industry as the Dependent Variable V

	1	2	3	4	5	6
V (t−1)	0.237***	0.235***	0.226***	0.245***	0.222***	0.241***
	(22.038)	(11.857)	(20.488)	(27.420)	(17.102)	(28.329)
FAY	−0.140	−0.409	−0.203**	−0.865**	−0.128*	−0.369*
	(−1.417)	(−1.350)	(−2.017)	(−2.011)	(−1.666)	(−1.645)
FAY^2		0.068		0.077*		0.061
		(1.282)		(1.855)		(1.575)
Vapcgr	−0.297	0.201	−0.124	−0.155	−0.206	0.011
	(−1.025)	(0.347)	(−0.546)	(−0.483)	(−0.849)	(0.035)
Infla	−0.859	−1.886	−0.403	−0.483	−0.873	−1.044
	(−0.844)	(−0.944)	(−0.628)	(−0.644)	(−1.111)	(−1.016)
FDIY	−0.225		0.057	0.184	0.018	0.104
	(−1.162)		(0.387)	(1.503)	(0.122)	(0.776)
Exratio		−0.330	−0.164**	−0.157	−0.153*	−0.183*
		(−1.125)	(−2.241)	(−1.301)	(−1.704)	(−1.954)
CI			0.283	1.277**		
			(1.343)	(2.025)		
Ln (FXstdev)	0.127	0.196	0.125***	0.301**	0.116**	0.167*
	(1.545)	(1.459)	(2.718)	(2.105)	(2.139)	(1.915)
Hansen test p-value	0.036	0.009	0.241	0.793	0.115	0.075
AR (2) test p-value	0.493	0.023	0.294	0.322	0.193	0.050

Notes: Columns 1–6 present the results of the estimation of equation 7.6. The numbers in parentheses are t values. There are 108 observations and twenty-seven industries. Acronyms are explained in the text. *$p < 0.10$ **$p < 0.05$ ***$p < 0.01$.

CHAPTER 8

Assessment of the Empirical Results on the Finance-Industrial Growth Nexus

Why Has the Effect of Financial Deepening Been So Weak or Vanished?

Why have the presumed positive effects from financial deepening been so feeble in Korea? This chapter brings together and highlights a sequence of developments that have taken place in the real and financial sectors over the past three decades to find answers to this vexing question.

One might argue that by the early 1990s, Korea's financial sector had reached a mature stage of development characterized by "too much finance," where most of the benefits of financial growth—including efficiency improvements—evaporated. This study does not agree. Korea may have developed a broader and deeper financial sector, but as illustrated in this chapter, this study does not find any evidence of a financial system that has overgrown in Korea.

At the outset, it should be noted that no matter how competitive and efficient a financial system is, it cannot counteract the adverse impact of structural changes that wear away the potential for long-term growth. In Korea, these changes consist of a declining birth rate and an aging population, compounded by the high cost of developing (rather than imitating) new growth industries, the deterioration of the global trading environment, and the social and political conflicts aggravated by growing distributive inequity.

From the perspectives of this study, however, a succession of both internal and external financial crises—beginning with the 1997 financial meltdown that brought the country to the brink of insolvency—has been one of the most severe constraints on the role of finance. The series of crises has infused businesses of all sizes and financial institutions of all types with a great deal of fear of being exposed to another debilitating financial crisis. This fear has made Korea's chaebol and other large firms very cautious about assuming the risks of large investments with borrowed money, whether in old or new industries. These firms have streamlined their investments to concentrate on the industries (including services) where they have competitive advantages, and they have shifted to internal and equity from debt financing.

Having been subjected to a succession of severe restructurings dictated by reforms and market opening, banks and NBFIs also have become conservative in credit risk management. This risk aversion, combined with the deleveraging of large firms, has made banks reduce their lending to large nonfinancial corporations while catering to the credit needs of SMEs and households much more than before. Since the productivity of these two sectors is relatively low, the growing share of household and SME lending by banks and NBFIs has helped weaken the favorable effects of financial deepening.

The dominance of services in a national economy is a universal characteristic of economic development. As per capita income rises, the service sector's share of GDP continues to increase. If Korea follows the pattern of industrial growth in the advanced economies, the service sector's share of total value added will rise to more than 70.0 percent from the 2018 level of 55.4 percent.

In line with this trend, nonfinancial firms, as well as financial institutions and markets, have adapted themselves to the growing demand for services. Corporate groups and other large firms have reorganized their growth strategy to enlarge their investment in service industries, including those related to retail, wholesale, and financial business, and to shift away from manufacturing. In addition, financial intermediaries and markets have allocated a growing share of their lendable resources to service providers.

This change in the growth strategy has resulted in a reallocation of resources from a productive sector (manufacturing) to inefficient industries like services. Unless Korea's policymakers succeed in reforming the service sector to increase its productivity, given the tendency of finance to follow rather than lead industrial developments, the productivity differential will continue to reduce the positive effects of financial development on allocative efficiency and growth of the economy. Deregulation, opening, and diversification of financial institutions and markets will not help reverse the likely outcome.

Deceleration of Investment and Productivity Growth

A large number of empirical studies using country panel data show that by encouraging competition, reducing the cost of capital, and allocating capital efficiently, a well-functioning financial system can nurture productivity growth at both the firm and industry levels. An example of this more positive assessment is provided by Era Dabla-Norris, Erasmus Kersting, and Geneviève Verdier (2010). In contrast, Naceur and coauthors (2017) cannot confirm the findings of earlier studies.

Our analyses in this chapter confirm that similar ambiguous developments have taken place in Korea. Fixed investment relative to GDP, which was as high as 40 percent in the 1990s, has suffered a sizable and persistent decline. The fall is especially striking when compared to the continued growth of the financial sector.[1]

Figure 8.1 illustrates changes in both gross fixed investment and facilities investment as a share of nominal GDP since 1970. Both types of investment display a similar pattern of change. As a result of the ravages of the financial crisis of 1997, both plunged precipitously in 1998, more so in the case of gross fixed investment.[2] During the crisis period, gross fixed investment fell to below 30 percent of GDP from almost 40 percent before the meltdown. The percentage has remained relatively unchanged ever since.

After recovering from the 1997 crisis, facilities investment's share of GDP also dropped—from almost 14 percent a year earlier to below

---

1. The drop in TFP growth following the 2008 global financial crisis has been widespread and persistent across advanced and emerging economies, as well as low-income countries. And that decline, alongside weak investment in the case of advanced economies, has been the main contributor to output losses relative to trends before the crisis.

2. According to the Bank of Korea's classification, gross fixed capital investment consists of investments in construction, facilities, and intellectual property products. Our analysis excluded the last component because its time series data was unavailable for earlier periods.

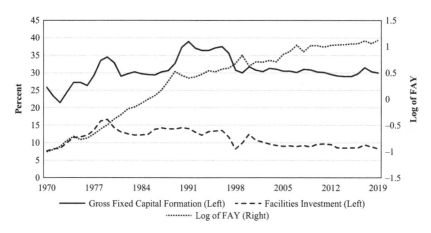

Figure 8.1. Gross Fixed and Facilities Investment as Shares of GDP
Source: Economic Statistics System of the Bank of Korea.

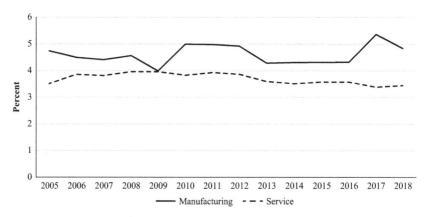

Figure 8.2. Manufacturing and Service Facilities Investment as Shares of GDP
Source: Economic Statistics System of the Bank of Korea.

10 percent, where it has remained ever since, except for 2000. Figure 8.2 presents the share of GDP for manufacturing and service investment since 2005. In particular, manufacturing investment suffered a sharper drop than gross fixed investment during the 2008 global financial crisis. After that, they remained relatively stable until 2016, when they started to diverge.

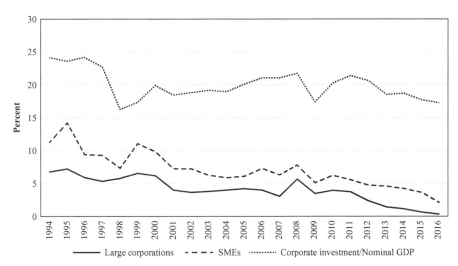

Figure 8.3. Share of Gross Fixed Investments in Total Assets of the
Manufacturing Sector
Source: KIS-VALUE: Database of NICE Information Service Co. Ltd.
Notes: The sample is explained in the text. Total assets consist of current assets (cash, deposits, and
other short-term financial assets) and noncurrent assets (tangible fixed assets, such as property, plants,
and equipment). Gross fixed investment refers to changes in total tangible fixed assets as a proxy.

Figure 8.3 presents estimated gross fixed investments of large firms and
SMEs in the manufacturing sector. The sample consists of 1,468 large
firms and 8,061 SMEs in the manufacturing sector that were listed in the
stock market or subject to external audit in 1994–2016.[3] The estimates
show that manufacturing investments as a share of total assets of large
firms fell below one percent in 2016 from a high of almost 7 percent in
the 1990s. SMEs also reduced their investments.

Deceleration of Total Factor Productivity Growth

Since the 1997 crisis, there has also been a steady deceleration in TFP
growth for industries overall. The average annual growth rate, which was
3.7 percent in the 1980s, dropped to 2.0 percent in the 1990s and to
1.7 percent in the early 2000s, before tumbling to 0.5 percent between
2011 and 2016 (Korea Development Institute 2017). Other TFP estimates

---

3. For a similar estimation of investments by large firms and SMEs, see Ro and
Kim 2014.

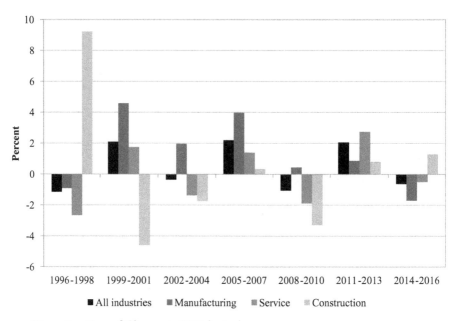

Figure 8.4. Rate of Change in TFP by Industry
Source: Korea Productivity Center 2019.

by the Korea Productivity Center (2019) differ but show a similar decline during the 2011–16 period, as shown in Figure 8.4.

In the manufacturing sector, the fall in TFP growth appears to have been much steeper. According to estimates by the Korea Productivity Center (2019), the three-year average TFP growth was 4.59 percent in 1999–2001. It continued to slide thereafter, dropping below -1.00 percent in 2014–16. Nevertheless, except for the 2011–16 period, TFP growth in manufacturing has always been higher than in the service sector and, except for the 1996–98 crisis and the 2014–16 periods, higher than that in the construction sector.

Causes of the Deceleration of Investment and Productivity Growth: Risk Aversion, Deleveraging, and Hysteresis

The deceleration of investment and productivity growth has several causes. Here we discuss risk aversion, deleveraging, and hysteresis. Since the early 1990s, the Korean economy has weathered a series of domestic, regional, and global financial crises. These have taken a heavy toll on the growth of outputs, investments, and productivity, though they have not had an as significant bearing on financial growth. The 1997 crisis was a stark reminder to nonfinancial corporations and financial institutions alike of how risky and unsustainable investment-led growth could be when it is financed mostly by borrowed money.

RISK AVERSION AND DELEVERAGING

Numerous large and small firms, as well as banks and NBFIs, were liquidated or merged with healthier ones during the 1997 crisis. Surviving corporations were required to lower their debt-to-equity ratios to below 200 percent, a drastic change. The government cleaned up the balance sheets of the banks and NBFIs that it had rescued, taking over most of their non-performing loans. At the same time, both corporations and financial institutions had to become much more prudent in assessing the primary risks of the underlying assets and liabilities they held, using newly introduced state-of-the-art risk-management technology (chapters 3 and 4 discuss this in greater detail).

When the crisis was over, policymakers and pundits expected that with their healthy balance sheets, the rejuvenated firms would become much more competitive than before. They would be ready for vigorous investment in the new technology-intensive industries on which Korea pinned its hopes for the future. Surviving financial institutions would have restored the soundness of their balance sheets to provide fresh financing to support the revival of the corporate sector. However, this was not to be.

Even before the worst of the 1997 crisis was over, a series of homegrown financial difficulties began battering the economy. A slump touched off by the burst of the dot-com bubble in 2001 hit the country hard. Excessive risky lending by credit card firms followed the slowdown and precipitated a credit card crisis in 2003 that involved four million delinquent borrowers in a country with a population of less than fifty million, as well as a massive increase in nonperforming assets on the part of credit card issuers.

By the time the credit card crisis was over, the country was thrown into a real estate boom stoked by the large expansion of bank credit for housing finance that came in the wake of the 1997 crisis. The housing market boom burst when the global financial crisis began in 2008. The collapse of the real estate bubble forced a large number of savings banks that were heavily loaded with housing loans to close in 2011.

For almost a decade following the 2008 crisis, the Korean economy was unable to regain its pre-1997 dynamism. This was in part due to a slowdown of growth in its major trading partners, but mostly to internal political strife and the absence of a consistent growth strategy from successive governments.

In the process of enduring and adjusting to the dislocations caused by the two major financial crises, a succession of domestic financial imbalances, and the boom-bust cycle in real property markets, Korea's large firms, including the chaebol, have come to realize the perils of debt financing.

By the early 2000s, Korea had reached the stage of development where it had to push the technology frontier outward to remain competitive in global markets. The push required a large amount of investment in a number of uncharted industries whose use of advanced technologies was intensive.

But the chaebol and other large corporations that should have been at the vanguard of the new technological push were so gripped by the fear of deteriorating the balance sheets that they were not prepared to take the risks involved in the new investments. Instead, they were content with expanding investments in old industries where they had been successful in the past and venturing into service industries.

Although banks and many NBFIs had built substantial financing capabilities with the growth of deposit liabilities, having suffered from the credit crisis and the boom and bust in real estate, they were reluctant to finance investment in unproven growth industries.

The 2008 liquidity crisis and the subsequent slow growth of the global economy further deepened the aversion to risk taking and debt financing. Under these circumstances, it is not surprising that banks and NBFIs have had little incentive to encourage or provide financial support for industrial borrowers to be forward-looking in reorganizing their investment strategies.

This lack of incentive, combined with the inherent passivity of following, rather than leading, real-sector developments, has led to inefficient allocation of resources by banks and NBFIs. This inefficiency, combined with the slow growth of investment in technology-driven industries and the weakening role of the financial sector, has precipitated a sustained decline in the growth of real output and productivity since the early 2000s.

HYSTERESIS

In a country embroiled in crisis after crisis and experiencing the attendant slow growth for more than two decades after 1997, the consequential economic malaise and discontent appear to have permeated every sector of society to propagate a syndrome of hysteresis.

There is a vicious circle in which a series of financial crises dampens the prospect of future growth, which in turn prompts firms to cut back or postpone investment. Procyclicality then kicks in, and banks and other financial institutions start to reduce their lending, which worsens the pessimistic outlook and weakens the ability of the financial sector to deflect or absorb the impact of internal or external shocks.[4]

The economic and psychological consequences of financial crises then manifest themselves in a long-term economic decline characterized by slow growth and difficulty in returning to the precrisis growth path.

Allocative Inefficiency of the Financial System

SURGE IN BANK LENDING TO SMES AND HOUSEHOLDS WITH LOW PRODUCTIVITY

Indirect Finance

Given the domination of manufacturing at the industry level by the chaebol and other large corporations, the decrease in lending to them was bound to bring on a similar reduction in the volume of bank loans allocated to SMEs. The share of direct money banks' loans to the manufacturing sector fell to about 35 percent in 2019 from close to 60 percent in the 1990s before 1997, resulting in a subsequent increase in the share of loans to the service sector: up to more than 57 percent in 2019 from about 38 percent in 2000 (Figure 8.5).

The service sector is densely populated by SMEs. In 2018, 82 percent of a total of 3.8 million SMEs were engaged in producing a variety of services, accounting for more than 59 percent of the service sector output in 2018. Labor productivity and TFPs of the service sector have consistently been lower than those of manufacturing. Given the differential, it is easy to see why a large increase in lending to the service sector has acted as a significant factor in the depressing of overall growth of productivity and output of the economy.

---

4. Because of the pro-cyclicality of the financial system, financial development has been shown to amplify swings in the business cycle. In extreme cases, it can cause a complete breakdown of intermediation channels between savers and investors. See Borio, Furfine, and Lowe (2001).

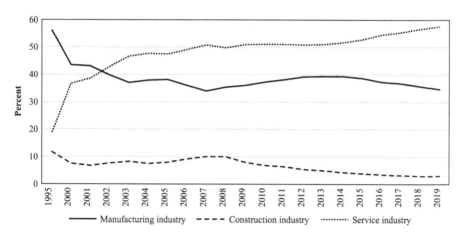

Figure 8.5. Shares of Loans of Deposit Money Banks by Industry
Source: Economic Statistics System of the Bank of Korea.
Note: Deposit money banks are commercial or specialized banks.

Figure 8.6 shows the gap in labor productivity between the manufacturing and service sectors that has been widening since the 1990s. By 2018 the labor productivity of manufacturing was 4.8 times higher than that of service. Except for the 1997 crisis period, TFP growth in manufacturing has always been positive, whereas that in the service sector has been negative since 2002, excluding the 2008–2010 period (Figure 8.4).

For households, as discussed in chapter 3, the deregulation of consumer lending in the wake of the 1997 crisis set off a rapid pace of expansion of indebtedness. At the end of 2001, total outstanding household loans extended by depository corporations and other financial intermediaries stood at 44 percent of GDP (see Table 3.1). It continued to grow at an annual rate of more than 20 percent on average, surpassing 63 percent of GDP in 2007. By the end of 2019, it was over 80 percent of GDP.

Much of the household debt consists of mortgage loans. By 2019, the share of these loans had shot up to almost 60 percent. This increase reflected mostly an explosion of the speculative demand for housing. On the supply side, it meant a roughly equal rise in the availability of financing for the construction of houses and other real properties. Despite the widespread concern of a systemic risk that the household loan growth has posed, little is known about its effects on the growth and productivity of

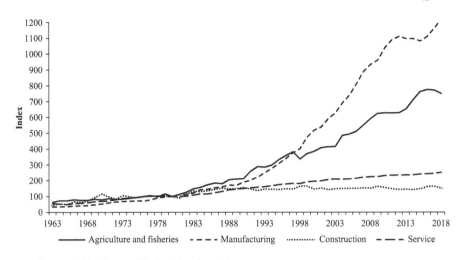

Figure 8.6. Indexes of Labor Productivity
Sources: Economic Statistics System of the Bank of Korea and Korea Statistics.
Notes: The base year is 1980. Labor productivity is measured as the value-added per worker.

the economy in Korea, mainly due to limited availability of the data needed for rigorous analysis.

In a panel study covering fifty-four countries over the 1990–2015 period, Marco Jacopo Lombardi and coauthors (2017) report that household debt stimulates consumption and growth, as households adjust spending and saving for consumption smoothing in the short run. But after a year, the favorable effects begin to wear off, as the burden of debt repayment kicks in to slow growth. More specifically, an increase of one percentage point in the ratio of household debt to GDP reduces growth by the same percentage in the long run. When an economy crosses the threshold of a 60 percent ratio of debt to GDP, the negative effects on consumption pick up, and over 80 percent of the adverse impacts on growth amplify. Joung Ku Kang (2017) presents similar results in his analysis of Korean data over the 2010–15 period.

Evidence suggests that credit booms are likely to damage the economy by reducing total factor productivity growth, as the expansion of the financial sector disproportionately benefits projects such as housing construction with high collateral but low productivity (Cecchetti and Kharroubi 2015).

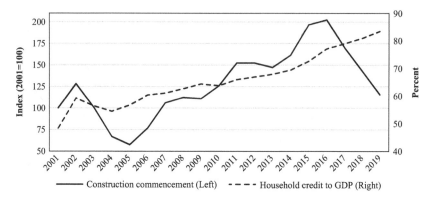

Figure 8.7. Index of Housing Construction Commencement and Household Loans as Share of GDP
Sources: Economic Statistics System of the Bank of Korea and Korea Statistics Information System.
Note: Household loans are the total loans extended by deposit money banks and other financial institutions from Table 3.1.

Except for a few large construction firms, most small and medium-size builders simply did not have credit ratings high enough to access bank lending after the 1997 crisis. As an alternative means of financing, housing and real estate developers have relied on a presales scheme, whereby buyers finance construction by making three installment payments during the building period. The program means that the buyers supply practically all of the financing for housing construction. Hence, empirical analyses could treat mortgage or household loans as part of total bank financing extended to the construction sector. There is a close correlation between an index of housing construction commencement and the ratio of household credit to GDP (Figure 8.7).

Figures 8.4 and 8.6 illustrate that both labor and total factor productivities in the construction sector have been the lowest of any industry throughout the period under discussion. These low productivities imply that the growing allocation of bank loans to the household sector—with much of the money used to finance housing construction—has been partly responsible for slowing the growth of labor and total factor productivities in the economy.[5]

---

5. Government financial support for SMEs and the deregulation of household lending have been dictated by the need to address policy objectives other than growth, so

Direct Finance

In a financially mature economy, it is a natural for corporations to raise relatively more of their external financing from capital markets than banks, which tend to specialize in consumer and SME lending. The decrease in risk tolerance, together with deleveraging in the wake of the 1997 crisis, has also led the chaebol and other large firms to migrate to the equity market and rely on internal financing in their efforts to build a better buffer against future crises (see Figure 4.2).

From the perspectives of this study, the shift in corporate financing raises an important question: has it offset the deterioration in the allocative efficiency of banks and NBFIs and, in so doing, made any significant contribution to the growth of business groups and large firms? Several pieces of evidence suggest that it has not.

First, as shown in this chapter, there is no evidence to suggest that a relative increase in direct finance has benefited the industries relying heavily on the capital market more than those depending on bank financing to boost growth. Instead, the evidence implies that the growth performance of firms does not vary according to their funding structure. Therefore, the allocative efficiency of the financial sector as a whole has deteriorated, as the relative increase in direct finance has not compensated for the inefficiency of the banking industry.

Second, nonfinancial corporate firms, mostly large corporations, have been raising funds by issuing various types of capital market instruments and at the same time investing in them. In 1995, before the 1997 financial crisis, total assets amounted to 21 percent of liabilities consisting of the three types of instruments (Table 8.1). The share rose to 27 percent in 2005 and to more than 30 percent after 2010.

Third, although the available data are rather sketchy and cover a relatively short period, the large industrial groups have made inroads into service industries. According to estimates from the Fair Trade Commission, since 2007 the number of manufacturing affiliates of the five largest chaebol increased by 36 percent, whereas the number

---

they cannot be criticized for the resulting loss of efficiency. All we are saying here is that the structural change in bank financing in favor of households and SMEs has been a factor in slowing economic growth since the 1997 crisis.

Table 8.1. Financial Assets and Liabilities of Nonfinancial Corporations (trillion won, percent)

	1995 (1968 SNA)		2000 (1968 SNA)		2005 (1968 SNA)		2005 (1993 SNA)		2010 (2008 SNA)		2015 (2008 SNA)		2018 (2008 SNA)	
	Assets	Liabilities	Assets	Liabilities	Assets	Liabilities	Assets	Liabilities	Assets	Liabilities	Assets	Liabilities	Assets	Liabilities
Bonds	34.8	151.7	37.2	234.2	79.8	242.4	109.2	230.3	43.3	415.3	65.5	548.3	76.9	512.1
Equity and investment fund shares	18.2	102.2	43.3	190.2	78.5	356.4	239.3	921.5	599.3	1,561.7	701.8	1,885.7	726.6	2,063.0
Financial derivatives	-	-	-	-	3.0	-	3.0	2.2	8.1	15.8	5.7	6.4	1.9	5.0
Total	53.0	253.9	80.5	424.4	1,613	598.8	351.5	11,54.0	650.7	1,992.8	773.0	2,440.4	805.4	2,580.1

Source: Economic Statistics System of the Bank of Korea (https://ecos.bok.or.kr/EIndex_en.jsp).

Notes: Assets' shares of liabilities are 20.9 percent for 1995, 19.0 percent for 2000, 26.9 percent for 2005 (1968 SNA), 30.5 percent (1993 SNA), 32.7 percent for 2010, 31.7 percent for 2015, and 31.2 percent for 2018.

Table 8.2. Affiliates and Total Assets of the Five Largest Chaebol
(number of firms and trillion won)

	2007 (A)	2017 (B)	B − A	B / A
Manufacturing	88	120	32	1.36
Nonmanufacturing	139	249	110	1.79
Total	227	369	142	1.62
Assets	613	975.6	362.6	1.59

Sources: Fair Trade Commission 2007 and 2017.

of nonmanufacturing ones increased by almost 80 percent (see Table 8.2).[6]

GROWTH OF EXTERNAL LENDING

Starting in the early 1990s, total savings as a share of GDP fell sharply, reaching a record low of about 32 percent in 2002. Since then it has recovered, topping 35 percent in 2019. Gross investment as a proportion of GDP has been unstable and lower than that of savings since 1998 (Figure 8.8).

This gap has matched a persistent surplus on the current account balance. Part of the surplus has been absorbed by the central bank to build foreign exchange reserves, and the remainder has been lent to foreign borrowers (Figure 8.9).

The cumulative total of annual current account surpluses from 2000 to 2018 amounted to more than 33 percent of indirect finance at the end of 2018. This surplus has increased the capacity and scope of external financial intermediation between domestic savers and foreign borrowers, as opposed to the internal channeling of savings to investment.

Table 8.3 presents the holdings of international bonds, stocks, and other financial instruments by domestic residents and the holdings of domestic securities by foreign investors. Before 1997, Korea was heavily dependent on foreign loans and investment in domestic securities for the financing of

---

6. The share of retail and wholesale business in total sales revenue of the large corporate groups rose to 11.4 in 2017 from 8.4 in 2009 (see table 7 in Wi 2018). The share of the financial services jumped to 13.8 from 7.8 percent over the same period. In contrast, the share of manufacturing dropped to 49.2 in 2016 from 55.0 percent in 2010.

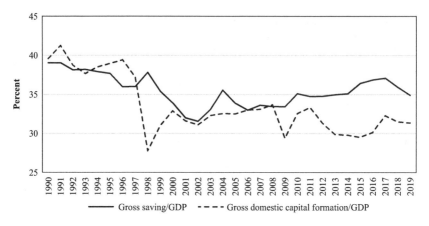

Figure 8.8. Total Savings and Gross Investment as Shares of GDP
Source: Economic Statistics System of the Bank of Korea.

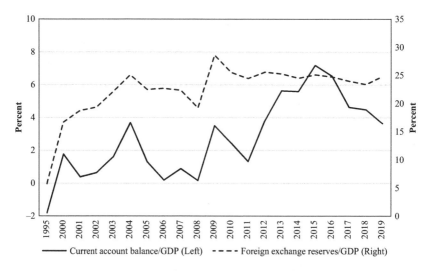

Figure 8.9. Current Account Balances and Foreign Exchange Reserves as Shares of GDP
Source: Economic Statistics System of the Bank of Korea.

domestic investment, so much so that the volume of foreign securities held by local investors was relatively small—averaging about 42 percent of foreign holdings of domestic financial assets.

After the 1997 crisis, this percentage began to surge, rising to 92 percent by 2004. After that, for over a decade, the level fluctuated between 74 percent and 84 percent before jumping to over 100 percent in 2015 to

Table 8.3. International Investment Position ($ million)

	Assets (A)	Liabilities (B)	A − B	A /B
1995	99,306.7	145,435.5	−46,128.8	68.3
2000	180,877.9	217,332.7	−36,454.8	83.2
2005	368,168.8	512,040.3	−143,871.5	71.9
2010	693,788.6	826,441.1	−132,652.5	83.9
2015	1,143,988.2	939,527.4	204,460.8	121.8
2016	1,245,118.7	964,020.5	281,098.2	129.2
2017	1,461,618.5	1,199,920.7	261,697.8	121.8
2018	1,546,329.9	1,110,167.6	436,162.3	139.3
2019	1,699,728.4	1,198,782.5	500,945.9	141.8

Source: Bank of Korea.

Notes: Assets include portfolio investments, financial derivatives, trade credits and advances, loans, and other equity in foreign countries by domestic citizens. Liabilities consist of portfolio investments, financial derivatives, trade credits and advances, and loans in the domestic country by foreigners.

142 percent in 2019, which made Korea a net international creditor for the first time. Much of the increase in external credit has had its sources in the current account surplus and the slowdown in domestic investment and economic growth, which has slashed the demand for foreign financing.

The growing amount of Korea's foreign lending implies that the country's financial system has not been able to channel all of the domestic savings to firms to invest. The excess savings has increased the room for financial institutions and markets to engage in, and expand the scale of, international intermediation between domestic savers and foreign borrowers, much like the central bank's process of accumulating foreign exchange reserves.

In open economies with a current account surplus, such cross-border intermediation is not unusual. But in emerging market economies—where investment opportunities are likely to be more abundant and the rate of return to capital higher than in advanced economies—persistent outflows of domestic savings reflect inefficiency in financial intermediation, in addition to other structural flaws.

The inefficiency may also underscore the passivity of the financial sector in responding to the weakening demand for business investment. This lack of proactiveness raises the question of whether the banking sector could have been more aggressive in courting business borrowers. The chaebol and large corporations are the most creditworthy and highly sought after borrowers.

Given their industrial dominance, it would be in the interest of banks to double their efforts to keep these coveted clients in their loan portfolios. But even long after the corporate restructuring was complete, banks failed or were not eager to attract corporate borrowers. By that time, the corporate borrowers had developed a cushion of internal savings and easier access to capital markets for financing, while large crowd consumers and SMEs were lining up for bank loans.

CHAPTER 9

Effects of Financial Deepening on Income Distribution

This chapter investigates whether the effects on the income distribution of the sweeping reform of the financial sector can be isolated and, if so, how large their quantitative magnitudes have been.[1] The chapter begins with a review of the literature. It then presents an analysis of panel data on incomes and household debt measured by loans from banks and NBFIs. The data are from the Korea Labor and Income Panel Study (KLIPS) for the 2000–16 period. The specific goal is to determine whether, and how much, financial growth contributed to improving household access to bank financing.

More specifically, we analyze Korea's household survey data to establish whether financial growth has contributed to expanding access by the poor to external financing and, if it has, whether the expansion has increased their income and thus improved distributive equity over time. The analysis includes an investigation of whether the change in accessibility has played any role in generating different rates of growth in quintiles of income to alter the distribution of income.

Literature Survey

Raghuram Rajan and Luigi Zingales (2003b) raise questions as to whether finance benefits only the rich, stating that "financial markets are simply

---

1. This chapter draws on Kwak and Park (2019).

tools for the rich to get richer at the expense of the general public." Most people would not hesitate to agree with this as regards Korea, as they believe that the rich are the most-favored clients of financial institutions. They may also believe that whatever its contribution to growth and efficiency of the economy may have been, financial growth has been one of the factors increasing inequality in income and wealth.

Its popularity notwithstanding, this view is not widely incorporated in economic theories. Instead, they provide conflicting predictions about the effects of financial development and liberalization on the distribution of income. Reflecting the diverse perspectives in theory, a large number of country-specific and cross-country panel studies provide equally contradictory empirical results. In short, it is challenging to reach a consensus on the nexus between financial deepening and income distribution.

One proposition is that the linkage between the two is nonlinear because it resembles the Kuznets inverted-U relationship between economic growth and income distribution (Greenwood and Jovanovic 1990). The nonlinear hypothesis is based on the observation that during the early stages of financial development, it is costly for low-income households and SMEs to access financial intermediaries. This is because they cannot provide the tangible collateral, credible credit history, or political connections that banks demand for lending.

Many of these potential borrowers who are denied access to bank financing are unable to undertake indivisible investments beyond their initial wealth, and thus they cannot take advantage of profitable investment opportunities that would improve their earning capacities. The limited access thus tends to intensify income inequality. This is even more the case if the wealthy capture financial industries characterized by an oligopolistic market structure.

As the financial sector grows and acquires a more efficient infrastructure, financial institutions can lower their transaction costs and improve their management of credit and market risk. This enables them to loosen the credit constraint on low-income small borrowers. Financial growth allows banks to increase their capacity to accommodate the credit needs of these newcomers to the financial sector. This change in the bank lending structure, which favors new entrants relatively more than the incumbents, first lessens but then gradually stabilizes income inequality.

Contrary to the view of the inverted relationship, Oded Galor and Joseph Zeira (1993), Abhijit Banerjee and Andrew Newman (1993), and

Philippe Aghion and Patrick Bolton (1997) develop theoretical models in which the capital market imperfections and indivisibilities of human capital act as a critical constraint on improving income distribution. When the credit of low-income families and SMEs with few assets is rationed, they cannot enter profitable occupations that have setup costs. Hence, they are denied upward mobility. In turn, this widens income inequality in both the short and long run. An important implication of this view is that to the extent that financial development alleviates the severity of capital market imperfections, financial deepening may improve income distribution even at the early stages of financial development.

Several empirical studies show that the inverted relationship Jeremy Greenwood and Boyan Jovanovic derive is not robust in the long term. For example, the inequality decreases with the progress in financial development from the early stages onward (Clarke et al. 2006; Beck, Demirgüç-Kunt, and Levine 2007).

Departing from the distributive inferences of the linear and nonlinear hypotheses, Rajan and Zingales (2003) emphasize the quality of political and legal institutions as a critical determinant of the positive effect of financial growth on income distribution. They argue that although financial development is a precondition for greater access to external financing by the poor, it does not necessarily improve distributive equity. This is because even in a financially mature economy with a sophisticated financial infrastructure, those in power (by which the authors mean wealthy individuals and large firms) exercise political influence. They use their influence to oppose the deregulation and market opening that would relax credit constraints on households and firms that might then compete for access to bank financing. The opposition perpetuates the systematic discrimination against, and rationing of credit for, low-income households and SMEs, which deteriorates income distribution.

Finally, there is the question of whether it is possible to identify the stage of financial development at which the positive effects of financial deepening on income distribution tapers off and eventually stabilizes. Neither the linear nor the nonlinear hypothesis has much to say on this point.

The debate about whether there can be too much finance for economic growth has stimulated interest in empirical analyses of whether there is a threshold beyond which financial development could widen income inequality. Donghyun Park and Kwanho Shin (2015) and Michael Brei and coauthors (2018) present evidence that once a threshold is reached, financial development could cause greater inequality for a host of reasons, but the turning point appeared to vary from country to country and changed over time.

A literature survey by Brei and coauthors (2018) points to many possible causes of the diminishing effect suggested by many authors. These causes include rising fees for asset management, a growing demand for household credit, higher wages and better benefits in creating and distributing risky assets, and the information advantages inherent in financial industries that magnify rent extraction. However, the relative significance of these causes has not been estimated. Moreover, the trajectories of income inequality, once the threshold is reached, differ for bank- versus market-based financial development. The subsequent increase in income inequality is much steeper in market-based financial systems.

The overriding theme running through all the hypotheses described above is that the degree of accessibility by low-income individuals and SMEs to bank and market financing determines the direction and magnitude of the effects of financial deepening on income distribution.

But how is access to be measured? Beck, Demirgüç-Kunt, and Soledad Martinez Peria (2006) identify three types of measures: physical access, eligibility, and affordability. The relative importance of these measures ultimately depends on the severity of financial market imperfections that stem from information asymmetry, transaction costs, and regulations. Nonetheless, because of the nonexistence of or gaps in the data needed to estimate these indicators, most empirical studies use a variety of aggregate measures of financial deepening as the primary determinant of access to bank lending or capital market financing. These measures include the ratios to income of bank debt and of bond and equity market capitalization.

The quantitative measures are understandably deficient in that they do not capture the multifaceted nature of financial development. For instance, they overlook the incongruous fact that a repressed financial regime may grow rapidly. Still, development strategies may allocate most of the lendable resources to firms in strategic sectors to support growth. This limits the access of households and SMEs to the financial sector. Quantitative growth may not improve the allocative efficiency of a financial system, nor would it be associated with financial stability.

Ratna Sahay and coauthors (2015) develop a more comprehensive index that takes into account the depth, access, and efficiency of both financial institutions and markets. The International Monetary Fund constructed a database of these indicators and has updated it.

A World Bank report adds other dimensions of financial development to show that the fostering of more efficient resource allocation by financial market liberalization is as important as the direct provision of financial services to the poor in reducing poverty and income inequality (2008, chapter 3).

Following up on that report, Sami Ben Naceur and Ruixin Zhang (2016) added two other dimensions of financial development: financial stability and capital market liberalization. Using a sample of 143 countries and covering the period 1961–2011, their empirical investigation finds that four of the five dimensions of financial development can significantly reduce income inequality and poverty. The exception is financial liberalization, which tends to exacerbate inequality and poverty. This contradicts the view of the World Bank study.

Overview of Income Distribution in Korea

For almost ten years after the 1997 crisis, the distribution of income in Korea deteriorated. The Gini coefficient rose from 0.283 in 1997 to 0.312 in 2007. The bursting of the real estate bubble and the 2008 global financial crisis were followed by sustained improvement until 2015, when the coefficient began worsening again.

From the perspective of this study, one of the most important structural changes in Korea's financial system has been the unbalanced allocation of credit extended by banks and various NBFIs to households belonging to different income quintiles. The study shows a steep decline in the share of borrowers represented by the disadvantaged—defined as those belonging to the first, or lowest, quintile. This group's share went from 13 percent in 1999 to below 10 percent in 2016 (the data here and below are from KLIPS). The fifth quintile gained the most, with its share soaring to 50 percent from 37 percent over the same period.

The decline in access to the financial system measured by the average bank credit or debt-to-income ratio in the first quintile was steeper yet, falling from 3.6 percent in 1999 to 1.4 percent in 2016. This unbalanced allocation has had a great impact on worsening the distribution of income.

Even after liberalization took off, following the 1997 crisis, it appears that financial institutions did not abandon their old practice of favoring loan customers with dynastic wealth and those who had political connections or long-term relations with them. The institutions appear to have continued to pass over low-income households and SMEs without proper credit histories and collateral.

This limited access by disadvantaged borrowers is likely to have been partly responsible for exacerbating income inequality. It has constrained financing for investment by these borrowers, thereby lowering their relative earning capacities. The financial constraint may also have reduced spending on education and health care for younger generations, further diminishing intergenerational distributive equity.

Most of all, the discrimination against the poor has meant that the bulk of household loans has been allocated to wealthier households for housing and other real estate investments, allowing them to speculate and amass substantial capital gains from the continuing rise in housing prices. The liquidity crisis that began in 2008 ended the property boom, but only a year later, housing prices started to soar again. This rising trend suggests that the rich have been able to accumulate substantial capital gains over the years.

The opening of the financial market and deregulation of capital accounts spurred financial development through a reduction in the cost of capital by allowing for risk sharing between domestic and foreign agents and by providing additional financing sources. Since most large and well-established firms are able to rely on both foreign and domestic financing, their owners and employees are more likely to have benefited disproportionately from the development and opening of the capital market, compared to the self-employed and SMEs.

Foreign direct investment usually increases the demand for skilled workers. As a result, the financial deepening associated with capital account liberalization has tended to widen the income gap between the richer and poorer, as well as the wage gap between skilled and unskilled workers, with negative implications for equity in income distribution.

The complexity of the nexus between financial deepening and income distribution suggests that a priori, it is difficult to determine the extent to which financial depth could lead to more equitable income distribution. The issue is an empirical one, and empirical studies require a large amount of microeconomic data on the behavior of households and financial institutions. Although the gaps in much of the data needed narrow the scope of this study, its empirical tests present numerous clues that shed light on the causal relationship between financial deepening and income distribution.

A Model for Financial Growth and Income Distribution

Since the early 2000s, when financial deregulation started gathering force, the growth of direct finance has been phenomenal—increasing to more than 169 percent of GDP in 2019 from 102 percent in 2000. The growth of indirect finance has been relatively moderate, rising from 86 percent of GDP in 2000 to 137 percent in 2019. Because of the lack of data on the household holdings of capital market instruments, this study uses the loans of households from banks and NBFIs as a proxy for household access to external financing. The financial growth is measured by the ratio of indirect finance to nominal GDP (IFY), as KLIPS data show that very few households in any income group use the capital markets for financing.

Along with the growth of indirect finance, the intensification of competition among banks and NBFIs and the migration of firms to capital markets have led banks to restructure their lending operations by allocating a relatively larger share of loanable funds to the self-employed, SMEs, and households. These developments raise three questions:

1. To what extent did financial growth increase the relative accessibility to loans from banks and NBFIs (henceforth, banks) by borrowers across different income groups during the study period (2000–16)? Put differently, were households in the two lowest income quintiles able to borrow more than before, relative to households in the higher quintiles?
2. What was the effect of the change in the relative accessibility to bank loans on household income in different income quintiles?
3. Did changes in household income improve or reduce the equity of income distribution? More specifically, this study probes whether financial deepening enhances the ability of households in the bottom quintile to borrow from banks and, if it does, whether those poorer families can increase their share of total household income.

To find answers, we developed a model based on the premise that financial growth alters the distribution of income through its effects on the access of households in different income brackets to bank financing—which in turn has an impact on the changes in households' earning capacities. The answer this study finds confirms what many Koreans believe: financial deepening has been likely to worsening distributive income equity, as it has failed to improve the access of low-income households to external financing.

The model divides the analysis into a two-stage investigation. The first stage analyzes the extent to which financial deepening was responsible for changes in the access of households in different income quintiles to the banking system during the study period. The debt-to-income ratio is a proxy for accessibility, where the debt is measured by the total amount of loans each household obtained from banks and NBFIs. Equation 9.1 describes the first-stage investigation.

The second stage explores whether, and by how much, these changes in access led to changes in household income in the different income quintiles. This examination, which is depicted in equation 9.2, is intended to quantify the effects of financial development on income distribution.

We estimate the two equations with individual household panel data from KLIPS for the period 2000–16. This survey contains information on 89,439 households.

The data set includes outliers beyond the range of what is expected under normal circumstances. To avoid distortions caused by these extreme values, we removed households with an annual nominal income of less than 100 thousand won (about $115, adjusted for purchasing power over the period) and with outstanding debt of more than fifteen times the income (equivalent to 0.5 percent of all debt-to-income ratios). We also excluded households where the gender of the head of household changed (which was generally the result of death or divorce). After these exclusions, the number of households in the sample was 53,489. Table 9.1 provides details on their characteristics.

First-Stage Analysis of Financial Development and Access to Bank Loans

A reduced form of the first equation of the model is specified as follows:

$$DTI^*_{it} = \sum_{j=1}^{5} \beta_j (IFY_{t-1} * D_{jit-1})$$
$$+ \sum_{j=1}^{5} \delta_j D_{jit-1} + \beta_c X_{it} + \beta_g GFC_t + u_i + f_t + e_{it} \qquad 9.1$$

Table 9.1. Summary Statistics

Variable	Explanation	Mean	SD	Min.	Max.
Inc	Annual household nominal income (10,000 won)	3,811.8	3,600.0	10	110,000
DTI	Debt-to-income ratio	0.802	1.655	0	15
IFY	Indirect finance–to-GDP ratio	1.106	0.131	0.874	1.273
Edu	Years of schooling of the household head	11.304	4.360	0	26
Male	Sex of household head	0.841	0.366	0	1
Seoul	Dummy variable for living in Seoul	0.473	0.499	0	1
Age	Age of household head	51.686	14.307	16	95
Ownhm	Dummy variable for home ownership	0.611	0.487	0	1
Land_gr	Average rate of change in land prices	2.404	2.117	−0.32	8.98

Source: KLIPS.

Notes: There were 53,489 observations. For sex, 1 is male and 0 is female. SD is standard deviation. Min. is minimum. Max. is maximum.

Dependent variable:

DTI^*_{it} (a latent variable of the debt-to-income ratio [DTI] of household i in time t, which is a measure of access to the banking sector at time t).

Explanatory variables:

IFY_{t-1} (the ratio of indirect finance to GDP at time $t-1$, which is a time-varying aggregate measure of financial growth),

D_{jt-1} (a dummy variable for households belonging to income quintile j at time $t-1$),

GFC (an indicator variable for the global financial crisis period 2008–9, where 1 is that period and 0 is all other periods in the study), and

X (a set of control variables, including Age (age of household head), Edu (years of schooling of household head), Male (sex of household head, where 1 is male and 0 is for female), Ownhm (a dummy variable for homeownership), Seoul (a dummy variable for living in Seoul), and Land_gr (the average rate of change in the land price index, which is a macroeconomic control variable)).

Fixed effects:

u_i (individual fixed effects) and
f_t (time fixed effects).

Equation 9.1 assumes that the debt-to-income ratio (DTI) depends on the interaction terms of the IFY with quintile income group dummies IFY*D_j, quintile dummies D_j, a set of control variables X, and GFC. For a variable representing financial growth, we choose the IFY rather than the FAY (a ratio of total finance to GDP), mainly because few households in the KLIPS survey invested in bonds, stocks and other capital market products, and issued these instruments for funding. GFC is included to detect whether any structural changes in bank lending occurred during the global financial crisis period.

As for household debt, an increase in the loan-to-income ratio in any given income quintile reflects an increase in either the demand for household loans (assuming that there are no borrowing constraints) or the supply. The loan data did not allow us to distinguish between demand- and supply-side changes. However, as banks traditionally ration credit in screening household borrowers in terms of their creditworthiness and collateral, it is reasonable to assume that an increase in the loan-to-income ratio mostly results from changes in supply-side factors.

In estimating equation 9.1, the value for debt is censored for households with negative debt as follows:

$$DTI_i = \begin{cases} DTI_i^*, & \text{if } DTI_i^* \geq 0 \\ 0, & \text{if } DTI_i^* < 0, \end{cases}$$

Where

DTI* is a latent—that is, unobservable—variable of the observable variable DTI_i.

We estimate equation 9.1 by a correlated random effects (CRE) Tobit model. The model addresses the data censoring as well as the incidental parameters problem, which refers to the bias of the fixed effects estimators of nonlinear panel data models—such as the one represented by equation 9.1, where dummy variables explain the fixed effects (see Lancaster 2000, Greene 2004, and Wooldridge 2010).[2]

---

2. The incidental parameters problem arises in a Tobit model with a large number of cross-section units and a small number of time units when individual fixed effects are explained in terms of dummy variables. Such a dummy approach is liable to create a severe estimation bias. This is because there are too many parameters that increase with the rise in the number of observations to be estimated, so the parameter estimates can

In the CRE Tobit model, individual fixed effects u_i are described by $\bar{X}_i$, which is an average over time of all explanatory variables for each household i. In this specification, we assume that given X_i, the distribution of u_i is such that the mean is $\beta_0 + \bar{X}_i \lambda$ and the error term is $a_i \sim N(0, \sigma_a^2)$, where a_i is uncorrelated with $IFY_{t-1} {}^* D_{jit-1}$. These assumptions for u_i are called CRE assumptions.

Unobserved aggregated time effects f_t are explained by year dummy variables, as the number of years is fixed and small compared to the number of individual households. Note that since the number of years does not increase with the increase in sample size, it does not cause the incidental parameters problem.

Finally, equation 9.1 is also estimated by a pooled Tobit model that does not impose a random-effects assumption of normality—$a_i \sim N(0, \sigma_a^2)$—but uses the average over time of covariates $\bar{X}_i$ as an additional explanatory variable and f_t. The model is estimated to see the robustness of the results of the CRE Tobit model.

Table 9.2 reports the coefficient estimates and their standard errors of equation 9.1.

Given the large sample size, the normality assumption of the CRE Tobit model is crucial for obtaining the precision, rather than the consistency, of the estimates. It ensures that the estimates of the pooled Tobit model do not differ (beyond the sampling error) from those of the CRE Tobit model, because both estimators are consistent.

In analyzing the effects of change in the IFY on the DTI in both the CRE and pooled Tobit models, in contrast to a linear regression model, the coefficients of the IFY cannot be interpreted as measuring the average marginal effects of financial growth on the debt-to-income ratios of individual households in different income quintiles. In these models, the estimates of the average marginal effects are adjusted by multiplying the coefficients by a scaling factor: $\Phi\left(\dfrac{X\beta}{\sigma}\right)$.[3]

---

never converge to their true values when the sample size increases. In this study, there are as many as 3,655 households, so there are just as many individual fixed effects parameters to estimate. Joseph Altonji and Rosa Matzkin (2005) and Jeffrey Wooldridge (2005, 2010) show that the use of a correlated random effects model resolves the incidental parameters problem.

3. For the estimation of the average marginal effects and the definition and derivation of the scaling factor, see Wooldridge (2016, 538–39).

Table 9.2. Heterogeneous Effects of IFY on DTI

	2001–16		2009–16	
	Pooled	CRE	Pooled	CRE
IFY*D1	−1.461***	−2.186***	−3.723**	−3.501***
	(0.324)	(0.299)	(1.788)	(1.489)
IFY*D2	−0.984***	−1.036***	−1.789	−1.879
	(0.342)	(0.285)	(1.864)	(1.379)
IFY*D3	0.195	0.165	−0.549	−0.357
	(0.327)	(0.270)	(1.818)	(1.314)
IFY*D4	0.647**	0.647**	−0.204	0.209
	(0.333)	(0.273)	(1.778)	(1.262)
IFY*D5	1.990***	2.085***	0.191	0.395
	(0.315)	(0.259)	(1.564)	(1.100)
Land_gr	−0.028*	−0.034***	−0.205	0.009
	(0.016)	(0.013)	(0.315)	(0.816)
GFC	−0.177	−0.158		
	(0.243)	(0.202)		
Edu	0.048***	0.054***	0.018	0.030
	(0.019)	(0.016)	(0.049)	(0.039)
Male	0.475***	0.506***	0.645***	0.595***
	(0.475)	(0.076)	(0.215)	(0.162)
Seoul	0.150	0.176	0.615**	0.745***
	(0.141)	(0.116)	(0.298)	(0.221)
Age	−0.011**	−0.010**	−0.011	−0.008
	(0.006)	(0.005)	(0.013)	(0.010)
Ownhm	0.628***	0.623***	0.672***	0.617***
	(0.043)	(0.036)	(0.100)	(0.071)
Observations	53,489	53,489	24,226	24,226
Households	3,655	3,655	3,654	3,654
Ln (likelihood)	−76,432	−69,824	−33,010	−28,789

Notes: The years 2009–16 represent the period after the 2008 financial crisis. Pooled and CRE refer to Tobit estimation methods. All numbers reflect year and individual fixed effects. Standard errors are clustered by household level and reported in parentheses. To save space, coefficient estimates on dummy variables and other control variables are not reported. Due to the convergence issue, some outliers (such as people with incomes greater than 99.9 percent) were removed from the sample. The acronyms are explained in the text. * $p < 0.10$ ** $p < 0.05$ *** $p < 0.01$.

Table 9.3. Marginal Effects of IFY on DTI

	2001–16		2009–16	
	Pooled	*CRE*	*Pooled*	*CRE*
$\Phi\left(\dfrac{X\hat{\beta}}{\hat{\sigma}}\right)1*\hat{\beta}_1$	−0.365 (0.25)	−0.678 (0.31)	−0.782 (0.21)	−0.910 (0.26)
$\Phi\left(\dfrac{X\hat{\beta}}{\hat{\sigma}}\right)2*\hat{\beta}_2$	−0.413 (0.43)	−0.456 (0.44)	−0.662 (0.37)	−0.752 (0.40)
$\Phi\left(\dfrac{X\hat{\beta}}{\hat{\sigma}}\right)3*\hat{\beta}_3$	0.090 (0.46)	0.078 (0.47)	−0.231 (0.42)	−0.154 (0.43)
$\Phi\left(\dfrac{X\hat{\beta}}{\hat{\sigma}}\right)4*\hat{\beta}_4$	0.317 (0.49)	0.317 (0.49)	−0.096 (0.47)	0.100 (0.48)
$\Phi\left(\dfrac{X\hat{\beta}}{\hat{\sigma}}\right)5*\hat{\beta}_5$	1.075 (0.53)	1.105 (0.54)	0.105 (0.55)	0.209 (0.53)
Observations	53,489	53,489	24,226	24,226
Households	3,655	3,655	3,654	3,654
Ln (likelihood)	−76,432	−69,824	−33,010	−28,789

Notes: The years 2009–16 represent the period after the 2008 financial crisis. All numbers reflect year and individual fixed effects. Pooled and CRE refer to Tobit estimation methods. The average values of scale factor—$(\frac{1}{N_k}\sum_{i=1}^{N_k}\left(\frac{X_i\hat{\beta}}{\hat{\sigma}}\right)$—for k = 1, 2, 3, 4, or 5 are reported in parentheses. To save space, coefficient estimates on dummy variables and other control variables are not reported. The acronyms are explained in the text. * $p < 0.10$ ** $p < 0.05$ *** $p < 0.01$.

Table 9.3 presents the values of the average marginal effects—$\Phi\left(\dfrac{X\hat{\beta}}{\hat{\sigma}}\right)*\hat{\beta}_{j*D_{jit-1}}$—of all income quintiles of both the CRE and pooled Tobit models for the whole and the post crisis sample periods. Those of the CRE Tobit model are plotted in Figure 9.1. For example, in the first income quintile, the average marginal effect for the whole sample is:

$$\Phi\left(\dfrac{X\hat{\beta}}{\hat{\sigma}}\right)*\hat{\beta}_{1*D_{jit-1}} = 0.31 * (-2.186) = -0.678.$$

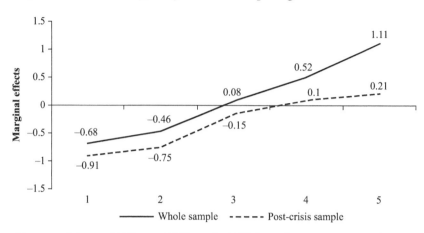

Figure 9.1. Marginal Effects of IFY on the DTI Ratio by Income Quintile
Source: Authors' estimation.
Note: The average marginal effects for the five income quintiles are from the pooled Tobit model estimations in Table 9.3. The period 2009–16 is after the 2008 financial crisis.

The average marginal effects of change in the IFY on the DTI are negative for the first and second quintiles in both the CRE and pooled Tobit models, whereas the same effects are positive for the fourth and fifth brackets. These differences in the signs of the adjusted coefficients account for significant differences in the effects of change in the IFY on the DTI in the five income quintiles.

For instance, an increase of one standard deviation in the IFY (0.131 in Table 9.1) lowers the DTI by 0.09 (0.68*0.13 = −0.09) in the first quintile, while the same increase in the IFY raises the DTI by 0.14 (1.11*0.13 = 0.14) in the fifth quintile in the CRE Tobit model.

Figure 9.1 shows that the average marginal effect increases monotonically in ascending order of the income quintile during the whole sample period. That is, households in higher quintiles gain greater access to bank loans as the financial sector deepens. This result is consistent with the view that banks are biased against low-income households in their lending and that, as a consequence, they allocate much of the increase in credit generated by financial deepening to wealthier households.

However, during the post crisis period, the average marginal effects in all quintiles except the first fell significantly (particularly in the fifth), but they are statistically insignificant in both Tobit models (Table 9.4). This finding suggests that the impact of financial development measured by the

Table 9.4. Effective Differences in IFY between 1st and Other Quintiles of Income of DTI

	2001–16		2009–16	
	Pooled	*CRE*	*Pooled*	*CRE*
IFY*D1-IFY*D2	−0.477	−1.149***	−1.934	−1.630
	(0.437)	(0.285)	(2.338)	(1.855)
IFY*D1-IFY*D3	−1.655***	−2.351***	−3.174	−3.152*
	(0.426)	(0.373)	(2.285)	(1.794)
IFY*D1-IFY*D4	−2.108***	−2.833***	−3.520	−3.717**
	(0.429)	(0.375)	(2.253)	(1.758)
IFY*D1-IFY*D5	−3.451***	−4.271***	−3.915*	−3.904**
	(0.413)	(0.362)	(2.090)	(1.651)
Observations	53,489	53,489	24,226	24,226
Households	3,655	3,655	3,654	3,654
Ln (likelihood)	−76,432	−69,824	−33,010	−28,789

Notes: The years 2009–16 represent the period after the 2008 financial crisis. Pooled and CRE refer to Tobit estimation methods. All numbers reflect year and individual fixed effects. Standard errors are clustered by household level and reported in parentheses. To save space, coefficient estimates on dummy variables and other control variables are not reported. Due to the convergence issue, some outliers (such as people with incomes greater than 99.9 percent) were removed from the sample. The acronyms are explained in the text. $*p < 0.10$ $**p < 0.05$ $***p < 0.01$.

IFY on the accessibility of bank financing for households in higher income quintiles weakened mainly due to stagnation in the growth of the banking sector after the 2008 crisis (see chapter 1). For almost six years after the crisis, the growth of indirect finance was anemic. Since then, it has grown modestly, but at a pace much slower than that of direct finance (DFY).

Access to Bank Loans and Income Growth

The main finding of the preceding section of this chapter is that, as far as the availability of bank financing is concerned, much of the benefit from financial growth has gone to households in higher income quantiles. This partiality raises an important question: has banking institutions' apparent discrimination against the poor contributed to any significant deterioration of income distribution equity in Korea?

To verify that deterioration, this section develops a model in which income per household is a function of the availability of bank financing specified in the linear regression model of equation 9.2. We estimate this model to quantify the marginal effects of changes in the DTI on individual household incomes in the five income quintiles.

$$lnInc_{it} = \gamma_0 + \sum_{j=1}^{5} \gamma_j (\widehat{DTI}_{it-1} * D_{jit-1})$$

$$+ \sum_{j=1}^{5} \delta_j D_{jit-1} + \gamma_c X_{it} + u_i + v_i \cdot time_t + f_t + e_{it} \qquad 9.2$$

Dependent variable: $lnInc_{it}$ (log nominal income of household i in year t).
　Main explanatory variable:
　$\widehat{DTI}_{it-1}$ (a fitted value of the debt-to-income ratio of household i in
　　year t − 1 and obtained from the estimation of equation 9.1 in
　　Table 9.2).
Control variables:
　X (the set of control variables in equation 9.1).
Fixed effects:
　u_i (individual fixed effects),
　f_t (aggregate time effects), and
　v_i (individual-specific time trend).

　In equation 9.2, the fitted loan-income ratio $\widehat{DTI}$, rather than the DTI itself, enters as a regressor—which serves as the variable linking financial growth and quintile income growth and ultimately determining the distribution of income. Other regressors are $\widehat{DTI}$'s interaction terms with quintile income dummies (D_{jit}) and a set of control variables X. As in equation 9.1, D_{jit} are included as additional independent variables.

　To obtain consistent estimates for γ_j (j = 1, 2, 3, 4, and 5) in estimating equation 9.2, it is necessary to address the possibility that $\widehat{DTI}_{it-1}$ is correlated with an unobserved part of individual household income represented by u_i, as well as with an unobserved part of the growth of the income represented by $v_i \cdot time_t$. The existence of these correlations could bias the estimates of γ_j. For instance, if households with the unobserved factors that are associated with high income are also the ones with high DTI, γ_j would be overestimated.

　Similarly, if households with the unobserved factors that are associated with high income growth over time are also the ones with high DTI, γ_j would be overestimated. We remove these potential biases by converting equation 9.2 into the first-difference form of equation 9.3. Using this form also helps reduce the difficulty of estimating the parameters in equation 9.2 that arise from the fact that u_i and $v_i \cdot time_t$ include a large number of unobserved factors.

Since equation 9.3 is a typical panel data model with individual fixed effects, it can be used to estimate the same parameters γ_j in equation 9.2.[4]

$$\Delta lnInc_{it} = \sum_{j=1}^{5} \gamma_j \Delta(\widehat{DTI}_{it-1} * D_{jit-1})$$
$$+ \sum_{j=1}^{5} \delta_j \Delta D_{jit-1} + \gamma_c \Delta X_{it} + v_i + \Delta f_t + \Delta e_{it} \qquad 9.3$$

Note that the first differencing does not change the sign or size of the parameters of equation 9.2. This means that we could use equation 9.3 to estimate the same parameters γ_j and δ_j in equation 9.2. It also means that in equation 9.3, v_i, which enters as a covariate for individual fixed effects, explains $v_i \cdot time_t$ (individual-specific time trends), and Δft accounts for f_t in equation 9.2.

In estimating equation 9.3, aggregate time effects denoted by f_t should be controlled. Otherwise, they could bias the estimates of γ_j because they could be correlated with $\widehat{DTI}_{it-1} * D_{jit-1}$ as well as income. To remove the bias, aggregate time effects f_t in equation 9.3 are explained by year dummy variables.

The $\widehat{DTI}_{it-1}$ from the CRE Tobit model (equation 9.1 of the first stage of analysis) is substituted for DTI_{it-1} in equation 9.3. This substitution does not cause any bias, because $\widehat{DTI}_{it-1} = DTI_{it-1} + \hat{e}_{it-1}$ and $E(\widehat{DTI}_{it-1} | X) = DTI_{it-1}$. But the standard errors of the coefficients of $\widehat{DTI}_{it-1} * D_{jit-1}$ need to be corrected, as $\widehat{DTI}_{it-1}$ contains an error term: $\hat{e}_{it-1}$. The error term introduces the uncertainty known as the generated regressor problem (Pagan 1984), which is corrected by the bootstrapping method (Efron and Tibshirani 1993).[5]

---

4. The process of estimating equation 9.3 using a fixed-effects method is called a random growth (or random trend) model (see Baier et al., 2014; Wooldridge, 2016).

5. Bootstrapping is one way to estimate the estimator's variance by using repeated sampling from an approximating distribution. The basic idea is that inference about a population from sample data can be modeled by resampling the sample data and performing inference about a sample from resampled data. As the population is unknown, the true error in a sample statistic against its population value is unknown. In bootstrap resamples, the population in fact is the sample, and this is known; hence the quality of

Table 9.5. Heterogeneous Effect of DTI on Income by Income Quintile (estimation of Equation 9.3)

	2001–16		2009–16	
	1	2	3	4
$\widehat{DTI}*$D1	0.010	0.009	0.008	0.016
	(0.015)	(0.016)	(0.023)	(0.025)
$\widehat{DTI}*$D2	0.013	0.013	−0.003	0.002
	(0.012)	(0.012)	(0.020)	(0.021)
$\widehat{DTI}*$D3	0.027**	0.028**	0.013	0.015
	(0.012)	(0.013)	(0.022)	(0.023)
$\widehat{DTI}*$D4	0.031***	0.032***	0.048***	0.055***
	(0.010)	(0.010)	(0.015)	(0.015)
$\widehat{DTI}*$D5	0.026***	0.026***	0.037***	0.037***
	(0.008)	(0.008)	(0.014)	(0.014)
Edu	0.005	0.002	−0.006	−0.015
	(0.010)	(0.010)	(0.019)	(0.021)
Male	0.119***	0.101**	0.065	0.044
	(0.046)	(0.048)	(0.063)	(.073)
Seoul	0.075	0.071	0.038	0.061
	(0.076)	(0.080)	(0.105)	(0.122)
Age	−0.007**	−0.007**	−0.006	−0.008
	(0.003)	(0.003)	(0.004)	(0.004)
Ownhm	0.019	0.013	0.017	0.001
	(0.016)	(0.016)	(0.029)	(0.033)
Observations	46,491	46,491	16,692	16,692
Households	3,655	3,655	3,611	3,611

Notes: The years 2009–16 represent the period after the 2008 financial crisis. All numbers reflect year and individual fixed effects. Standard errors are clustered by the household level and reported in parentheses. To save space, coefficient estimates on dummy variables and other control variables are not reported. The acronyms are explained in the text. $* p < 0.10 ** p < 0.05 *** p < 0.01$.

Table 9.5 presents the estimation results of equation 9.3. In the whole sample, changes in the DTI have no statistically significant effects on household income in the first and second quintiles, but they have posi-

---

inference of the "true" sample from resampled data is measurable. For more details, see Efron and Tibshirani (1993).

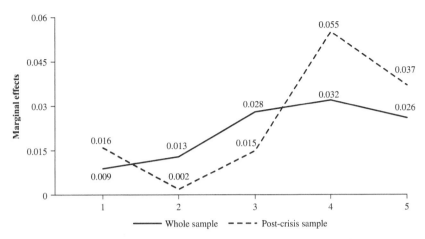

Figure 9.2. Marginal Effects of DTI on Income by Income Quintile
Source: Authors' estimation.

tive and statistically significant effects on the income in the other quintiles. For instance, using the estimates γ_1 and γ_5 in column 4, a one-unit increase in the DTI raises the household income of the fourth quintile by 5.5 and of the fifth quintile by 3.7 percent on average (Figure 9.2).

As shown in Table 9.2, the coefficients of the IFY in equation 9.1 are positive and statistically significant in the fourth and fifth income quintiles. Combining these coefficients with those presented in Table 9.5, we find that an increase in the IFY contributed to a significant increase in the average income of households in the fourth and fifth quintiles. In contrast, the same increase in the IFY did not increase average incomes in the lower income quintiles. However, we cannot draw the same conclusion for the post crisis period, because the effects of the IFY on the DTI are inconclusive. These findings for the whole sample period provide evidence that financial development since the early 2000s has contributed to redistributing income in favor of wealthier households in Korea.

Another finding for the post crisis period in Table 9.5 is the significant increase in the average marginal effects of the DTI on the household income in the fourth and fifth quintiles, compared with the effects for the whole study period. However, given the statistical insignificance of the average marginal effects of the IFY on the DTI in the post crisis period, it is unclear as to whether financial growth played a part in the increase.

Overall, the preceding analyses present evidence suggesting that the growth of the debt-to-income ratio has played a more important role in expanding the earning capacities of households in the higher income quintiles, compared to those in the lower quintiles. Financial growth has done little to improve opportunities for households in the first and second quintiles to increase their average incomes. This bias implies that, if anything, financial development may have been partly responsible for the deterioration of Korea's income distribution equity since the early 2000s.

Corroborative Evidence

To substantiate the view that financial development has led to an increase in income inequality, this study examines data from other sources of income and the composition of consumption and investment expenditures of individual households. This additional data analysis is intended to ascertain whether there are any structural characteristics or constraints unique to low-income families that could shed light on the causes of the adverse effects of the DTI on household income growth in the first and the second quintiles.

For this purpose, this study uses information obtained from the Survey of Household Finance and Living Conditions (SHFLC), an annual survey conducted by Statistics Korea that, unlike the KLIPS surveys, compiles data on bank loans allocated to financing various types of spending.

According to the SHFLC data for the 2012–16 period, one of the most salient causes of the adverse effects of the DTI on income in the first income quintile was nonproductive use of the borrowed money for investments in housing and paying for living and housing rental expenses. Households in the first income quintile used, on an annual average, 27.8 percent of borrowed funds for living expenses plus monthly housing rental and rent deposits. This was accompanied by 30.5 percent for investment in housing and only 20.2 percent for business investment. Altogether, these households spent more than 68 percent of the borrowed funds on financing nonproductive expenditures that did not generate income.

A median of business investment per household financed by bank loans in the first income quintile was about 13 million won ($11,000 at the exchange rate at the time), and 20 million won ($18,000) on average during the SHFLC sample period. In the same quintile, the proportion of families that invested more than 20 million won in business with bank funding was 30.2–38.9 percent. In an economy where an investment of 100 million won ($88,000) is required to set up a stand selling beverages and food (Ko 2015), it is difficult to imagine what type of a start-up business low-income households could launch with a loan of 20 million won.

Because of poor or nonexistent credit records, a lack of collateral, and limited experience in managing a business, self-employed people and households running small businesses in the first and the second income quintiles are subject to greater credit rationing. They also pay higher interest rates than those in higher-income groups. These constraints then lower the probability of a venture's success.

A different sample survey of Korean Statistical Information Service shows that about 45 percent of new entrants in wholesale and retail trade or accommodation and food services went bankrupt within the first year. The failure rate jumped to 60 percent after three years and to more than 70 percent after five years.

According to the SHFLC survey, 50 percent of heads of households in the first income quintile were self-employed and engaged in wholesale and retail trade or accommodation and food services. The percentage was 37 percent in the second quintile. It would not be surprising if an equally large number of the self-employed included in the SHFLC survey met the same fate as many of those in the Korean Statistical Information Service survey.

CHAPTER 10

Consolidation of Financial Regulatory Authorities

The Evolution of Korea's Financial Regulatory System

Restructuring Financial Supervision and Regulation

This chapter takes up the restructuring of financial supervision and regulation, the strengthening of prudential regulation, improvement of the internal and external governance of financial institutions, capital market deregulation, and protection of consumers of financial services. Before the 1997 crisis, the supervision and regulation of financial markets and institutions were divided among four sector-specific institutions: one each for banks, NBFIs, insurance, and securities. As the country's central bank, the Bank of Korea was entrusted with the supervision of commercial and specialized banks. Financial liberalization in the 1990s, which blurred the lines between financial industries, brought to the fore the issue of whether a regulatory system composed of separate and independent sector-specific institutions is viable.

When the walls separating banking, insurance, and securities were broken down or lowered to allow financial firms to move into the traditional territories of other service providers, there was growing concern that such a diversified system might not be efficient. If nothing else, the conglomeration and diversification of financial services provided by banks and other financial institutions made it necessary to ensure close cooperation and coordination and facilitate information exchange among the separate regulatory institutions.

During the 1990s, some European countries chose to introduce a unified regulatory system. The United Kingdom had been working to consolidate its regulatory agencies before establishing a single supervising institution. Encouraged by the unification trend worldwide, Korean policy makers undertook a complete overhaul of financial regulation to create a unified system.

The Bank of Korea Act sets out the legal basis for bank supervision. First promulgated in May 1950, it was wholly revised as of December 31, 1997, in connection with the promulgation of the Act on the Establishment of Financial Supervisory Organizations (EFSO Act), which was designed to unify the separate sector-specific supervisory authorities.

Under the EFSO Act, the Financial Supervisory Commission was established in April 1998. The commission's executive arm, the Financial Supervisory Service (FSS), was created in January 1999 by consolidating the four financial supervisory authorities: the Office of Bank Supervision, Securities Supervisory Board, Insurance Supervisory Board, and Nonbank Supervisory Authority. The FSS was charged with the examination of financial institutions, along with enforcement and other oversight activities as directed by the commission, which was the FSS's supervising body.

The start of the administration of President Lee Myung-bak in 2008 led to a renaming and shuffling of duties. Under amendments to the Bank of Korea Act and EFSO Act promulgated on February 29, 2008, the Financial Supervisory Commission was integrated with the Financial Policy Bureau of what was then called the Ministry of Finance and Economy to become the Financial Services Commission. The posts of commission chairman and FSS governor were separated in March 2008 to create a division of labor between policy making and supervision.

The Financial Services Commission, as now structured, serves as a consolidated policy making body for all matters pertaining to the supervision of the financial system. It is responsible for formulating financial policies, supervising financial institutions and financial markets, and protecting consumers of financial services.

The primary function of the FSS, as now structured, is to be Korea's integrated financial regulator. It examines and supervises financial institutions under the broad oversight of the Financial Services Commission. It also undertakes other oversight and enforcement functions as charged by that commission and the Securities and Futures Commission.

How well has the new system worked so far? There are no generally accepted criteria for evaluating the relative effectiveness of a unified regulatory system, as is discussed in chapter 11. The Financial Services Commission has not been immune to corruption. It also failed to prevent the credit card loan and savings bank crises (see chapter 12). The system has been criticized for its lack of independence and disregard for consumer protection. The division of labor and legal statutes between the commission and the FSS has not been specified. So, not surprisingly, the system has been the subject of reform ever since it was established—as demonstrated by the frequent amendments to the EFSO Act, among other things.

Despite, or perhaps reflecting, continuing disputes about the need to rectify the structural flaws of financial supervision and regulation, particularly the lack of independence, the governments that came to power in 2008 and 2013 did not want to undertake a genuinely comprehensive system overhaul. Nor were they able to find a compromise among different proposals for reform, except for creating a new institution for protecting consumers of financial services.

Strengthening Prudential Regulations and Improving the Financial Sector's Internal and External Governance

Since the onset of the 1997 crisis, the government has undertaken various measures to fortify prudential regulations and reform the governance of financial institutions.

The first measure was to allow regulatory authorities to take the prompt corrective actions if a bank's financial conditions do not meet the standards of capital adequacy ratios and its composite grade on the score known as CAMELS (capital adequacy, asset quality, management, earnings, liquidity, and sensitivity to market risk) is less than the stipulated level. The corrective actions consist of three sets of progressively more stringent corrective procedures, as outlined in Table 10.1. The actions were initially applied to banks, merchant bank corporations, and securities

Table 10.1. Prompt Corrective Actions for the Banking Sector

| Measure | Conditions when measures were taken | | Decision maker | Details of measure |
	BIS ratio	Other		
Recommend management improvement	Below 8%	1. Above the third rate in CAMELS but below the fourth rate in terms of quality of assets or capital adequacy 2. It seems evident that the above cutoff conditions were not satisfied because of a large financial debacle	Governor of the FSS	1. Organizational restructuring 2. Cost reduction 3. Increasing the efficiency of business unit management 4. Restrictions on fixed-asset investment, entry into new businesses, and new financial investment 5. Management of insolvent assets 6. Recapitalization 7. Restriction of dividend payouts and special allowance for bad debt
Require management improvement	Below 6%	1. Below the fourth rate in CAMELS 2. It seems evident that the above cutoff conditions were not satisfied because of a large financial debacle	Governor of the FSS (after FSC vote)	1. Closure or consolidation of existing business units or restriction on new ones 2. Retrenchment of organization 3. Restriction on holding risky assets and management of assets 4. Restriction on the deposit rate 5. Restructuring of subsidiaries 6. Requirement of management turnover

(continued)

Table 10.1 (Continued)

| Measure | Conditions when measures were taken | | Decision maker | Details of measure |
	BIS ratio	Other		
				7. Partial suspension of banking operation
				8. Planning of mergers and acquisitions or transfer of banking business
				9. Measures specified in Clause 2, Article 34 of the Act on the Structural Improvement of the Financial Industry
Order management improvement	Below 2%	1. Unsound financial institutions specified in Clause 3, Article 2 of the Act on the Structural Improvement of the Financial Industry	FSC	1. Write off shares
				2. Prohibition of execution of banking operations by management and nomination of managers
				3. Mergers and acquisitions with other banks
				4. Suspension with other healthy banks for less than 6 months
				5. Transfer of contracts

Source: Financial Services Commission (http://www.fsc.go.kr/eng/index.jsp).

Note: The actions shown are as of March 1999. BIS ratio is the Bank of International Settlements' ratio of bank soundness. The rates of CAMELS are explained in the text. FSS is the Financial Supervisory Service. FSC is the Financial Services Commission.

companies, starting in April 1998. This application was subsequently extended to include insurance companies and mutual savings banks (in June 1998) and credit unions (in December 1999).

The second measure was to expand (through the Financial Services Commission) the scope of regular disclosure items to the level dictated by the International Accounting Standards to strengthen banks' disclosure systems.

The third measure was to strengthen loan classification standards, as well as provisioning requirements, according to international practices (Table 10.2).

Table 10.2. Loan Classification Standards and Required Provisions

	Before July 1998	*As of December 2011*
Definition		
Normal	—[a]	—[a]
Precautionary	3–6 months past due	1–3 months past due
Substandard	More than 6 months past due, secured	More than 3 months past due, secured
Doubtful	More than 6 months past due, unsecured	3–12 months past due, unsecured
Estimated loss	Expected losses	More than 12 months past due, unsecured
Loan loss reserve requirement		
Normal	0.5%	Above 0.85%
Precautionary	1%	7%
Substandard	20%	20%
Doubtful	75%	50%
Estimated loss	100%	100%
Provisioning for outstanding guarantees	Not required	20% of substandard, 50% of doubtful, and 100% of estimated loss

Source: Financial Statistics Information System of the Financial Supervisory Service (http://www.fss.or.kr/fss/eng/main.jsp).

Notes: Normal, precautionary, substandard, and doubtful refer to quality of loans. Estimated loss refers to loss of loan payments.

[a] Not applicable.

In addition, forward-looking asset quality classification standards were introduced for commercial banks at the end of 1999. They were based on the debtors' ability to generate sufficient future cash flows rather than on their past payment records. Similar standards were introduced for merchant banks in June 2000 and insurance companies in September 2000.

Furthermore, the asset categories subject to loan-loss provisions were broadened to include commercial paper, guaranteed bills, and privately placed bonds in trust accounts. And the evaluation standard for marketable and investment securities held by banks was changed from the lower of cost or market method to mark to market.

In tandem with the changes in prudential regulation, the Financial Services Commission strengthened direct regulations limiting exposure of banks and merchant bank corporations, among others (Table 10.3).

Table 10.3. Ceilings on the Credit Exposure of Financial Institutions

	Commercial bank	Merchant bank corporation	Insurance company
Credit exposure to a single borrower	Up to 20% of bank capital	Up to 20% of bank capital	—[a]
Combined credit exposure to firms affiliated with the same chaebol	Up to 25% of bank capital	Up to 25% of bank capital	Up to 3% of total assets
Total large credit exposure	Up to 5 times bank capital	Up to 5 times bank capital	Loans and securities holdings up to 5% of total assets
Credit exposure to large shareholders of financial institutions	Up to ownership shares of respective shareholder with maximum 25% of bank capital	Up to ownership shares of respective shareholder with maximum 25% of bank capital	—[a]

Source: Financial Statistics Information System of the Financial Supervisory Service (http:// www.fss.or.kr/fss/eng/main.jsp).

Note: Large shareholders are those owning 10 percent or more of total shares with voting rights.

[a] Not applicable.

The definition of exposure for a single borrower was broadened to include not only loans and payment guarantees in the conventional sense, but also all direct and indirect transactions that carry credit risks—such as corporate bonds and commercial paper holdings.

In May 1999, the combined exposure for firms affiliated with the same chaebol was tightened to 25 percent of a bank's capital from 45 percent. Additionally, the total exposures of more than 10 percent of a bank's capital to a single borrower or a group of firms affiliated with the same chaebol was limited to five times that of bank capital.

Finally, the exposure for large shareholders of a bank, defined as those holding 10 percent or more of the shares, was limited to the equity shares of respective large shareholders with a maximum 25 percent of bank capital. The primary purpose of these exposure limits is to prevent chaebol-affiliated financial institutions from taking too many risks and to reduce their exposure to risks affecting other subsidiaries of the same chaebol.

The most dramatic and effective measure of governance reform in the financial sector is no doubt the closure of insolvent institutions. Indeed, the closure of nonviable banks opened a new chapter in Korea's financial history, considering that not a single commercial bank had been closed in the four decades before the 1997 crisis.

Since January 1998, under the Act on the Structural Improvement of the Financial Industry, the supervisory authority mandated equity write-offs against shareholders deemed responsible for bank insolvencies. To encourage shareholders and internal auditors to assume a more significant role in monitoring management, the Financial Services Commission removed many of the restrictions imposed on exercising minority shareholder rights.

Since 1999, financial institutions are required to have 50 percent of their board members be outside directors. In addition, banks and securities and insurance firms were required to make financial disclosures quarterly instead of semiannually.

Since January 1, 2005, class action lawsuits to protect shareholders from stock price manipulation, insider trading, and false financial disclosures have been allowed under the Securities-Related Class Action Act. For a variety of reasons, few cases have been filed. Members of the legal profession and others have lobbied intensively to expand the scope and ease of class action suits (see Soonghee Lee 2014; Jin Yeong Chung et al. 2019).

The Financial Services Commission also implemented a sanction system in which, if necessary, civil and criminal liabilities can be imposed on directors. Equivalent sanctions can be imposed on the external auditors and examiners of the supervisory authorities for dereliction of duty.[1]

Capital Market Deregulation

Financial deregulation and market opening in the wake of the 1997 crisis set the stage for rapid growth; diversification of bonds, equities, and other derivative products; and proliferation of capital market institutions. Yet supervision and regulation of money and capital markets were not revised to cope with these market developments.

Financial firms were restricted to a limited range of activities such as commercial and investment banking and insurance until 2009. Before the capital market deregulation was initiated, diverse capital market institutions and financial investment companies—such as stock brokerages, asset management firms, futures companies, and trust companies—offered similar services and products but were regulated by fourteen different laws.

There had been a long debate about streamlining these laws to foster the competition among and consolidation of these institutions.[2] It was claimed that the consolidation would facilitate the emergence of sizable global-scale investment banks and the better protection of consumers. However, there were also concerns that it could increase the market share of shadow banking and aggravate the problems associated with it.

There was certainly a need to increase the scope of deregulation covering capital market institutions. The debate culminated in the enactment of the Capital Market Consolidation Act (CMCA), which took effect in February 2009. The act integrated the fourteen financial laws, including those on securities and futures exchanges, into a single regulatory framework.

---

1. A prime example is a lawsuit against former officials of the Korea First Bank by a group of minority shareholders, which resulted in an award of 40 billion won to be paid by the former officials (two presidents, a director, and an auditor) to the bank for wrongful behavior and managerial failures.

2. A Capital Market Consolidation Act was discussed before the 2008 financial crisis as part of the initiative to make Seoul a global financial hub and create megabanks. However, the act was not promulgated until August 2007. It took effect in February 2009.

The CMCA had a dual purpose. It was part of further deregulation that had two goals: to foster the competition in financial markets by allowing financial firms to provide a broader range of financial services and capital market institutions to move into their competitors' territories, thus enabling them to deal in multiple markets; and to protect the interests of consumers of financial services. Investment companies were no longer limited to one type of financial business but were allowed to market all financial services and products for which they obtained a license.

The CMCA made it possible for brokerage firms, asset management firms, futures companies, and trust companies to compete not only with each other but also with banks and insurers. Before the act, such companies were permitted to sell only a narrow range of services and products. By consolidating the fourteen financial laws, the act aimed to facilitate the mergers and portfolio diversifications of banks and other financial service providers.

It was expected that the act would allow financial companies to grow larger and benefit from economies of scale as well as increasing competition across the entire spectrum of financial markets. However, there have been relatively few mergers and acquisitions across traditional product lines, and diversification has been limited. The effects of the CMCA may have been counteracted by new regulations for consumer protection and a reduction in capital account liberalization triggered by the crisis.

So far, the legislation has not been successful in creating investment banks that are large and efficient enough to compete in global markets. In the wake of the 2008 crisis, policy makers have had few incentives for another big-bang financial reform to complement the CMCA. Instead, they have moved on to tightening the control of capital inflows.

The 2008 crisis led to some reorientation of policy toward capital flows and foreign currency exposure by introducing a set of macroprudential tools. The crisis was a reminder that the regulatory and policy authorities lacked adequate instruments for coping with the volatility of capital flows. Of particular concern was preventing foreign investors from overreacting and heading for the exits and foreign banks refusing to roll over short-term loans when the signs of a crisis emerge. At the same time, Korea's policy makers have found some justification for their renewed tightening of capital account transactions in the International Monetary Fund's revised position that supports some types of capital control if capital flow volatility puts financial stability at risk (see the discussions by Fund staff members in Ostry et al. 2010 and Habermeier et al. 2011).

Protection of Consumers of Financial Services

As for consumer protection, the CMCA includes measures to grade the risks of financial products, require firms to sell only products with a risk level appropriate for the individual customer, and not recommend a product unless the customer asked about it first.

However, the CMCA has been ineffective in providing better protection for consumers. In recognition of this, and after blaming the FSS for its inability to assume more responsibility in this regard, the government of President Geun-hye Park, which came to power in 2013, proposed the creation of a new agency that would be independent of the FSS. This agency would increase both the scope of coverage and the effectiveness of protection. However, this proposal was abandoned, mainly due to the objections from the FSS on the grounds that the new agency would weaken its role as the principal financial regulator.

The protection of consumers of financial services surfaced as a crucial item on the reform agenda in the wake of the 2008 crisis. Although a decade has passed, Korea has yet to create a full-fledged system for consumer protection in the financial sector. A financial consumer protection bill, first introduced in the National Assembly in July 2010, was not signed into law because the ruling and opposition parties failed to agree on the creation of an independent protection agency or a similar institution to be established within the purview of the FSS.

Subsequently, the government submitted legislation on the Financial Consumer Protection Act on February 22, 2012, but it was rescinded when the 18th National Assembly ended. The government submitted the bill again with some modifications on July 6, 2012, but once again it was rescinded. Afterward, the government made further legislative efforts to create a single piece of legislation on financial consumer protection, which would systematically regulate financial products and their sale under the principle of applying the same rule to the same functions.

Moon Jae-in, who has been president of Korea since May 2017, has made an issue of consumer protection, so there is some expectation that legislation will be forthcoming in this area. In fact, on May 23, 2017, a government bill was submitted to the National Assembly, while representatives of the ruling and opposition parties proposed similar bills.

However, the one area in which action has been taking is internet banking. Legislation covering internet-only banking became effective on January 17, 2019. Among other things, under this law, nonfinancial businesses can own up to 34 percent of an internet bank. The limit for ownership of different types of banks is 4 percent.

As of November 2019, a financial consumer protection bill, approved by the National Policy Committee of the National Assembly, was under consideration. It contains sales regulations that would be applied to all financial products and establishes a legal basis for penalizing firms that violate its provisions.

CHAPTER 11

Role of the Financial Supervisory System in Safeguarding Financial Stability

The Effectiveness of Macroprudential Policy

Role of Macroprudential Policy

One of the main objectives of creating a unified financial regulatory system was to improve the effectiveness of supervision in safeguarding financial stability in a liberalized system. This chapter and chapter 12 assess the extent to which the new regulatory system has been successful in this regard. This chapter is devoted to evaluating the role and effectiveness of Korea's macroprudential policy. Such policies are defined as policy regimes in which policy makers dynamically adjust the parameters of prudential supervisory instruments (microprudential tools) to contain systemic risks.

This chapter focuses first on analyzing the effectiveness of two measures in mitigating the real estate boom-and-bust cycle in the 2001–07 period. These measures are the ratio of the loan to the appraisal value of real estate purchased (LTV) and the ratio of debt to income (DTI), defined as the principle and interest payments on all loans divided by income.

In contrast to a long-held view, it is now widely accepted that consumer price stability is not a sufficient condition for financial stability. Financial imbalances in the form of booms and busts in asset markets, excessive leverage in financial institutions and households, and increased maturity and currency mismatches on the balance sheets of financial institutions can pile up in a noninflationary environment. These imbalances can destabilize the financial system and even trigger a crisis, which in turn causes serious disruptions to real-sector development.

Experience with managing financial crises has demonstrated that the potential risk associated with financial imbalances can be substantial, and central banks and regulatory authorities now recognize the need to supplement their tool kits with new policy instruments. One such instrument is macroprudential policy.

There is a growing literature on macroprudential policy. However, this has not led to a consensus on such policies' scope and effectiveness.[1] Although it is generally agreed that the efficiency of monetary policy would be improved by macroprudential supervision, there is a lack of understanding of the contours of a new system for the coordination of the two policy regimes. This is because the new system needs to be calibrated to avoid potential conflict, which could cancel out the effects of the two because macroprudential policy has macroeconomic spillovers, whereas monetary policy affects the risk-taking behavior of participants in the financial market.

The objectives of macroprudential policy are to lean against the wind when systemic risks are building up and to stem the risks associated with interconnections and spillovers in the financial system (Committee on the Global Financial System 2010; Hannoun, 2010). To be sure, these objectives are not mutually exclusive. This is because greater resilience in a financial system improves its ability to adjust to financial cycles (Crockett 2000; Borio 2003).

To recap, the microprudential objective is to limit the idiosyncratic risk that individual financial institutions are exposed to, while macroprudential policy safeguards the stability of the entire financial system. The systemic risk that the macroprudential approach focuses on is endogenous, as it is determined by the collective behavior of individual institutions—whereas the idiosyncratic risk is exogenous.

---

1. For a literature survey, see Galati and Moessner 2011, and Kahou and Lehar 2017. The International Monetary Fund (2018) has started to publish the results of its annual survey on the macroprudential policy of its member countries, with the objective of covering macroprudential measures taken by countries.

The 2010 survey by the Bank for International Settlements on the use of macroprudential instruments in thirty-three countries shows that in most cases, the objective was to enhance the resilience of the financial system rather than to moderate financial cycles, and the evidence on the effectiveness of macroprudential measures is not conclusive (Committee on the Global Financial System 2010). In part, these findings are supported by the experience with a macroprudential policy directed at managing the housing market boom and bust in Korea.

Effectiveness of Macroprudential Policy: The Housing Market Boom and Bust

LTV AND DTI REGULATIONS, 2002–18

In the years following the 1997 crisis, Korea's financial regulators have been charged with mitigating, if not preventing, boom-and-bust cycles in housing and other real estate markets.[2] As the first line of action, the regulators have invariably relied on two of the recalibrated microprudential tools: the LTV and DTI. These instruments were adjusted to regulate the supply of mortgage loans at financial institutions whenever there were signs of overheating or cooling-off in the housing market.[3] Implementation of these instruments entails a quantitative control of the availability of sectoral, as well as aggregate, bank credit rather than adjusting the cost of bank borrowing.

The next section of this chapter examines the modus operandi and effectiveness of the two instruments in bringing the boom-and-bust cycle in the housing market under control.[4] Since 2002, Korea's financial regulatory authorities have intervened in the bank loan market twenty-three times by using the LTV and DTI. In managing the two instruments, the financial regulatory authorities have built up a highly complex and discrete regime for their implementation, in which different ratios are ap-

---

2. This section draws on Yung Chul Park 2010.

3. If these two instruments prove to be ineffective, the supervisory authorities may—although they never have in Korea—resort to another type of instrument, which is reserved for tempering procyclicality in bank lending. This includes countercyclical capital charges, dynamic loan-loss provisioning, and capital conservation rules for banks.

4. For details of the changes in mortgage lending regulations, see Igan and Kang 2011, Soon-Taek Chang 2010, and Kim Yung Do 2018.

plied to different financial institutions, loan maturities, values of house collateral, types of housing (house or apartment), speculative areas (Seoul, other metropolitan areas, or regions), and even different classes of borrowers at banking institutions.

The rationale behind the construction of such a complex system was to take into account some of the structural characteristics unique to a national housing market that consists of a large number of regional markets segmented by income; living conditions; and access to public transportation, as well as cultural and educational institutions.

In looking at the regulatory history, it is essential to note that Korea has a liquid market for apartments, which are standardized in terms of size and actively traded. In particular, smaller ones are easily marketable, making them a tradable investment asset and a good substitute for financial assets.

Table 11.1 details the use of LTV and DTI regulations during 2002–18. The data underscore how detail-oriented the financial regulatory authorities—the Financial Supervisory Commission (which, as explained in chapter 10, changed its name in 2008 to the Financial Services Commission; FSC) and Financial Supervisory Service—have been in relying on the two instruments in taming the boom-and-bust cycle in the housing market. In 2002, the authorities introduced for the first time the LTV, capping it with a ceiling of 60 percent to contain the incipient housing boom that was feared to be getting out of control.

Thereafter, the authorities adjusted the ratio fifteen times until 2018. On ten occasions, the FSC tightened it to clamp down a housing market boom, while easing it five times (in 2004, 2008, 2013, 2014, and 2015) when the FSC saw a weakening in housing demand. In August 2005, the FSC fortified its arsenal of macroprudential tools by adding the DTI, which was tightened nine times and loosened six times to either suppress or stimulate housing demand.

INDEX OF THE LTV AND DTI REGULATIONS

To analyze the effectiveness of macroprudential policy in the context of Korea's long struggle to dampen volatility in the housing market, we constructed indexes of LTV and DTI regulations using a method devised by Deniz Igan and Heedon Kang (2011), which is a weighted average of the

Table 11.1. Timeline of LTV and DTI Regulations

Time	LTV	DTI
Sep. 2002	Inception	—[a]
Jun. 2003	Tighten	—[a]
Oct. 2003	Tighten	—[a]
Jun. 2005	Tighten	—[a]
Aug. 2005	—[a]	Inception
Mar. 2006	—[a]	Tighten
Nov. 2006	Tighten	Tighten
Feb. 2007	—[a]	Tighten
Aug. 2007	—[a]	Tighten
Nov. 2008	Loosen	Loosen
Jul. 2009	Tighten	—[a]
Sep. 2009	—[a]	Tighten
Oct. 2009	Tighten	—[a]
Aug. 2010	—[a]	Loosen
Mar. 2011	—[a]	Tighten
May 2012	—[a]	Loosen
Apr. 2013	Loosen	Loosen
Jul. 2014	Loosen	Loosen
Jul. 2015	Loosen	Loosen
Aug. 2016	Tighten	Tighten
Jun. 2017	Tighten	Tighten
Aug. 2017–Nov. 2018	Tighten	Tighten

Source: Igan and Kang 2011.
[a]No change.

two ratios.[5] As shown in Figure 11.1, the changes in the LTV-DTI index on the dates of implementation (Table 11.1) indicate changes in the stance of macroprudential policy—whether it is intended to be tight (causing a

---

5. In view of the fact that the DTI is a more powerful regulation than the LTV, it is given a larger weight (two-thirds). This weighting, which is somewhat arbitrary, is chosen to reflect more accurately the changes in the regulatory stance—the degree of tightness or looseness over time. The weighting does not change the conclusions of this chapter. See Table 11.2 for the numerical values of the indexes.

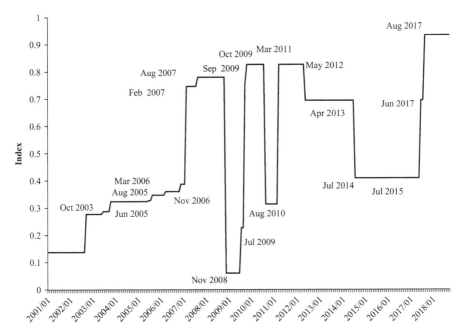

Figure 11.1. LTV-DTI Regulation Index, 2001–18
Source: Authors' estimation.
Note: The horizontal axis indicates January in each year.

rise in the index) or loose (causing a fall). Table 11.2 provides the numerical values of the index.

In what follows, this section presents—at the risk of being redundant—descriptive details of macroprudential policy since 2003, when it became apparent that the housing market was heating up, to show how reactive, rather than proactive, the authorities have been in their operations.

Tightening

In June 2003, the FSC lowered the LTV cap to 50 percent for mortgage loans that had a maturity of less than three years and were extended by banks and NBFIs in specific zones or areas affected by speculation. The LTV control turned out to be less than effective because banks were started to extend mortgage loans with a maturity of longer than three years to avoid the restriction, while NBFIs were not subject to the downward adjustment.

Table 11.2. LTV, DTI, and Regulation Indexes

Time	LTV	DTI	Regulation
1/2001–8/2002	0.41	0.00	0.14
9/2002–5/2003	0.82	0.00	0.28
6–9/2003	0.86	0.00	0.29
10/2003–5/2005	0.97	0.00	0.32
6–7/2005	0.98	0.00	0.33
8/2005–2/2006	0.98	0.03	0.35
3–10/2006	0.98	0.05	0.36
11/2006–1/2007	0.98	0.09	0.39
2–7/2007	0.98	0.63	0.75
8/2007–10/2008	0.98	0.68	0.78
11/2008–6/2009	0.04	0.07	0.06
7–8/2009	0.54	0.07	0.23
9/2009	0.54	0.86	0.75
10/2009–7/2010	0.76	0.86	0.83
8/2010–2/2011	0.76	0.09	0.31
3/2011–4/2012	0.76	0.86	0.83
5/2012–6/2014	0.76	0.66	0.69
7/2014–5/2017	0.30	0.46	0.41
6–7/2017	0.60	0.74	0.70
8/2017–9/2018	0.96	0.92	0.93

Notes: The LTV and DTI indexes are constructed using the method devised by Igan and Kang (2011). The regulation index is a weighted average of the LTV and DTI indexes.

To resolve the matter, in October 2003, the FSC increased coverage of the LTV regulation to mortgage loans with maturity of ten years or less and lowered the LTV cap to 40 percent on loans for buying apartments, which was then the primary source of housing speculation.

Loosening

After the tightening of the LTV rule, the rise in housing prices began to decelerate. But, unsure about whether the market lull could be sustained, the FSC took the cautious step of relaxing the rule by lifting the LTV cap only to 70 percent for mortgage loans with a maturity of longer than ten years.

Tightening Again

Beginning in the early months of 2005, housing prices began to soar again. In June 2005, this prompted the FSC to lower the LTV cap from 60 percent to 40 percent on mortgage loans with a maturity of longer than ten years for the purchase of apartments valued at more than 600 million won (about $600,000 at the 2005 exchange rate) in speculative zones. In November 2006, this restriction was applied to NBFIs with a higher ceiling of 50 percent.

Fortifying the LTV with the DTI, Starting in August 2005

To complement the LTV regulation, between August 2005 and August 2007, the FSC lowered the DTI four times at banks and NBFIs. At the inception of DTI in 2005, a relatively small segment of riskier borrowers buying apartments was subject to the ceiling of 40 percent in several districts of the Seoul metropolitan area that were prone to speculation. The affected borrowers were single people under the age of thirty and married people whose spouses had debt.

On March 26, 2006, the coverage of the DTI restriction was broadened to include borrowing for the purchase of smaller apartment units priced at 600 million won or more. A year after that, this was extended to include all apartment units, with the ratio set at 40–60 percent.

Only when the DTI was lowered and other taxes and regulatory measures were implemented in 2006 and 2007 did the growth of mortgage loans drop, falling to a level of 2.1 percent in 2007. But more than anything else, the onset of the global financial crisis in 2008 contributed to bursting the bubble, leading to sluggishness in the housing market for two years beginning in 2007.[6]

Loosening in January 2008

After the collapse of Lehman Brothers—which triggered a domestic liquidity crisis, deeper recession, and contraction of housing demand—policy makers recognized the need to relieve the burden on household

---

6. A Granger causality test shows that causality runs from household credit to housing prices. This causal relationship indicates the significance of procyclicality in household lending, with an expansion of household loans for housing finance inflating housing prices—which in turn drives the growth in housing loans.

borrowers of servicing their mortgage. This debt relief led to the removal of most of the speculative areas from the list of controlled regions in November 2008.

Although demand for housing was slowing, banks continued to extend new loans, including issuing new mortgages and renewing outstanding ones, for fear that any contraction would increase nonperforming loans. They chose to wait out the downturn in the hope that once the housing market recovered, their problems would disappear.

Back to Tightening

Beginning in July 2009, housing prices started rising again. In response, the FSC lowered the LTV to 50 percent for bank loans that financed the purchase of apartments worth more than 600 million won in the Seoul metropolitan area. In October, this regulation was extended to the loans of all financial institutions.

Neutral Stance between September 2009 and May 2012

The FSC saw the need to complement the LTV by tightening the DTI regulation in 2009. Thereafter, until the early months of 2013, housing prices remained relatively stable, allowing room for a neutral stance in macroprudential policy.

Tightening Again

For the next three years until August 2016, the FSC was reluctant to tighten the supply of mortgage loans any further lest doing so delay a full recovery of a housing market that appeared to be fragile—although beginning in mid-2013 housing prices rose. Only in August 2016 did the financial regulatory authorities reverse their policy and decelerate mortgage lending. They did so by tightening both the LTV and DTI three times by July 2017.

Effectiveness of the LTV and DTI Regulations

There is a vast and growing Korean literature that analyzes the effectiveness of the LTV and DTI regulations in stabilizing the housing markets in different administrative regions.[7] Most of the empirical studies adopt a

---

7. For a survey of the Korean literature, see Y. Lee and Lee 2018.

panel estimation of a reduced form equation that covers different administrative districts over different periods. The rate of change in the housing price index, as the dependent variable, is regressed against changes in the LTV and DTI and a host of control variables.[8] With a few exceptions, the studies all show that the two instruments have been effective in reducing the amplitude, if not preventing the onset, of a boom-and-bust cycle.

All the available empirical studies test the hypothesis that tightening the two ratios helps restrain price inflation in the housing market. This is under the assumption that the effects of tightening or relaxing the two ratios are transmitted through the market for household credit by changing the sectoral supply of mortgage loans. But few of the authors show whether such a credit channel exists or, if it does exist, whether it is operative.

Changes in the LTV and DTI ratios do not directly affect housing prices. Instead, they do so by changing the availability of bank credit for housing finance. To be credible, therefore, empirical studies need to test for a causal relation between the LTV and DTI regulations and the supply of housing finance. If an adverse effect is not found, then the positive impact of the changes in the capping rule on housing prices may not be as significant as existing studies show.

Also, none of the existing empirical studies control for the impact of tax levies and numerous other administrative directives that affect the demand for housing. Of course, there is no easy way of properly controlling for these discrete and often ad hoc market interventions in a panel estimation. Unless these deficiencies are rectified, the evidence of positive effects of the two types of macroprudential regulations on housing prices may not be free from statistical spuriousness.

Korea's experience demonstrates that, when faced with an incipient housing market price boom, the FSC has always resorted to the implementation of mortgage capping rules as its first line of defense. When this line is breached, other government ministries and agencies, including the national tax administration, have stepped in to dispense more direct and powerful tax and other administrative control measures.

---

8. The control variables introduced in Igan and Kang 2011 do not include tax regulations or administrative control.

For instance, the administration of President Roh Moo-hyun introduced twenty-nine new housing policies during its tenure (2003–7), whose topics ranged from housing acquisition and registration taxes to new town construction. The number of regulatory policies has not changed with the succeeding governments. The fact that the government has employed so many tax and other instruments suggests that policy makers have not had much confidence in the efficacy of the LTV and DTI policy.

Figure 11.2 shows that changes in both the house price index (HPI) for apartments in Seoul (which has always been an area afflicted by rampant housing speculation) and the volume of household loans allocated to Seoul are highly correlated with the changes in housing prices. The coefficient of correlation between the two series is 0.8. However, this result should not be taken as implying that there is a causal nexus going from regulatory capping to the HPI or its effectiveness.

Figure 11.3 presents changes in the LTV and DTI regulation index and the HPI. Figure 11.4 displays the regulation index, along with the volume of mortgage lending allocated to Seoul. A visual inspection of the

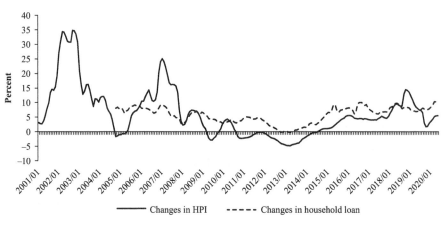

Figure 11.2. Changes in the Volume of Household Loans and the House Price Index

Sources: Economic Statistics System of the Bank of Korea and Kookmin Bank.

Notes: The horizontal axis indicates January in each year. "Household loans" refers to deposit money bank lending to households in Seoul. The house price index applies to apartment prices in Seoul (December 2015 = 100).

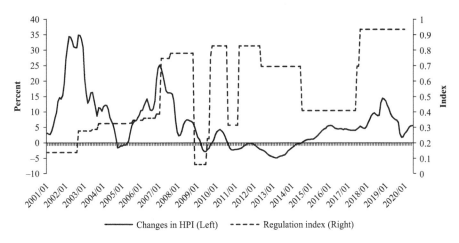

Figure 11.3. Changes in the House Price and Regulation Indexes
Sources: Economic Statistics System of the Bank of Korea and Kookmin Bank.
Note: The horizontal axis indicates January in each year.

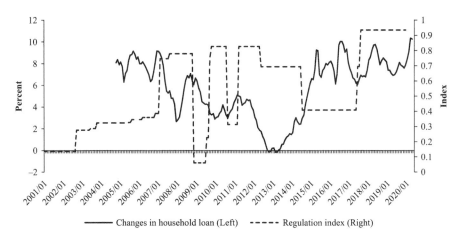

Figure 11.4. Changes in the Volume of Household Loans and the Regulation Index
Sources: Economic Statistics System of the Bank of Korea and Kookmin Bank.
Note: The horizontal axis indicates January in each year.

two figures suggests that the changes in mortgage loan regulations are not correlated with the changes in either the HPI or the volume of household loans. Instead, they move in opposite directions in several subperiods.

This observation is consistent with the findings of Igan and Kang (2011) that there is no evidence of a negative relationship between the growth of mortgage lending and the toughening of the LTV rule, possibly because of the slow-moving nature of the rule. However, this slowness may not apply to the DTI regulation, which is more closely linked to changes in household debt levels.[9]

The negative correlation between the changes in LTV and DTI capping and the availability of mortgage loans presented above underscores the need to broaden the scope of empirical examination to take into account the role of tax and other direct administrative interventions. With this need in mind, the following section discusses some structural impediments and other constraints that may have weakened the effectiveness of the regulations.

Constraints on Macroprudential Policy

One of the main reasons for the ineffectiveness of LTV and DTI regulations in changing mortgage lending is that they are plagued with the same flaws of diversion and evasion associated with the tools for traditional selective credit control. To administer the regulations, the authorities constructed a highly complex system in which they can impose different ratios on various financial institutions, borrowers, and speculative areas. This complexity of the rules has created incentives to take advantage of loopholes and regulatory ambiguities. We discuss these anomalies below.

CREDIT DIVERSION

When the financial regulators lower the LTV cap to reduce the supply of housing loans, housing speculators can easily supplement their mortgages with other loans or—in the case of wealthier households—with the proceeds from the sale of securities. Instead of approaching banks for loans,

---

9. This is the conclusion reached in Kim Yung Do 2018. For more positive assessments in other countries, see Kahou and Lehar 2017.

large firms can issue bonds and equities to finance real estate investments. Since mortgage lending is part of total housing finance, house buyers can secure other sources of financing to make up for the cut in the mortgage loans as long as they expect housing prices to rise continuously.

BALLOON EFFECT

The rationale behind the use of various LTV and DTI ratios across different borrowers and financial institutions appears to be the assumption that housing markets are disparate, fragmented, and segmented regionally. Thus, just because housing speculation begins one area, other areas are not necessarily likely to follow suit. Individual market–specific regulations, therefore, would be more effective than nationwide controls.

However, when a city is divided into speculative, speculation-prone, and stable districts, as is the case in the Seoul metropolitan area, real estate investors often move to less-restricted areas in the expectation that the prices of properties there will also rise. This expectation can become a self-fulfilling prophecy if enough speculators move into the same markets. This balloon effect could exacerbate a boom in one market so that it becomes nationwide housing speculation, nullifying much of the efficiency of a sector-specific contractionary LTV and DTI policy.

PROCYCLICALITY

Changes in the LTV-DTI regulation index, as pictured in Figure 11.1, show how reactive the supervisory authorities have been in changing the ceilings of mortgage loans whenever the housing prices are perceived to threaten the stability of the housing market. In doing so, the authorities do not seem to pay much attention to whether the price movements reflect a change in the trend or short-run fluctuations around it.

This reactive response has allowed market participants to forecast with a fair degree of accuracy when and how the authorities would react to price changes in the housing market. For example, on seeing a housing market boom on the horizon, market participants would conclude that regulators will soon toughen mortgage regulations. The participants then rush to borrow as much as possible before more stringent restrictions are imposed.

A subsequent rise in housing prices increases the collateral value of a purchased house, which allows banks to lend more while complying with the regulations and thus weakens the effect of the tighter regulations. Banks may have to cut the LTV ratio further.

In the opposite case, when the housing market is in a slump, market participants stop borrowing and leave the market even before the loosening of the regulatory policy, if they believe that the stagnation will continue. The regulators then have to relax the LTV and DTI again. If the additional easing is less than expected, households and speculators will not return to the market in the belief that there will be another round of loosening. Instead, they will wait—which may require a further increase in the LTV and DTI.

CONFLICTS BETWEEN MONETARY AND MACROPRUDENTIAL POLICY

There are potential conflicts between macroprudential and monetary policies that could undermine the scope and efficiency of the LTV and DTI regulations. As shown in Figure 11.5 and Table 11.2, since 2009, there has been no evidence suggesting that the Bank of Korea and the financial

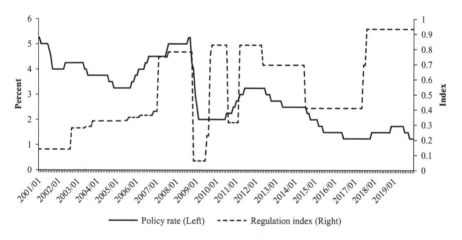

Figure 11.5. Changes in the Policy Rate and Regulation Index
Sources: Economic Statistics System of the Bank of Korea and Kookmin Bank.
Notes: The horizontal axis indicates January in each year.

regulatory authorities have sought to coordinate their policies. The Bank of Korea has maintained a relatively easy monetary policy to counter a slowdown in growth with little prospect of inflation. In contrast, the financial regulators have adjusted the regulation index eight times.

Under these circumstances, suppose that the regulatory authorities lower the ceilings of the LTV and DTI to stave off an incipient housing market boom and there is no change in the monetary policy stance, which will keep the level of total bank lending unaffected. In such a case, banks will be able to extend more of other types of business and consumer loans using funds that might otherwise have gone to housing finance. If the expected real return on housing investments is higher than the returns on other assets, many borrowers taking out nonmortgage loans will divert the bulk of their loan proceeds to housing investment.[10]

This diversion suggests that reducing the LTV on mortgage lending will not be effective unless the Bank of Korea tightens monetary policy to reduce the growth of aggregate bank credit. But the bank may not find any reason to do so when consumer prices are stable.

In an actual case of the policy changes at the two institutions, in August 2010, the Bank of Korea raised the policy rate to guard against signs of growing inflationary pressure, while the FSC increased the DTI on specific mortgage loans to increase the sagging demand for housing. The tighter monetary policy may have frustrated the financial regulators in their effort to revive the housing market.[11]

There is a clear need to improve the coordination of monetary and macroprudential policies. Still, given the different objectives and approaches of the monetary and regulatory authorities, coordination between them has been difficult to institutionalize.[12]

---

10. A housing market boom often overlaps with land speculation. Business borrowers may decide to use a fixed investment loan to build a plant on a larger piece of land than otherwise to take advantage of the boom.

11. During the first seven months of 2010, consumer prices rose by about 1 percent, whereas housing prices in some parts of the Seoul metropolitan area began to fall in the second quarter of 2010.

12. The regulatory authorities may have not developed the expertise or culture of macroprudential policy, while the central bank cannot exercise supervisory control at the level of individual institutions. These institutional constraints could hamper the coordination between the two policy authorities.

Does this difficulty mean that to control the growth of aggregate bank credit, financial regulatory authorities should be given greater freedom in using macroprudential tools such as countercyclical capital requirements, leverage restrictions, and general dynamic provisioning?

Should the regulators also assume responsibility for detecting signs of real-asset speculation well before it gets out of control and for identifying turning points in cyclical developments? Suppose that regulators are allowed to use tools to help institutions lean against the wind, such as controlling total bank credit growth. Such control constitutes monetary policy. The regulators and the central bank will then end up managing a similar policy, running the risk of aggravating duplication and competition in the conduct of macroeconomic forecasting and policy setting.

The potential confusion and conflict underscore the need to construct a policy coordination mechanism between the regulators and the central bank. But because the government is heavily involved in the conduct of macroprudential policy, such a mechanism might undermine the bank's independence. That is, there is a conflict between having unified financial regulation and an independent central bank, unless regulators are required to work within the framework of monetary policy. But that approach also has its drawbacks.

CHAPTER 12

Moral Hazard, Regulatory Forbearance, and Corruption in the Financial Regulatory System

Moral Hazard and the 2003 Credit Card Loan Crisis

It may seem incredible, but immediately after recovering from the 1997 financial crisis, Korea was thrown into another financial turmoil in 2000–2003. This was precipitated by a credit card lending boom that ended in a painful bust, and it was followed by a crisis triggered by the failure of 15 of 106 savings banks in 2011. The two homegrown crises could have been prevented had the deregulation of these two financial industries specialized in consumer lending been carried out in an orderly way, complemented by proper financial supervision. This chapter discusses some of the lessons Korea learned from managing the resolution of the two crises.

The credit card loan crisis had a significant impact on Korea's financial system, but unlike the financial crisis of 1997, it did not pose any serious systemic risk. This is because credit card firms accounted for only a small share of consumer credit and were not allowed to borrow from abroad. The crisis was brought under control relatively quickly by an injection of central bank liquidity into the banking system and other regulatory interventions.

As shown in Table 12.1, at the height of the credit card lending boom in 2002, the number of credit cards per the economically active population jumped to 4.6 from less than 2.0 in 1999. Between 1999 and 2002, the volume of credit card loans plus cash advances grew more than 3.6 times. Many developments, including an expansionary macroeconomic policy drawn up to boost domestic demand for growth, added fuel to the credit card lending boom. The bursting of the dot-com bubble in the developed world in 2001 brought a mild recession to Korea, further slashing the investment demand that had been battered by the 1997 crisis.

To revive the sagging economy, in 1999 Korea's policy makers gave tax deductions for purchases made with credit cards, lifted the restriction on the maximum monthly cash advances on the cards (which had been limited to 700 thousand won, or $588.49), and removed the restriction on credit card issuers from expanding their non-traditional credit card activities (that is, making cash advances and card loans).[1] Expansionary monetary policy, together with the government's promotion of credit card use, set off a surge in buying goods and services with credit cards: from 1999 to 2002, the number of credit card billings almost tripled, to 46 percent of private consumption (Table 12.1).

At the same time, the slowdown in investment dampened the business demand for bank loans at a time when banks were inundated with liquidity. To make up for the decline in the demand for corporate loans, the banks took advantage of relaxations on consumer lending after the 1997 crisis. As a result, the banks increased their mortgage and consumer lending, allowing households to invest in housing and other types of real estate, and SMEs and the self-employed to obtain working capital.

Despite the easing of restrictions on consumer loans, commercial banks were not prepared to cater to the credit needs of households that lacked collateral and proper credit records. However, a flourishing business served those who did not meet traditional bank standards. Commercial banks and corporate groups chose the credit card business as a way to enter the retail credit market. Doing so was attractive because card issuers were subject to relatively loose regulation and were reaping high returns. Issuers were allowed to charge 20 percent or more on cash advances and loans. Unfortunately, these high returns were somewhat illusionary. This is because in the early stages, the delinquency rate was relatively low. As a result, issuers did not make provision for the substantial losses that they faced.

---

1. The main objective of the new credit card policy was to curtail cash transactions for tax evasion and other illegal payments, but according to Yun (2004), this policy change was in part designed to stimulate consumption.

Table 12.1. Credit Card Market

Year	No. of credit cards issued[a] (millions)	Credit card loans and cash advances[b] (trillion won)	Credit card purchases (% of private consumption)	Total credit card assets (% of household credit)	Cash payment fees and revenues on credit card loans (% of credit card revenue)
1999	39.0 (1.8)	13.8 (55.1)	15.5	6.4	79.9
2000	57.7 (2.6)	29.5 (69.2)	24.9	11.1	62.5
2001	89.3 (4.0)	36.9 (51.4)	39.1	10.8	53.8
2002	104.9 (4.6)	50.9 (44.3)	45.7	11.6	44.3
2003	93.9 (4.1)	27.3 (17.5)	43.9	6.1	57.5
2004	86.0 (3.6)	15.4 (18.5)	41.0	3.2	32.1
2005	86.5 (3.5)	15.7 (25.8)	44.8	3.0	28.0
2006	92.5 (3.8)	17.5 (35.0)	47.3	3.0	18.2
2007	88.8 (3.7)	18.4 (38.8)	—[c]	2.9	19.9
2008	96.2 (4.0)	24.0 (33.0)	—[c]	3.5	18.7
2009	107.0 (4.4)	29.9 (35.8)	—[c]	4.1	17.6
2010	116.6 (4.7)	37.6 (34.8)	—[c]	4.7	18.9

Source: Financial Statistics Information System of the Financial Supervisory Service (http://www.fss.or.kr/fss/eng/main.jsp) and, for credit card purchases, Tae Soo Kang and Guonan Ma (2007).

[a] The numbers in parentheses in this column are number of credit cards issued per economically active person.

[b] The numbers in parentheses in this column are percentages of total assets.

[c] Not available.

By 2000, there were twenty-five credit card issuers. Practically all commercial banks offered card services directly or indirectly (by setting up credit card subsidiaries). Some of the chaebol, which had limited banking experience, established monoline credit card companies. They succeeded in capturing as much as 76 percent of domestic credit card transactions by 2002. The four largest credit card issuers were Samsung, LG, KB (Kookmin Bank), and BC (a joint venture of Korea Telecom (KT) and Woori Bank).

The credit card business is profitable only when it achieves economies of scale. Constructing the infrastructure for data processing, credit analyses, and account payments and settlements requires a large initial investment (Yun 2004). More importantly, credit card issuers need to build a sufficient cardholder base to attract retailers that will accept their cards for payments. As a consequence, credit card issuers were engaged from the beginning in intense competition for a significant market share. In fact, they were so eager to expand their customer base that they often resorted to such practices as soliciting new credit card customers on the streets with offers of high rebates.

Solicitors were paid the equivalent of $10 for signing a new cardholder. Scrutinizing the applicant's credit record was not necessary to get paid. There were 31,000 solicitors at the end of 2000. As a group, they rounded up 10.6 million new credit card holders, accounting for 58 percent of the 18.3 million newly issued credit cards that year (Financial Supervisory Service 2001).

Competition for a larger market share contributed in part to lowering industry-wide screening and underwriting standards (see, for example, Tae Soo Kang and Ma 2007.) More importantly, the competition led issuers to lend a disproportionately large share of their loanable funds to the least creditworthy borrowers, including households, the self-employed, and others who were denied access to loans at banks. Inevitably, the credit quality of the issuers' loan portfolios began to deteriorate.

To compensate for the fact that they did not know about or pay much attention to the creditworthiness of their cardholders, issuers charged high interest rates on their loans and high fees for cash services. The high lending rates came back to haunt the credit card companies, as the rates ultimately led to the bursting of the bubble of credit card loan market.

On the funding side, the moral hazard for institutional investors came into play in amplifying the boom. In raising funds, credit card companies borrowed from banks and issued debentures, commercial paper, and asset-backed securities (ABS). Compared to other types of financial products, these carried higher interest rates. Although the high yields reflected the higher default risk that credit card firms were exposed to, institutional investors ignored the riskiness. The largest investors—investment trust companies (ITCs), pension funds, and insurance companies—acted as if their holdings were guaranteed by the commercial banks and industrial groups that owned the credit card issuers. This moral hazard syndrome was contagious in that it motivated credit card issuers to borrow and lend much more than they would have otherwise. This aggravated the boom and made the bust more costly.[2]

During the credit card lending boom from 2000 to 2002, the share of cash services and loans in total credit card assets rose to more than 55 percent on average. In 2001, the estimated return on credit card companies' assets was six times higher than the average return for commercial banks (Yun 2004).

The credit card loan boom could last only so long. Given the high cost of loans and cash services, many of the borrowers could not service their debt at a time when the economy was slowing. The debt snowballed, with many borrowers having several credit cards and using one to borrow money that would repay another.

The number of credit card defaulters started to soar (Figure 12.1), and so did the volume of bad credit card loans (Figure 12.2)—which squeezed the profits of the credit card issuers (Figure 12.3).

The massive increase in the volume of credit card loans and delinquent accounts was enough to send a warning signal that the end of the boom was near. In response to the growing default risk, credit card companies began imposing tighter screening standards for new applicants for cards and loans, as well as for the renewal of existing loans. This tightening created a liquidity crunch, which sent more accounts into arrears. Concerned about these growing financial woes, institutional investors with massive exposure to card companies waited for the right moment to unload their investments.

---

2. In some respects, the unfolding of the boom-and-bust cycle in Korea reveals similar problems associated with the "originate-to-distribute" model of mortgage lending that contributed the subprime crisis in the United States.

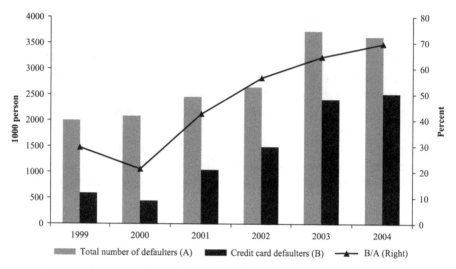

Figure 12.1. All Credit Defaulters and Credit Card Defaulters
Source: Financial Statistics Information System of the Financial Supervisory Service.

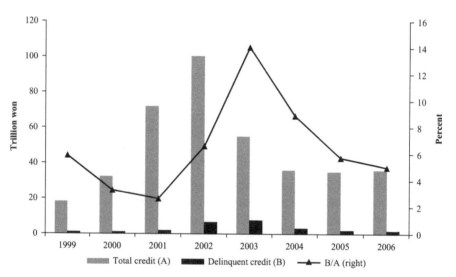

Figure 12.2. All and Delinquent Credit Card Credit
Source: Financial Statistics Information System of the Financial Supervisory Service.

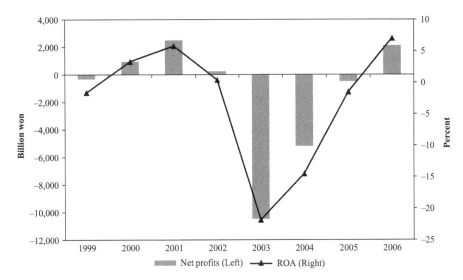

Figure 12.3. Net Profits and ROA of the Credit Card Industry
Source: Financial Statistics Information System of the Financial Supervisory Service.

Moody's Investors Service's downgrading of Korea's sovereign rating in February 2003 and an accounting scandal at SK group (then Korea's fourth-largest chaebol) that broke in March disrupted money and capital markets. This precipitated a sharp fall in the share prices of ITCs that were heavily invested in credit card company stocks. Fearing losses, investors began cashing in their ITC shares.

Because of the restriction on borrowing, ITCs had to liquidate assets to meet redemptions. As a result, ITCs could not invest as much as they previously had in the debentures and ABS issued by credit card companies. Their withdrawal from the market created a severe liquidity crunch in the credit card industry, pushing up its funding costs even as delinquency rates on card loans and cash advances were rising. By early 2003, many of the credit card companies had been pushed to the edge of insolvency.

A liquidity drought at both credit card companies and ITCs posed a systemic risk to the financial system. To avert a crisis, the Bank of Korea injected 4 trillion won (equivalent to $3.36 billion at the time) into the banking system, and the state-owned Korea Development Bank (KDB) bailed LG out by lending it almost 1.5 trillion won ($1.26 billion), more than a quarter of KDB's creditor claims. The government also pressed the chaebol (including Samsung, LG, and Hyundai) to recapitalize their credit card subsidiaries, and it leaned hard on the banks with card units (such as Kookmin, Woori, and Shinhan Banks) to inject funds into their credit card affiliates.

Under the emergency package announced on April 3, 2003, banks and the chaebol with credit card businesses were required to put up an additional 3.8 trillion won ($3.19 billion) collectively to boost the capital of their credit card affiliates. The package also mandated that banks, brokerage firms, and insurance companies arrange bridge loans amounting to 4.2 trillion won ($3.52 billion) collectively to rescue ITCs. At the same time, institutional investors holding credit card debt were required to roll it over indefinitely to give the debt issuers more time to pay.

In no small measure, the regulatory failure to detect the signs of a credit card lending boom and take corrective action aggravated the crisis. Among other things, no explicit capital requirement had been put in place to provide credit card companies with a cushion against the contingent liability arising from the securitization of their loans.

Mutual Savings Bank Crisis in 2011: Moral Hazard and Regulatory Forbearance

Mutual savings banks are community banks established to provide financial services to low-income households, the self-employed, and SMEs with limited access to commercial banks. In 1997, there were 231 savings banks.

Like the credit card crisis in 2003, the savings bank crisis was homegrown and did not pose a significant threat to the stability of the financial system. This is because the savings bank industry was small, accounting for about 5 percent of the total assets and capital of the entire banking system. Also, savings banks are not allowed to borrow or lend foreign currency.

In the aftermath of the 1997 crisis, many of these banks were closed or merged with others, which reduced their number to 116 by the end of 2002. Over the next eight years, 18 more banks merged with others or were shut down. The remaining 106 savings banks, which had combined assets of 86.4 trillion won (about $77.97 billion) at the end of June 2010 (Figure 12.4), suffered a loss of 6,049 billion won ($5.46 billion) during fiscal 2011 (the year ending June 2012), as shown in Figure 12.5.

The financial woes of the relatively small banks had been known for some time but did not become an issue until January 2011, when the Fi-

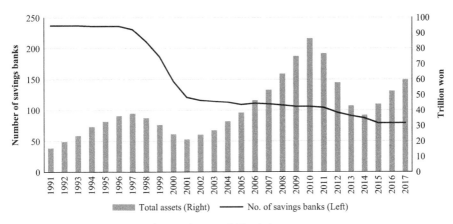

Figure 12.4. Savings Bank Numbers and Total Assets
Sources: Financial Statistics Information System of the Financial Supervisory Service and, for the period before 1997, Bank of Korea.

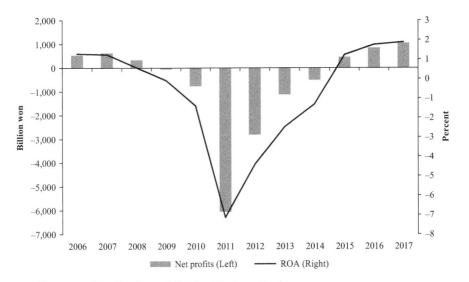

Figure 12.5. Net Profits and ROA of Savings Banks
Source: Financial Statistics Information System of the Financial Supervisory Service.

nancial Supervisory Commission (FSC) suspended the operations of Samhwa Mutual Savings Bank when its Bank for International Settlements (BIS) ratio fell below zero. Samhwa was the fourth largest savings bank in terms of assets at the end of June 2010. This started a run on other ailing savings banks, forcing the suspension of seven more—including

Busan Savings Bank, which owned five affiliate savings banks. The bank, based in the country's second-largest city, Busan, was the largest group of savings banks in Korea. It appears that regulators knew about its scale of NPLs, which had reached alarming proportions, but failed to act. This was because they were more concerned about a possible bank run that any closing or restructuring might trigger.

Korea's policy makers and regulators must have known about the savings and loan associations (S&L) crisis in the 1980s in the United States. Yet they appear not to have taken advantage of the lessons of that event in constructing Korea's regulatory framework.

Mounting losses and NPLs at Busan Savings Bank first emerged as an insolvency problem. The situation turned into a criminal case involving the bank's senior managers, who were engaged in illegal lending to its owners and building projects and bribing regulators and powerful politicians to avoid penalties and suspension. It degenerated into a corruption scandal and a political crisis, which forced the National Assembly to initiate its own investigation.

The pervasiveness of corruption among the regulators took the public by surprise, as it was unprecedented.

Savings banks acquire more than 80 percent of their loanable funds from savings deposits. To compensate for their competitive weaknesses vis-à-vis commercial banks and other depository institutions in funding, they were allowed to charge higher interest rates on their loans and offer higher interest rates on deposits. Deposits are protected up to fifty million won per account at a bank by the deposit guarantee system.[3] The high interest rates, coupled with the guarantee, attracted a large number of depositors seeking safety and high yields. On an annual average during the 2000–2010 period, deposits at savings banks grew twice as fast as those at commercial banks, yet this rapid growth did not prevent the demise of the savings bank industry.

In the wake of the 1997 crisis, commercial banks began moving into household lending on a large scale to replace corporate lending. The proportion of household loans in commercial banks' total loans climbed to about 50 percent by 2005 from less than 30 percent in 1998 (see Figure 4.1). Not only commercial banks, but also a growing number of credit card

---

3. This means that depositors could own guaranteed deposit accounts at many different banks.

companies and moneylenders were moving into the consumer loan business, cutting into the market share of savings banks. By 2005, savings banks' loans to household borrowers had fallen to less than 25 percent of their total loans. With the loss of their traditional business, savings banks were forced to seek new business by devoting a large share of their total loans to real estate investments.

After the 1997 crisis, savings banks also had to adjust to a trend of bank consolidation. Individually, they were too small in terms of asset volume and were confined to too small a geographical area to realize scale economies. To overcome these disadvantages, some of the large savings banks set out through cross-bank stock holdings to form a horizontally integrated alliance with other banks operating in different localities.

The formation of such alliances offered the benefits of scale economies by offering joint new services and products and consolidating the data processing systems and back-office functions among the participating banks. It also allowed individual savings banks to have more efficient risk diversification, participate in project financing, and enlarge their service areas. By the end of June 2010, eleven groups that collectively contained thirty-one savings banks had been established. It appeared that policy makers supported such horizontal integration, which was expected to improve the soundness and safety of savings banks through consolidation.

Riding on the back of a booming real estate market, savings banks belonging to the alliances were growing rapidly and generating hefty profits. However, the groups had a critical weakness: the credit and market risks of all participating savings banks were consolidated into one entity. The savings banks in the groups were engaged in cross-lending among themselves and pooled their funds to make large loans to special-purpose companies (SPCs), through which they financed housing and other real estate projects that required large and long-term investments. In so doing, they were transforming themselves into mortgage lenders and property developers, with the attendant risk of exposing themselves to the vagaries of real estate markets. The cooperative arrangements on joint lending meant, therefore, that the failure of a group-wide project or the insolvency of a participating bank could endanger the solvency of other banks in the group.

Group formation did not affect either profit or asset quality as long as real estate prices were rising. However, once the real estate boom collapsed, as it did following the 2008 liquidity crisis, many savings banks—in particular, those belonging to a group—were piling up losses that threatened not only their own but also their entire group's financial soundness.

In retrospect, the crisis could have been contained had regulators refused to ease the lending constraint at savings banks. Through alliances, savings banks were able to achieve a measure of consolidation. Still, it did not help them to finance large-scale property developments because they were constrained by the lending limit of eight billion won to a single borrower. It was not surprising, therefore, that savings banks mounted intense lobbying efforts to revoke this regulation. They succeeded in 2006.

The FSC relaxed the lending rule so that those savings banks with a BIS ratio higher than 8 percent and a share of NPLs below 8 percent were exempt from the eight billion won lending ceiling for up to 20 percent of their capital. This relaxation gave many savings banks more leeway to diversify their loan portfolios from household to property lending.[4]

Freed from the limit, savings banks began making large loans to special-purpose companies that they had set up to provide project financing. Because their primary funding source was savings deposits, they were borrowing short and lending long, creating maturity mismatches. By 2010, corporate loans accounted for almost 90 percent of savings banks' total lending, and more than 50 percent of their total loans were extended to construction firms or real estate rental companies, or for real estate and project financing.

The 2008 liquidity crisis dealt a severe blow to and hastened the downfall of the savings bank industry. The crisis further depressed the real estate market, which had already been cooling off. As property prices plummeted, the proportion of unpaid mortgage loans soared, and the expected cash flows from project financing did not materialize at many savings banks.

Official data on delinquent credit are shown in Figure 12.6. At the end of June 2010, 11 percent of total loans were non-performing.[5] In particular, loans extended to property developers that were in arrears for more than a month rose to more than 25 percent of total loans (see Figure 12.6).

---

4. The conditions proved to be difficult to enforce because of the unreliability of balance sheets and income statements, many of which were being falsified.

5. This is a very conservative official estimate made by the FSC. The market believed the true share to be much higher, given the widespread practice of cooking the books at savings banks.

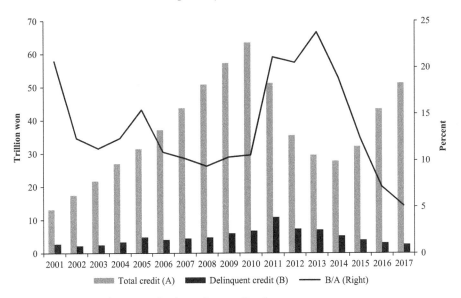

Figure 12.6. Delinquent Credit at Savings Banks
Source: Financial Statistics Information System of the Financial Supervisory Service.

By the end of June 2010, two savings banks, the Samhwa Mutual Savings Bank and Daejeon Savings Bank, had become insolvent and had negative BIS ratios. The former was suspended in January 2011 (Table 12.2) and the latter was acquired by Busan Savings Bank.

At this point, a logical step might have been to close the insolvent savings banks. Instead, regulators adopted a stance of regulatory forbearance because they did not have sufficient deposit insurance funds to pay off depositors.[6]

Also, regulators did not want to admit they failed in the proper supervision of savings banks. Prompt corrective actions (PCAs) were deferred for some of the troubled savings banks. Instead, the regulators induced larger savings banks to acquire the troubled banks by allowing them to open up to five branch offices outside of their designated regions.[7] Busan Savings Bank, which ultimately was suspended, had acquired troubled savings banks in 2008. It saw a sharp increase in its

---

6. On average between 2003 and 2010, the Korea Deposit Insurance Corporation's deposit insurance fund for mutual savings banks suffered annual deficits of 353 billion won.

7. In addition, the savings banks that had acquired troubled banks were not subject to regular on-site examinations by the FSS for three years.

Table 12.2. Suspended Savings Banks in 2011–15

Year	Suspended Savings Banks
2011	15: Samhwa, Busan (2 banks), Joongang-Busan, Domin, Jeonju, Bohae, Kyungeun, Daeyoung, Tomato, Prime, Parangsae, Jeil (2 banks), Ace
2012	9: Solomon, Hankuk, Mirae, Hanju, Tomato (2 banks), Jinheung, Kyungki, W Savings
2013	5: Seoul, Yeongnam, Shilla, Smile, Hanwool
2014	1: Haesol
2015	1: Goldenbridge

Source: Financial Statistics Information System of the Financial Supervisory Service (http://www.fss.or.kr/fss/eng/main.jsp).
Note: In 2014, seven savings banks were merged.

deposits and project financing, but the acquisition did not help it to survive.

It was also found that many regulators were too close to the people they were supposed to be regulating. Retired savings bank examiners from the FSS were often hired by savings banks to help lobby on their behalf. Because savings banks knew that regulators were likely to opt for regulatory forbearance instead of closure, it is not surprising that they spent an enormous amount of money paying off regulators in return for leniency in their inspections. Savings banks were conspiring with the regulators to sweep their problems under the rug in the hope that the problems would go away.

After the suspension of Busan Savings Bank and Samhwa Mutual Savings Bank in 2011, investigations conducted by the Busan prosecutors' office exposed many lending irregularities and instances of corruption. A host of shareholders and senior managers of Busan Savings Bank were indicted for financial crimes involving nearly 7.7 trillion won ($6.94 billion). Samhwa's senior executive officers were prosecuted for lending 200 billion won ($180 million) illegally.

It was also revealed that these banks had lobbied top government officials and politicians to prevent their businesses from being shut down. Bank officials tipped off employees' relatives and valuable customers about their bank's impending suspension to help them withdraw their deposits in advance. Regulators claimed that they had not known about this, and the FSS was subjected to mounting public criticism and mistrust. Prosecutors charged five FSS employees for suspected collusion with savings banks.

Prosecutors indicted a commissioner of the Board of Audit and Inspection (BAI), who was suspected of having exercised his influence to help Busan Savings Bank avoid being forced to exit from the savings banking industry. He had received hundreds of millions of won in exchange for overlooking the group's illegal lending and other wrongdoings in early 2010, when the BAI was investigating it.

A commissioner of the Korea Financial Intelligence Unit (KoFIU) attached to the FSC was arrested for having taken tens of millions of won in bribes from a troubled savings bank in 2008, in return for his promise to use his influence to help the bank escape punishment for its illegal loans.[8]

In retrospect, there is little doubt that regulatory forbearance deepened the crisis. Regulators refrained from exercising proper supervision and regulation of the savings bank industry and from closing insolvent banks. Instead, they turned a blind eye to accounting irregularities and increases in NPLs. The stance of regulatory forbearance pervaded moral hazard at savings banks. Knowing that the regulators were unwilling to put them out of business, these banks did not have any incentive to restructure themselves. Instead, they became more reckless in their lending and lobbied regulators and politicians (to whose campaigns they made large contributions) to conceal their problems.

---

8. None other than the former FSS's governor reportedly asked the head of BAI to go soft on the investigation of the troubled Busan Savings Bank. He pleaded that the corruption in the savings bank industry be covered up lest the investigation cause a bank run. The governor turned out to have been a lobbyist for the troubled savings bank. The Asia Trust Fund, which Jong-chang Kim had created before his appointment, had a 5 percent stake in Busan Savings Bank. Kim claims that he stepped down as an outside director of the fund and sold his shares in the bank when he became governor of the FSS. But further suspicions arose that Busan Savings Bank made up for the losses of Asia Trust Fund and that Kim actually remained the largest shareholder of the fund through a proxy. For a summary of Kim's role, see "Former Top Financial Regulator Indicted over Savings Bank Scandal" 2011.

CHAPTER 13

The 1997 Financial Crisis

The 1997 crisis was as dramatic as it was unexpected. As late as October of that year, no one was predicting that in only two months, Korea would be pushed to the brink of financial collapse. The country was reduced from being the world's eleventh-largest economy to begging for a lifeline from the IMF. It was a moment of national shame.

Korea suffered from a capital account crisis from which it could not extricate itself on its own. The causes, triggers, and dynamics of the crisis differ from those of crises in other countries that suffered a similar meltdown, but the crisis was no less virulent.

A capital account crisis is defined as a sequence of disruptive macroeconomic adjustments that starts with large capital inflows, often dominated by short-term foreign loans and portfolio investments relative to the absorptive capacity of the economy. This is then followed by their sudden stop or reversal (Yung Chul Park 2006). When this happens, the economy in question shifts into a bad equilibrium.

A sudden reversal of capital inflow freezes financial markets, causing a drought in foreign currency liquidity.[1] The evaporation of liquidity causes a banking crisis in which the contraction of bank credit in turn causes a sharp increase in NPLs and the collapse of real economic activity.[2] The economy is then forced to repay its external debt by running

---

1. In countries where households and firms cannot borrow from abroad in their own currencies, liquidity in this chapter refers to foreign currency liquidity.

2. In emerging economies, a reversal of capital inflow causes a currency crisis that puts the nominal exchange rate on an implosive trajectory or—in a regime with a fixed ex-

current account surpluses, either by exporting more or by curtailing import demand.

Korea fell victim to overreaction and herding by foreign creditors alarmed by the Thai financial crisis, which had broken out earlier in 1997. The general fear triggered self-fulfilling expectations that Korea would not be immune to a similar crisis. This change in market sentiment shifted Korea to a bank-run equilibrium. The country's strong economic fundamentals might not have justified such a sudden swing. A firm commitment by the IMF or any other international institution ready to serve as a lender of last resort could have prevented the shift. That would have mitigated the costs and burdens of the crisis. However, Korea could find no such lender.

In the run-up to the 1997 crisis, Korea had few of the macroeconomic vulnerabilities associated with a current account crisis. The country was known for fiscal prudence, high private savings rates, and low inflation. Its exchange rate was misaligned, but not so much as to trigger a speculative attack. Korea's current account deficits pointed to a productive and growing economy, as they reflected an excess of investment over savings.[3]

Korea had indeed been plagued by many structural distortions in its financial and corporate sectors, as well as by the policies bent on control, for an extended period. These weaknesses had existed for decades and were not unique to Korea. They were masked by rapid growth of the economy. Foreign creditors knew of their existence but had ignored or discounted them because they were not considered severe—certainly not severe enough to impair the fundamentals of the economy. As long as the Korean economy was growing rapidly, foreign creditors believed that their loans would be guaranteed by the government and were prepared to lend as much as domestic banks and corporations were willing to borrow. If there were imprudent borrowers, they were matched by equally reckless lenders.

How, then, did the country come under such a virulent speculative attack that was both highly contagious and persistent? As foreign exchange

---

change rate—provokes a run on foreign exchange reserves. A capital account crisis in an emerging economy is a run on foreign exchange reserves, its banking system, or both.

3. Although Korea's macroeconomic performance had worsened in the mid-1990s, the extent and depth of the 1997 crisis could not be attributed to structural weaknesses or a deterioration in economic fundamentals.

reserve holdings started to decline and economic growth to slow, foreign lenders began to question whether Indonesia, Thailand, and Korea were susceptible to financial crises like the ones that had plagued Latin American economies before. A trigger was provided by the crises in Thailand and Indonesia, and Korea succumbed to a contagion of those meltdowns.

The crisis of 1997 was both dramatic and unforeseen. From October to December 1997, Korea was reduced from one of East Asia's superperformers to an economy surviving on overnight loans from international money markets. What was so surprising about the crisis was that as late as October, no one, including the international credit rating agencies, could have predicted that in only two months, Korea would be pushed to the brink of financial collapse. But with the spread of the Thai crisis, which broke out in June 1997, a painful crisis was already looming large, as Korea was borrowing from abroad beyond its debt-servicing capacity.

Borrowing Short and Lending Long in Dollars

Economic growth from 1994 to the beginning of 1997 had been mostly fueled by the rapid growth of business investment, which rose to 40.3 percent of GDP in the fourth quarter of 1996 from 37.1 percent two years earlier.[4] This increase resulted in a current account deficit of a little over 4 percent of GDP in 1996. One of the developments that boosted investment was the partial deregulation of capital inflows, which gave banks, NBFIs, and large corporations greater access to low-cost foreign credit than before. This induced a surge in foreign capital inflows—which in 1994–96 rose to an annual average of 47 percent of GDP from less than 30 percent during the preceding three-year period. Short-term external liabilities had climbed to 245 percent of foreign exchange reserves at the end of the third quarter of 1997 (Figure 13.1).

A large fraction of Korea's capital inflows was channeled into financing the long-term investments of the chaebol. Banks and NBFIs were borrowing short and lending long in foreign currency, thereby exacerbating currency and maturity mismatches on their balance sheets (Figure 13.2). This was a significant factor in making Korea susceptible to a capital account crisis.

---

4. Another cause was the strengthening of the yen, which brought about a sharp increase in export earnings that in turn stimulated a great deal of capital investment in 1994–96.

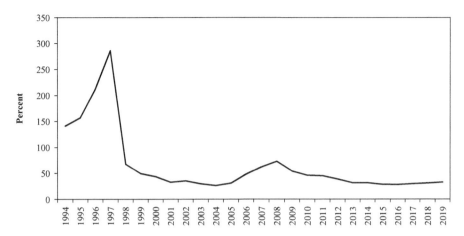

Figure 13.1. Short-Term External Debt as a Percentage of Foreign
Exchange Reserves
Source: Economic Statistics System of the Bank of Korea.

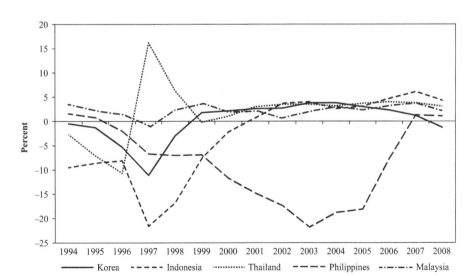

Figure 13.2. Aggregate Effective Currency Mismatch
Sources: Goldstein and Turner 2004 and Goldstein and Xie 2009.

Table 13.1. Foreign Reserves of the Bank of Korea (billions of $)

	1996	1997						1998
		Mar.	Jun.	Sept.	Oct.	Nov.	Dec.	Jan.
Official foreign reserves	33.2	29.2	33.3	30.4	30.5	24.4	20.4	23.5
Deposits at overseas branches	3.8	8.0	8.0	8.0	8.0	16.9	11.3	11.0
Other	—ᵃ	—ᵃ	—ᵃ	—ᵃ	0.2	0.2	0.2	0.2
Total	29.4	21.1	25.3	22.4	22.3	7.3	8.9	12.4

Source: Economic Statistics System of the Bank of Korea (https://ecos.bok.or.kr/EIndex_en.jsp).
Notes: Official foreign reserve holdings are based on the IMF's definition. Deposits at overseas branches are deposits made by the Bank of Korea at the overseas branches of domestic commercial banks. In November, when domestic commercial banks were unable to repay their loans from foreign banks, the Bank of Korea supported them by making foreign currency deposits at their overseas branches.
ᵃ Not applicable.

The investment boom supported by foreign credit could last only so long. The slowdown in export growth beginning in the third quarter of 1995—in part because of the yen's depreciation from its mid-1995 peak and worsening of the terms of trade—burst the investment bubble in 1996. Inevitably, the number of corporate bankruptcies began to soar, and so did the volume of NPLs at banks and NBFIs. From December 1996 to June 1997, NPLs as a proportion of total bank loans almost doubled (Yung Chul Park 1998).

By the first week of September 1997, Korea's economic slowdown had already dragged on for nearly two years, and foreign banks' rollover rates of their short-term loans to Korean financial institutions were falling, as were foreign exchange reserves. Despite mounting pressure for depreciation since the early months of 1997, the Korean government made a stand at 1,000 won per dollar, intervening heavily in the market. By the end of November, usable reserves had fallen to $7 billion (Table 13.1).

Between July and November, the central bank sold $12.2 billion in the spot market and made forward sales amounting to $7 billion to defend the won. As a result, during the same period, the Bank of Korea's reserve holdings fell by $10 billion. The government further strained investors' credulity during this time by failing to divulge the actual level of the Bank of Korea's foreign reserves or its forward market commitments. It asserted that the Bank of Korea held about $30 billion in reserves, a figure that investors found implausible. The actual level of usable reserves had already dropped below $22 billion at the end of March.

This difference arose from the exclusion of about half of the foreign currency operations of the banking sector that were handled by overseas branches whose transactions were not reflected in domestic monetary indicators. Had the monetary authorities taken into account the short-term external liabilities of overseas branches, they would have realized that the amount of foreign reserves was sufficient to buffer against a potential liquidity run.

When Korea's credibility plummeted, merchant banks—pressured to obtain foreign currency to repay their debts—began buying foreign currency in the spot market with call loans from commercial banks. The dire financial situation was aggravated further by the downgrading of Korea's sovereign credit ratings. In January 1997, Moody's gave Korea a rating of A1, and the S&P rating was AA–.

On November 28, Moody's lowered its rating to A3, and on October 24, S&P changed its rating to A+. Before the end of 1997, Moody's readjusted its rating downward twice and S&P did so three times.[5] Whenever the sovereign credit rating was downgraded, the premium on Korean securities denominated in dollars rose, worsening market sentiment. In response, the rating agencies adjusted their ratings downward again, thereby generating a vicious circle of declining ratings and market sentiment.

When the crisis that had broken out in Thailand spread to Korea, neither Korea nor the IMF was prepared or able to deal with what was mainly a capital account crisis. When Korea's reserves were depleted toward the end of the second quarter of 1997, in the absence of any regional arrangement or foreign central banks that were ready to provide short-term US dollar liquidity, the country had no choice but to ask for IMF's rescue financing. But it was unwilling to do so because of domestic political opposition and the harsh policy conditions that came with it.

---

5. In terms of sovereign credit ratings, Moody's rating for Korea had been A1 since April 1990. The S&P rating had been AA—since May 1995. On August 6 (dates are according to New York time), S&P reaffirmed its rating but changed the outlook to negative. On October 24, S&P lowered its rating to A+ and kept the negative outlook. Moody's dropped its rating two notches to A3 but considered the outlook stable on November 27. As with the sovereign credit ratings, Moody's adjusted its sovereign credit rating downward twice, and S&P did so three times before the end of 1997.

By September 1997, foreign banks' rollover rates of short-term loans had fallen to alarming levels, and the Bank of Korea had lost most of its reserves, tipping Korea into a crisis. Even then, policy makers continued to intervene in the foreign exchange market as if they had plenty of ammunition to defend the won. Toward the end of October, it became clear to policy makers and market participants that the financial situation was going out of control. With a sense of panic increasing by the day, the government made public its decision to approach the IMF for assistance on November 19.

On December 3, the IMF announced its rescue package for Korea, which consisted of $21 billion from its resources and $37 billion from other multilateral sources. The IMF would phase in the disbursement of funds conditional on Korea's meeting the targets of policy reforms that included seventy-three structural policy commitments, many in areas not relevant to crisis management.

Initially, the IMF disbursed $9.1 billion, but the amount was not enough to impress the market. On December 24, $10 billion of the backup financing was added to the IMF disbursement, together with the bail-in of foreign creditors who agreed to lengthen the maturity of their short-term loans.

The IMF program for crisis resolution consisted of tight or neutral fiscal policy; contractionary monetary policy with high interest rates and a sharp devaluation, achieved by adopting free-floating exchange rates; and structural reforms in trade, the regulatory system, the labor market, and public enterprises. Many observers felt that the rationale for this program and the effectiveness of the IMF were dubious. The program accelerated the steep downfall of the economy, trapping it in a vicious circle with credit contraction, collapsing output, and mounting bad debt. It was the wrong prescription (Radelet and Sachs 1998).

Recovery

The IMF's program intensified a steep downfall of the economy as it accelerated the sagging demand for investment spending. The investment-to-GDP ratio dropped to 25 percent in 1998 from 36 percent in 1997. To the surprise of many, however, the crisis was short-lived. Six months after Korea accepted the IMF conditions, market sentiment began to turn in

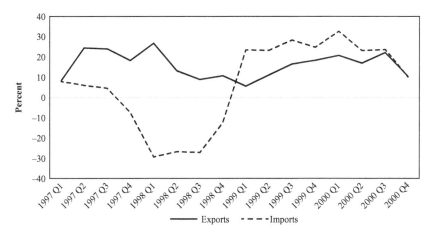

Figure 13.3. Quarterly Export and Import Growth
Source: Economic Statistics System of the Bank of Korea.

the country's favor, which restored a measure of financial stability. The quarterly data on the rates of growth of exports and imports shown in Figure 13.3 detail the pattern of recovery, with Korea reaching a trough as early as the second quarter of 1998.[6]

While domestic demand was sluggish, a large real depreciation of the won that amounted to more than 27 percent buttressed a quick surge in net exports, generating a substantial current account surplus on the order of 12 percent of GDP. The return of foreign investors, combined with a significant increase in exports, paved the way for a quick recovery.

The rebounding of the growth rate was no less dramatic than its free fall: Korea's economy grew by 9.5 percent in 1999 and by 8.5 percent in 2000. Over time, the recovery process gained additional momentum. The adjustment process in Korea that can be inferred from changes in the growth rate seems to be generally consistent with the stylized V pattern observed from previous crisis episodes (Figure 13.4).

The rapid recovery also made it possible for Korea to pay back all of the loans that it had obtained from the IMF and other multilateral sources for the crisis resolution well ahead of their due dates. It first repaid the

---

6. Despite the large current account surplus, foreign debt climbed to 47.3 percent of GDP, largely because of the need to borrow from abroad to replenish the foreign reserves depleted in 1997.

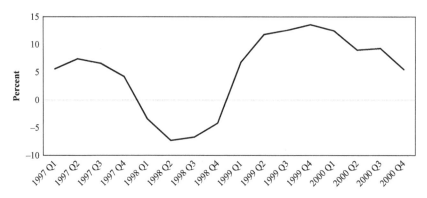

Figure 13.4. Quarterly Real GDP Growth
Source: Economic Statistics System of the Bank of Korea.

multilateral debt before closing out the $19.5 billion loan from the IMF in August 2001, thirty-four months ahead of schedule.

Financial Restructuring

As part of the IMF's conditions for providing rescue financing in December 1997, the government embarked on a drastic restructuring of the financial and corporate sectors. During the first phase, which lasted until June 2001, the Financial Supervisory Commission closed sixteen of the thirty-three banks (Table 13.2).

The restructuring was much more extensive for NBFIs, many of which were owned or controlled by chaebol. By June 2001, 929 NBFIs had disappeared. Twenty-two of thirty merchant banks were forced out of business. As for other NBFIs, sixteen securities companies, fourteen investment trust companies, and twenty-two insurance companies had to close their doors. Additionally, more than half of the mutual savings banks and fourteen of the twenty-five leasing firms were dissolved. Government financial supervision had been almost nonexistent until the onset of the crisis.

The restructuring was costly. By the end of June 2001, when the critical phase of the restructuring was complete, the government had spent 137.5 trillion won—mostly to recapitalize ailing banks, repay depositors at liquidated banks, and purchase NPLs. To be specific, 53.0 trillion won was used for recapitalization, 38.2 trillion won for the purchase of NPLs, and 20.0 trillion won for the payment of deposit insurance claims. The

Table 13.2. Restructuring of Financial Institutions

	Total institutions, 1997 (A)	Resolution					New entry	Total institutions, 2009
		License revoked	Merger	Other	Subtotal (B)	B as % of A		
Banks	33	5	11	—[a]	16	48.5	1	18
NBFIs	2,069	169	196	564	929	44.9	147	1,287
Merchant bank corporations	30	22	7	—[a]	29	96.7	1	2
Securities companies	36	5	8	3	16	44.4	27	47
Insurance companies	50	10	6	6	22	44.0	25	53
Investment trust companies	31	6	8	—[a]	14	45.2	50	67
Mutual savings banks	231	113	28	1	142	61.5	17	106
Credit unions	1,666	2	137	553	692	41.5	14	988
Leasing companies	25	11	2	1	14	56.0	13	24
Total	2,102	174	207	564	945	45.0	148	1,305

Source: Public Fund Management Committee of Republic of Korea (2009).

Notes: Total institutions in 1997 are as of the end of the year. Total institutions in 2009 are as of the end of June of that year. "Resolution" refers to the restructuring that took place in the period November 1997–June 2001. "Other" includes dissolution, bankruptcy, and suspension.

[a] Not available.

Table 13.3. Public Funds Injected by Source (trillion won)

	Recapitalization	Capital contributions	Deposit repayment	Asset acquisitions	Acquisition of NPLs	Total
Bonds issued	35.5	11.2	15.3	4.2	20.5	86.7
Funds recovered	3.3	1.0	4.2	3.6	15.7	27.8
Public funds	14.2	—ᵃ	0.5	6.3	2.0	23.0
Total	53.0	12.2	20.0	14.1	38.2	137.5
	(63.5)	(18.6)	(30.3)	(17.7)	(38.5)	(168.6)

Source: Public Fund Management Committee of Republic of Korea (2009).

Note: The table shows funds injected in the period November 1997–June 2001, with the totals as of the end of 2009 in parentheses.

ᵃ Not available.

total amount was equal to 25 percent of Korea's 2002 GDP. Thereafter, an additional 30 trillion won were needed (Table 13.3).

In retrospect, the high cost raises a fundamental question: could Korea have found a less costly way of restructuring and shared some of the expenses with external lenders? It could have if the country had approached the IMF earlier than it did. In addition, the IMF could have worked out a program for bail-ins and persuaded its American and European members of the need to make available a large amount of liquidity at the beginning of the crisis to assure foreign creditors that their loans would be repaid.

Corporate Restructuring

In 1998, under the broad framework of a debt workout, the government created four approaches to corporate restructuring. These were applied according to the firm's restructuring capacity. First, four of the top five chaebol, which were considered to have the capacity to absorb the resulting losses, were allowed to pursue a self-directed restructuring. Second, financially unhealthy affiliates of the medium-size chaebol (the sixth to the sixty-fourth largest), which were deemed to be unable to successfully restructure on their own, entered into corporate workouts or corporate reorganization with financial institutions. Third, the Daewoo Group, the remaining chaebol in the top five, was dissolved in 1999 and was subject to a corporate workout. And fourth, SMEs that were too weak to bear the costs of restructuring were supported by their creditor financial institutions. During the crisis, thirty of the top sixty-four chaebol with a corporate debt of 250 billion won or more were forced to undertake some form of corporate restructuring.

However, restructuring was slow to gain momentum, as troubled firms and their creditors both sought to protect their interests. The managers of distressed firms had strong incentives not to disclose accurate information on their firm's financial status, as they wanted to maintain control. Creditors were motivated to apply lenient accounting standards to meet the capital adequacy requirement.

The government mobilized public funds to expedite the restructuring of troubled firms. During 1998–2001, the Korea Asset Management Corporation purchased NPLs that collectively amounted to 48.3 trillion won from the top sixty-four chaebol for 17.4 trillion won. Aided by government support, financial institutions swiftly achieved financial health and were able to carry out creditor-led corporate restructuring.

The government required banks to roll over loans to viable SMEs, and it provided 33 trillion won of guarantees for loans to small firms and additional budgetary support of 2.2 trillion won through a variety of programs. It also reduced the income tax and corporate tax by half for newly established SMEs during their first five years.

Lessons

In its postmortem on the Asian crisis, the IMF drew many lessons from its policy prescriptions that, in East Asia's view, were misguided and might have inflicted higher than necessary costs and pains on the three Asian countries (Lane 1999; Yung Chul Park 2006, chapter 8). Since the IMF will continue to be called upon to resolve future crises in emerging economies, it is worthwhile to review the pitfalls of the IMF crisis management program for Korea. We look specifically at the design of conditions for macroeconomic policy adjustments and structural reforms and at making the disbursement of financial assistance conditional on meeting fiscal targets and structural performance criteria.

SURVEILLANCE

By the middle of 1996, almost a year before the outbreak of the Thai crisis, many foreign investors were nervously asking themselves if financial meltdowns such as those that had befallen Mexico in 1995 and 1982 were in the making in Asia (Yung Chul Park 1998). With the miracle years over, Korea was finding it increasingly difficult to refinance its foreign loans, and its foreign exchange reserves were dwindling.

The IMF was slow to recognize the deterioration of investor confidence and failed to advise the Korean authorities to take proper precautionary measures to fend off an impending crisis. This was because the IMF had not established an efficient way to monitor economic developments in its member countries in an increasingly integrated East Asia. As the countries in the region opened their markets for goods and services and liberalized their capital account transactions, they found it increasingly difficult to insulate their economies from external shocks.

In the absence of a regional economic review, it is not surprising that the IMF did not recognize the possibility that the Thai crisis could spread to other countries in the region as fast as it did. In the aftermath of the crisis, the IMF acknowledged the need to improve its surveillance and undertook a series of institutional reforms to strengthen and broaden the scope of its regional surveillance.

SPEEDY RESPONSE

Once a capital account crisis strikes, there is little time to lose—given the speed with which capital flows out and currencies depreciate. Foreign creditors seek to be the first out the door when they believe a country lacks enough foreign exchange reserves to service its debt.

However, the Korean government was reluctant to admit that the country was in a crisis. Instead, policy makers waited until the last minute, by which time the situation had become desperate, before seeking IMF assistance. This meant that the economy was so much deeper in a crisis that it required a larger resolution program than would otherwise have been the case—more financial aid and more severe banking and corporate restructuring than would have been needed had Korea approached the IMF earlier. Korea decided to make that approach on November 19, 1997, and completed the negotiations for a standby loan about two weeks later. A similar delay took place in other countries affected by the crisis. It took six weeks from the devaluation of the Thai baht on July 2, 1997, for Thailand to deliver its first letter of intent to the IMF (on August 14), and that was followed by the IMF Executive Board's approval of the program a week later. In Indonesia, the first letter of intent was signed on October 31, 1997. On November 5, the IMF Executive Board approved a three-year standby loan of $10.14 billion.

Policy authorities in the three countries could not overcome their perception that involvement with the IMF created a stigma. The IMF did not take steps to allay such fears. And it could not unilaterally do anything to assuage the fears of foreign lenders and investors.

BAILING IN

During the Asian crisis, the IMF recognized the need to require private creditors to maintain their net lending to a debtor country through debt restructuring and controls on capital outflows. However, the IMF was concerned that imposing such a requirement could exacerbate the contagion that would, in the end, reduce—rather than increase—private financing (Lane 1999).

Nonetheless, the IMF set a precedent for bailing in in the midst of a raging crisis. It did this by imposing a de facto payment standstill in Indonesia and persuading international lenders to extend the maturities of their short-term loans to Korea toward the end of 1997. At the time of the crisis, the IMF was the only institution that could help creditors recover their loans. Drawing on this leverage, it could have been more aggressive in demanding the creditor bail in to reduce the cost of the crisis resolution, but it did not.

OVERLOADING SUPPLY-SIDE REFORM

During the Asian crisis, one of criticisms leveled at IMF programs was that they included overly extensive and complicated lists of structural reform measures. Many creditors and the general public did not believe that the governments of the three crisis countries had the administrative capacity or the will to carry the programs out—and certainly not on the strict schedule they had agreed to with the IMF. In the three countries, the numbers of structural policy conditions were enormous—at their peak, there were about 140 in Indonesia, more than 90 in Korea, and more than 70 in Thailand.[7]

---

7. The number of structural policy conditions for Indonesia hit a peak early and then declined, perhaps reflecting an initial effort to impress the markets with the extent of intended reform and then scaling back as market reaction proved disappointing and as

The imposition of structural reforms, irrespective of the ability and will of the countries to achieve them, was doomed to fail. Indeed, it backfired. There were two reasons for this.

The first reason was that many of the reforms were not critical to restoring macroeconomic stability in the short run, although they may have been necessary for improving efficiency in the long run. Furthermore, without careful prioritization and sequencing, most of the reforms could not deliver the needed outcomes.

The crisis countries simply could not make such preparations and implement so many reforms in so many sectors at the same time. Rather than emphasizing the need for the reform, the governments—those of Indonesia and Thailand, in particular—were reluctant to own the reform programs, partly out of fear that they would lose credibility. Instead, they chose political expediency and let it be known that they were required to comply with IMF conditions.

The second reason was that using structural reforms as a substitute for, or complement to, financial assistance undermined the credibility of the rescue package. The IMF sought to convince foreign lenders of the reliability of its plans with a long list of supply-side reforms aimed at improving allocative efficiency and export competitiveness. The underlying assumption was that the more effective the structural reform program, the more confident foreign creditors would be of repayment, and the smaller the liquidity support that would be required to resolve the crisis.

However, the foreign creditors knew all too well that many structural measures would take a long time to organize and execute, even if the policy makers were determined to follow through the reforms. Without knowing whether the reforms would be carried out, foreign creditors had little reason to wait for an outcome that was uncertain at best. Because the disbursement of IMF loans was conditional on the countries' meeting reform targets, foreign creditors wondered whether the countries would have enough money to cover the next payment of interest and principal if they failed to meet the reform target schedule.

---

evidence accumulated that implementation capacity or willingness would be lower than anticipated. See Goldstein 2003.

CHAPTER 14

The Post-1997 Corporate Governance Reform and Chaebol Investment Behavior

In February 1998, the newly installed administration of President Kim Dae-jung proposed a series of corporate reforms designed to enhance transparency, improve financial structure, streamline business activities, strengthen accountability, and stop cross debt guarantees (Ministry of Finance and Economy 1998, 21–28).

Enhanced transparency requires adopting new accounting and auditing rules in line with internationally accepted standards, as well as the establishment of an external auditors' committee. It also involves strengthening the legal protection of the rights of minority shareholders and the compulsory appointment of outside directors. In addition, two measures were implemented to enhance corporate governance: one requiring the separation of banks from industrial capital and the other imposing restrictions on intragroup investment.

Shareholder Rights, Directorships, and Disclosure

To improve the board of directors' decision-making process, the role of company directors was enhanced. Importantly, the responsibility of directors was reinforced through the introduction of the principle of their fiduciary duty. De facto directors, including controlling shareholders, became subject to the same legal obligations as elected directors. Moreover, beginning in 1998, listed companies (that is, those listed at the stock exchange) were required to appoint at least one outside director.

Although the increase of outside directors should have had a positive impact on corporate governance, in reality, the effect has been limited. One reason is that they have a low participation rate at board meetings (only 69 percent).

Moreover, many outside directors have not acted as independently as expected, because they are close associates of the family owners or managers. Jaehoon Kim and Hwa Ryung Lee (2015) showed that CEOs tended to appoint outside directors to whom they have close personal ties, such as being from the same hometown or having graduated from the same high school. As a result, outside directors rarely, if ever, cast a dissenting vote at board meetings, to avoid the risk of being replaced. This has given support to the perception that their role is nothing more than rubber-stamping. Many studies have addressed this issue (see, for example, Sungbin Cho 2005, 2006).

The reforms have improved disclosure and audits somewhat by penalizing not only the companies but also the auditors for accounting fraud. However, although the rules for disclosure and audits meet global standards, whether firms effectively implement them is another matter.

In any case, the courts will enforce them. For example, the Supreme Court set a judicial precedent by ruling that officials of companies that use false accounting methods could be tried for criminal activity. In a case involving Daewoo, the court upheld the imposition of a fine of 26 trillion won against the management for window-dressing in 2001, as well as the sentencing of Daewoo's founder to prison. Joongi Kim (2008) provides an extensive examination of this case.

Changes in Funding Sources

The reforms and, to a lesser extent, the restructuring were intended to improve the transparency and efficiency of the chaebol, by enhancing the role of the market in scrutinizing and regulating their investment and financing decisions. Specifically, there was a reduction of funding for investments channeled through the opaque internal capital markets of the chaebol, instead using more transparent and market-based external funding. Thus, the critical hypothesis is that if opaque internal capital markets are in operation, then a chaebol's investment is less constrained by its own cash flow (defined as net profits) than would otherwise be the case. A corollary is that if corporate reform were effective, then a chaebol's investment would become more sensitive to its cash flow for two reasons. The first is that the role of internal capital markets would become weaker, if not dysfunctional, following the reform. The second is that external funding would be better regulated by the market.

To assess these theories, we conducted an empirical evaluation using a framework closely related to those of Sangwoo Lee, Kwangwoo Park, and Hyun-Han Shin (2009)—hereafter LPS—and Krislert Samphantharak (2006). Details are available from the authors.

Our conclusions add to the body of literature that suggests the chaebol have become less dependent on internal capital markets and more able to access financing on their own.

Qualitative Assessment of Governance Reforms

According to a study by KDI that examined corporate governance (Youngjae Lim et al. 2003), Korea had an overall score of 0.80 out of 1.00 on an institution index that measured the substance of rules and regulations in various categories. This was just slightly below the U.S. score of 0.89. However, on an enforcement index, Korea's scores were significantly lower than those on the institutional index in all categories, which suggests that the rules and regulations had yet to be effectively enforced (Table 14.1).

Although it is clear that more work is needed to improve corporate governance in Korea, there are signs that the reform efforts have yielded tangible results. For instance, the market has been rewarding companies that have good governance by increasing their share prices (Black et al. 2005).

Although this is a sign that great strides have been made in recruiting and promoting professional managers, the question remains whether the reform has led to any measurable decrease in the influence of founding families, since they can effectively control the affiliates with very little direct ownership. For example, the Lee family directly owns about 5.5 percent of Samsung Electronics, Korea's largest company, but the family effectively controls it by controlling companies such as Samsung Life Insurance and Samsung C&T (the Samsung holding company) that own significant blocks of Samsung Electronics.

Owing to the major restructuring of Korea's corporate sector since the 1997 crisis, a number of the chaebol have been dissolved, the average debt-to-equity ratio of listed companies has significantly decreased, and transparency and corporate governance have improved as accounting and auditing standards have been brought closer to international best practices.

Table 14.1. Scores on Institution and Enforcement Indexes

	Institution index (A)	Enforcement index (B)	A – B
Disclosure and audits	0.79	0.50	0.29
Disclosure	0.88	0.47	0.41
Audits	0.63	0.53	0.10
Supervision and litigation by shareholders	0.72	0.39	0.33
Independence of supervisory bodies	0.50	0.47	0.03
Power of supervisory bodies	1.00	0.51	0.49
Litigation by shareholders	0.67	0.19	0.48
Accountability of managers	0.90	0.45	0.45
Shareholders' rights	0.88	0.34	0.54
Market for corporate control	1.00	0.56	0.44
Directors' or controlling shareholders' liability	0.83	0.45	0.38
Overall	0.80	0.45	0.35

Source: Youngjae Lim et al. 2003, cited in Organization for Economic Cooperation and Development 2004.

Note: Index scores range from 0.00 to 1.00. The institution index is constructed by examining a country's legal framework, while the enforcement index is based on the results of a survey of experts.

The Philosophy of Corporate Governance Reform

Underlying the government's reform efforts has been the idea that strong market discipline, rather than government intervention, should lead the restructuring process. Thus, creditors and shareholders are now empowered to monitor corporate governance; more rigorous bank accounting standards are in place; and the mergers and acquisitions have been encouraged.

Nonetheless, questions have been raised regarding the wisdom of imposing the so-called global standard on corporate governance in Korea. Sung-Hee Jwa (2003) doubted whether the global standard—which is, in fact, Anglo-American—would work effectively in Korea, a country that differs from the West in terms of history, culture, and institutions. Keun Lee (2003) raised a similar concern, finding that soon after the crisis, Korea had succeeded in bringing about changes in areas where the targets for reform could readily be quantified (that is, the number of outside directors and debt-to-equity ratio), but it has yet to improve the workings of boards of directors and corporate governance in general. These issues involve person-to-person relations in which informal institutions such as culture and the habits and mind-sets of actors play an essential role.

Indeed, despite the extensive efforts to reform corporate governance in Korea through the adoption of global standards, there is still skepticism about whether the reforms were adequately adapted to the Korean context.

The Effects of Corporate Governance Reform on Chaebol Investment Behavior

This section of the chapter provides empirical evidence on the effects of the corporate governance reform on chaebol investment behavior. Specifically, the analysis focuses on identifying the long-term impact on the role played by internal capital markets in funding chaebol investment before and after the 1997 crisis. The reforms—and, to a lesser extent, the restructuring—were intended to improve the transparency and efficiency of the chaebol by enhancing the market's role in scrutinizing and regulating their investment and financing decisions.

Since the onset of the 1997 crisis, Korea's corporate sector has made great strides toward soundness and efficiency. Chaebol debt-to-equity ratios of over 500 percent in the year preceding the crisis were brought down to the target level of 200 percent by the end of 2000, and intra-chaebol debt guarantees have been significantly reduced. More importantly, many large-scale spin-offs have resulted in streamlining business activities among the financially weaker chaebol, with a significant reduction in the number of poorly performing affiliates. We surmise that the decline in the number of affiliates and the exit of troubled firms has led to a reallocation of labor and capital to growing businesses.

The rehabilitation and profitability growth of the chaebol since the 1997 crisis demonstrates their improved soundness and efficiency. At the end of 2017, the assets owned by the top thirty chaebol amounted to 2,247 trillion won (146 percent of GDP). On average, these chaebol had twenty-eight affiliates. However, the number of affiliates of some chaebol had crept back to the pre crisis level. For instance, SK's affiliates had increased significantly, from thirty-nine in 2000 to ninety in 2017.

The increased and strengthened role of the market was expected to replace funding for investment channeled through the opaque internal capital markets of the chaebol with more transparent and market-based external funding. The availability of market-based external funding for investment would likely depend positively on a chaebol's cash flows, as the flows would be taken into account when the market assessed the risk and return profile of the chaebol investment.

The basic setup for the analysis is an investment equation for the chaebol that is estimated using firm-level data and tested by determining if the role of internal capital markets has weakened since the 1997 financial crisis relative to the pre crisis period. Given the limited data available on the internal financial transactions of chaebol firms, the analysis focuses on testing whether—after controlling for other determinants of corporate investment—chaebol investment behaviors differ significantly between the pre- and postcrisis periods or between the chaebol that own financial intermediaries as subsidiaries and those that do not.

The empirical framework is closely related to those of LPS (2009) and Samphantharak (2006). LPS examined whether the role of internal capital markets in Korea changed systematically following the 1997 crisis and found that internal capital markets operated effectively before the crisis but lost their significance after it. The authors estimated a standard investment function that related investment to Tobin's q, firms' cash flow, and groups' cash flow by using a panel sample of listed firms. They found that group cash flow was a statistically significant determinant of investment during the pre crisis period but not after the crisis. This is evidence of the disappearing role of internal capital markets for the chaebol. Samphantharak developed a structural model for investment by business groups that assumed costly external finance and tested the implications of the model for the emergence of internal capital markets in business groups using data from Thailand.

Specifically, equation 14.1 was estimated for chaebol firms:

$$I_{ijt} = \alpha Q_{ijt} + \beta LV_{ijt} + \gamma_o OC_{ijt} + \gamma_1 (DL^*OC)_{ijt} \\ + \gamma_2 (DF^*OC)_{ijt} + Constant\ terms \qquad 14.1$$

Where subscript i: business group,
   subscript j: individual firm,
   subscript t: time,
   I: investment,
   Q: Tobin's q (or industry q for nonlisted firms),
   LV: financial leverage,
   OC: firms' cash flow,
   DL: dummy variable for listed firms, and

DF: dummy variable for business groups that own financial
    intermediaries.

Constant terms include business groups and industry dummies.
These dummies are expected to capture the factors specific to each business group and a common industrial effect, respectively.

Although the specification is similar to those of LPS (2009) and Samphantharak (2006), it departs from them in two important ways.

First, both listed and nonlisted firms are included in the sample. We suspect that internal capital markets within the chaebol may have played a particularly vital role in channeling financial resources to nonlisted firms, which have far more concentrated ownership than listed firms. Therefore, focusing only on listed firms may fail to identify the full effect of the postcrisis reform on the changing behavior of the chaebol.

Second, we analyze whether the ownership of within-group financial intermediaries affected the operation of internal capital markets and investment decisions in any systematic way. If the postcrisis corporate reform has had the intended effect and, as a result, the role of internal capital markets has diminished, then the ownership of within-group financial intermediaries should have a significantly weaker impact on investment once other determinants are adequately controlled for.

Investment is measured by capital expenditure calculated from a firm's cash flow statement (rather than as a change in the fixed assets, as Samphantharak did). The definition of capital expenditure used in this study is close to that of capital expenditures given in the Compustat database, and it includes net expenditures for tangible assets such as machines, vehicles, tools, fixtures, and assets in construction. We believe that the use of the simple change in the fixed assets for investment is highly inadequate because it involves asset revaluations and depreciation that were actively undertaken after the 1997 crisis (Kyung-Mook Lim 2008). To control for size, we normalize the capital expenditures by the stock of fixed assets at the beginning of the year.

For independent variables, a firm's own cash flow is defined as net profits normalized by the stock of fixed assets at the end of the previous year. Tobin's q is constructed as the ratio of total market capitalization to the book value of capital. This variable is widely used to capture firm-specific investment opportunities. For nonlisted firms (for which no stock price data are available), industry q is used as the proxy for Tobin's q. Industry q is computed as a simple average of the Tobin's q of listed firms in the same industry to which the specific nonlisted firm belongs. Financial leverage is measured by the ratio of total debt to total assets.

The coefficients of prime interest are γ_1 and γ_2. Our prior is that $\gamma_2 < 0$ while γ_1 is unclearly a priori. Regarding γ_2, the underlying assumption is that the ownership of financial intermediaries facilitates the functioning of internal capital markets and helps relax the external financing constraints faced by the chaebol. Consequently, investment tends to be less sensitive to a firm's cash flow if the firm is a subsidiary of a chaebol that owns financial intermediaries ($\gamma_2 < 0$). Moreover, it is expected that γ_2 may become smaller in absolute value or even change its sign during the postcrisis period if the corporate governance reform has the intended effect on the transparency and efficiency of the chaebol.

In contrast, γ_1 is ambiguous for two reasons.

First, compared to nonlisted firms, listed ones are subject to various stock exchange regulations on disclosure and minority shareholder rights, as well as more robust scrutiny from the market. This may have been true even before the crisis. As a result, listed firms would face greater difficulty in transferring financial resources across affiliated firms, with a more limited role played by internal capital markets. This implies that the investment of listed firms will be more sensitive to their own cash flow ($\gamma_1 > 0$).

Second, listed firms would likely have better access to external funding (including access to international capital markets) than nonlisted firms, in part because of greater transparency and information disclosure. The greater availability of external funding implies that the investment of listed firms would be less sensitive to their own cash flow than is the case for nonlisted firms ($\gamma_1 < 0$). Thus, γ_1 will depend on which effect dominates. Also, the sign and size of γ_1 may differ before and after the crisis, depending on the effect of the corporate governance reform.

The firm-level data are from the Korea Information Service (KIS) database. The database contains comprehensive financial information not only for firms listed on the Korea Stock Exchange (KSE) but also for nonlisted firms that are required to be externally audited. Although the database includes information on firms listed on both the KSE and the Korea Securities Dealers Automated Quotations (KOSDAQ) stock markets, firms listed on the KOSDAQ market are excluded because their characteristics and behavior are quite different from those of chaebol firms. Data are available for 1994–2017, but several years are excluded from the sample used for the analysis to minimize the possible bias from outliers. Specifically, data for the crisis years 1997–98 and 2008–9 and for 2017 (a year of heightened political uncertainty because Korea's president was impeached) are dropped.

Business groups are defined based on ownership and managerial control. Firms are in the same group if they are wholly or partly owned and managed by the same individual or group of individuals, such as a family. To identify groups, we use information from the KIS database. In constructing the sample of firms affiliated with groups, we define groups as those that have existed every year for the whole study period (1994–2017) and that contain at least five externally audited affiliates. We exclude all of those that underwent corporate rehabilitation procedures, as well as those that became new chaebol as a result of a spin-off after the crisis.

Table 14.2 presents summary statistics for the thirty-one business groups in the sample. About 23 percent were listed on the KSE, and on average each has 1.2 within-group financial intermediaries.

The regression results shown in Table 14.3 are estimated using cross-section data for more than 145 firms obtained using period averages for all variables, except dummies. The use of cross-section data conforms to the purpose of assessing the long-run effect of the corporate governance reform and also produces more stable results.

The precrisis period data in the table show that γ_0 is positive and statistically significant, indicating that in general investment is sensitive to a firm's cash flow.

The fact that γ_2 is negative and statistically significant indicates that the investment responds positively, but far less sensitively, to cash flow in firms affiliated with a chaebol that owns financial intermediaries as subsidiaries. This result conforms to our prior that internal capital markets tended to ease external financing constraints faced by the chaebol during the pre crisis period. It is also consistent with the findings of Takeo Hoshi and coauthors (1991) that intermediaries affect the sensitivity of investment to cash flow in firms in business groups.

As expected, the coefficient of the interaction term for listed firms (γ_1) is positive but not significant, suggesting that the effects of weaker internal capital markets and greater access to external financing may have canceled each other out.

The results for the postcrisis period reported in Table 14.3 generally support our predictions. Investment has become generally less sensitive to firms' cash flow relative to the precrisis period (that is, γ_0 is far smaller

Table 14.2. Summary Statistics at the Group Level

Year	Average			Minimum			Maximum		
	Listed firms	Affiliated firms	Within-group intermediaries	Listed firms	Affiliated firms	Within-group intermediaries	Listed firms	Affiliated firms	Within-group intermediaries
1994	3.7	10.8	1.1	0	5	0	15	31	4
1995	3.8	11.6	1.2	0	5	0	15	34	5
1996	3.8	11.9	1.2	1	5	0	15	36	5
1997	3.9	13.0	1.5	1	5	0	16	40	7
1998	3.9	14.0	1.6	1	6	0	18	41	8
1999	3.9	13.7	1.5	1	6	0	17	35	8
2000	3.9	13.5	1.6	1	6	0	16	34	9
2001	3.5	13.5	1.5	1	5	0	12	40	8
2002	3.5	14.1	1.5	1	5	0	14	46	9
2003	3.5	14.9	1.5	1	5	0	13	48	8
2004	3.4	15.1	1.3	0	5	0	12	47	7
2005	3.5	14.6	1.0	0	5	0	12	45	7

Year								
2006	3.4	15.4	1.0	0	5	0	12	47	7
2007	3.5	16.2	1.1	0	5	0	12	49	8
2008	3.6	17.3	1.0	0	5	0	12	60	7
2009	3.7	17.1	1.1	0	6	0	13	55	7
2010	3.8	17.8	1.1	0	6	0	12	55	7
2011	3.9	19.0	1.1	1	5	0	13	58	8
2012	4.1	19.4	1.1	1	7	0	12	69	7
2013	4.0	20.0	1.1	1	5	0	12	68	8
2014	4.0	20.7	1.1	1	5	0	11	71	9
2015	4.0	20.7	1.1	0	5	0	12	74	9
2016	3.9	20.8	1.1	0	5	0	11	74	8
2017	3.9	20.6	1.0	0	5	0	11	84	9

Table 14.3. Estimation Results of Equation 14.1

	1994–96	1999–2016
Cash flow to fixed assets	0.98	0.19
	(6.4)	(3.7)
Tobin's q	−0.45	2.28
	(−0.8)	(0.4)
Leverage	12.2	−21.4
	(2.4)	(−0.7)
Dummy for listed firm x	1.02	1.04
Cash flow to fixed assets	(0.7)	(0.7)
Dummy for group with intermediaries x	−0.76	0.13
Cash flow to fixed assets	(−3.4)	(1.8)
Observations	143	145
Adjusted R squared	0.62	0.32

Notes: The precrisis period was 1994–96. The postcrisis period was 1999–2016. Both periods included industry and group dummies. We exclude outliers for all variables that appear to be beyond their sample mean by ±2 sigma.

than in the pre crisis period), which reflects the increased availability of, and access to, cheaper external finance.

More importantly, γ_2 is positive and statistically significant at the 10 percent level, which indicates that the ownership of financial intermediaries tends to increase the sensitivity of investment to a firm's cash flow during the postcrisis period. This is in sharp contrast to the negative and strongly significant coefficient of the same interaction term in the pre crisis sample. A possible explanation would be that the ownership of financial intermediaries has subjected the chaebol to systematically stronger scrutiny by the financial regulatory authorities, and that as a consequence, the role of internal capital markets is far more limited. In this case, the investment may depend more on the availability of external funding, which is sensitive to a firm's cash flow.

The coefficient of the interaction term for listed firms (γ_1) is of the same sign and size as in the precrisis sample and continues to be statistically insignificant.

In sum, the empirical analysis discussed above adds to the body of literature suggesting that the chaebol have become less dependent on internal capital markets and more able to access financing on their own, aided in part by the corporate governance reform for transparency and efficiency.

Chaebol Resurgence

As part of the structural reforms that Korea embarked on in the wake of the 1997 financial crisis, a large number of chaebol were either liquidated or dismantled. In addition, the survivors were subject to restructuring that required them to improve their financial soundness by lowering their debt-to-equity ratio to below 200 percent and streamlining their businesses, with a greater focus on a few core areas.

Two decades after the crisis, it appears that the chaebol no longer overborrow and certainly do not monopolize bank lending. However, they seem to have once again captured large shares of the output of the Korean economy.

As seen in Figure 14.1, market competition has weakened, with an increase in monopoly power by the top three companies since the early 2000s. Fair trade policies need to be strengthened to regulate monopolistic behavior such as cartels.

Also, as can be seen in Figure 14.2, during 1991–2016, the operating profits of the four largest chaebol have increased by over 16.4 times, while those of the national economy increased by 5.2 times.

It is generally acknowledged that the chaebol have become much more efficient and resilient to external shocks, and that they have been

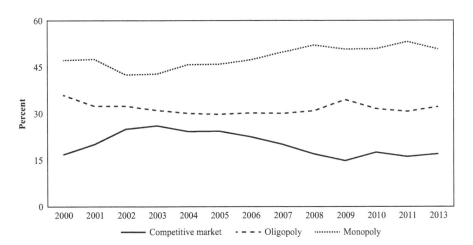

Figure 14.1. Market Concentration
Source: Fair Trade Commission.
Notes: Competitive market: CR3 (Market share of top 3) < 30%, Oligopoly market: 30% ≦ CR3 < 75%, Monopolistic market: 75% ≦ CR3. Vertical axis indicates the average market concentration of industries that are less than 30%, between 30% and 75%, and above 75% for each year.

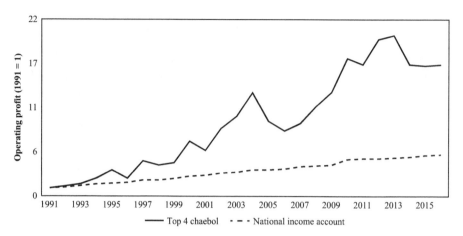

Figure 14.2. Operating Profits of the Top 4 Chaebol and the National Economy
Sources: Economic Statistics System of the Bank of Korea and KIS VALUE.

beneficial to the Korean economy. But the concentration of economic power in the hands of the large chaebol has brought back memories of their predatory behavior and other improprieties. Indeed, the total amount of illicit wealth accumulated by the family members of the top ten chaebol through unfair internal transactions (a practice known as "tunneling") was estimated to be 26.2 trillion won as of the end of 2015 (see Chong-hee Lee 2016).

The misgivings about the resurgence of the chaebol have deepened, as they have not been able to forsake their old, and often heavily criticized, ownership structure and management style. As has often been pointed out, the chaebol—even the largest ones—remain largely family controlled, with the opaque and confusing ownership structures. Market share is emphasized over profits.

The chaebol have also reverted to expanding their business lines into noncore and often unrelated businesses and to using the old strategy of expansion, which was a factor in their problems during the 1997 crisis. As a result, SMEs have been crowded out of industries where they traditionally had a strong foothold. The loss of market share by SMEs has led to a growing clamor for reinstating entry barriers against the chaebol in many of the traditional SME industries.

In 1979, the Korean government designated twenty-three industries as the exclusive business domain of SMEs. The designation effectively barred entry into these industries of the chaebol and other large firms. Over the next ten years, the number increased to 237 industries before declining gradually until 2006, when the system was abolished.

Responding to a growing demand for entry barriers, the former Presidential Committee for Shared Growth has taken up the issue of protecting SMEs and produced guidelines for designating industries to be reserved for SMEs. As of April 2018, the Committee had chosen 73 out of 234 industries proposed by SMEs for restriction (Noh 2018).

Conclusion

The 1997 Asian financial crisis was a major turning point in the development of the Korean economy. Its consequences have had a lasting impact. The wide and deep restructuring efforts after the crisis changed the Korean corporate landscape. Large numbers of insolvent firms were shut down, and highly leveraged and troubled firms were rehabilitated. A wide range of institutional reforms was implemented to improve Korea's corporate governance in terms of strengthening transparency and shareholder rights.

In the years since the crisis, chaebol have become globally leading multinational companies, not only improving their balance sheets but also increasing their profitability.

However, the success of the corporate restructuring and subsequent rehabilitation of the chaebol has brought new challenges. In addition to concerns that the chaebol are dependent on government subsidies or other preferential treatment, as they were before the crisis, there are growing concerns about the challenges posed by the fact that a few of the largest chaebol account for a disproportionately large share of the economy.

As this study shows, the expected gains from the corporate governance reform of the chaebol do not appear to have been realized, which implies that the postcrisis corporate reform did not have its intended effect—as argued by LPS (2009). Instead, the results are more consistent with the study by Youngjae Lim et al. (2003), which documented a significant gap between institution and enforcement (see Table 14.3). The results support concerns about whether global corporate governance standards were adequately adapted to fit the Korean context. It would seem that the important question now is not whether the chaebol are overleveraged or too dependent on the government and "too big to fail," but whether they are "too big to regulate."

CHAPTER 15

The 2008 Liquidity Crisis

Buildup and Causes

In the second half of 2008, less than a decade after recovering from the 1997 crisis, Korea succumbed to another crippling liquidity crisis and economic downturn. This time the crisis was not idiosyncratic. In contrast to its position during the 1997 crisis, Korea held 7.7 times more foreign exchange reserves than in 1997. There was a current account surplus, the won-dollar exchange rate was floating, and Korea's banks held a relatively small volume of nonperforming loans and an insignificant amount of toxic U.S. assets.

Overall, Korea's economic fundamentals were much stronger in 2008 than in 1997. However, once the global crisis broke out, being armed with what many people had claimed was an excessive level of foreign exchange reserves was not enough to spare the country from the collateral damage inflicted by the global financial crisis that had been touched off by the U.S. subprime lending debacle in August 2007.

As the effects of the global financial crisis reached Korea in the second half of 2008, the growing specter of another crash in the country's financial markets panicked foreign investors and lenders into moving out of Korea to the perceived safety of dollar-denominated assets. Because people believed that Korea was more vulnerable than other East Asian countries, the flight from Korea was greater than elsewhere in the region. In the end, Korea's relatively large and liquid financial markets made it easier for investors and lenders to leave.

Unable to stanch the run on its central bank reserves and stem the emerging capital account crisis on its own, Korea had to secure rescue financing from external sources. However, it was unthinkable for the Korean authorities to approach the IMF again. Instead, near the end of October 2008, Korea asked for—and received—a dollar-won currency swap line from the U.S. Federal Reserve amounting to $30 billion. Many investors operating out of Korea believed, rightly or wrongly, that the swap implied the United States had an interest in supporting Korea's effort to fend off speculation. The Fed's intervention was effective in helping turn around the market sentiment and restore financial stability (Baba and Shim, 2011).

After the collapse of Lehman Brothers in September 2008, Korean banks found it increasingly difficult to roll over their short-term foreign loans. At the lowest point, in November 2009, the renewal rate fell to below 40 percent, causing a significant drop in capital inflow and a 20 percent ($60 billion) loss of foreign exchange reserves. As dollar liquidity evaporated, the nominal exchange rate began depreciating, reaching 1,509 won to the dollar on November 24—down from about 1,000 won in April 2008. The won fell in value by almost 18 percent in October alone. At the height of the crisis, the sovereign spread jumped to 751 basis points on October 27, from a little over 200 in early May 2008. The credit default swap premium rose from 246 basis points to 699 over the same period.

The liquidity crunch resulted from a confluence of factors. They included panic and herding among foreign lenders, which were exacerbated by structural weaknesses of Korea's financial sector—mostly by the reemergence of a current account deficit in the first half of 2008.

At the end of 2005, the banking sector held $83.4 billion in foreign currency liabilities, equal to 44 percent of Korea's total external debt. Two years later, the amount had more than doubled to $194 billion, or 50 percent. NBFIs and private and public enterprises were equally active in borrowing from abroad. Their external debt jumped from $88.9 billion at the end of 2005 to $134.8 billion at the end of 2007.

The bulk of the increase in foreign debt consisted of short-term dollar liabilities. At the end of 2008, Korea's short-term foreign liabilities as a proportion of foreign exchange reserves had risen to 74 percent, way below 100 percent—which was then considered to be the limit for reserve adequacy, according to the Guidotti-Greenspan-Fischer (GGF) rule. What

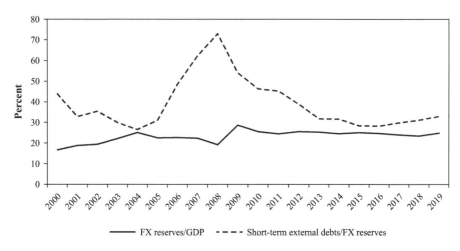

Figure 15.1. Foreign Exchange Reserves as a Percent of GDP and Short-Term External Debts as a Percent of Foreign Exchange Reserves
Source: Economic Statistics System of the Bank of Korea.

was startling to foreign investors was the rapidity with which the proportion soared: between 2005 and 2008, Korea's foreign exchange reserves as a percentage of short-term foreign liabilities more than doubled (Figure 15.1).

Concurrently, the loan-to-deposit ratio at banking institutions had risen steadily since 2001, reaching over 125 percent by the time the crisis erupted (Figure 15.2). Together with the emerging current account deficit, there was growing concern that these changes could cause a sharp increase in maturity and currency mismatches on bank balance sheets, making banks vulnerable to a sudden reversal of capital inflows.

Liberalization of Capital Outflows and Growth of Investments in Foreign Securities

The Korean won, which had started gaining value against the U.S. dollar in late 2005, continued to appreciate, falling below 920 won per dollar toward the end of 2006. Faced with an erosion of export competitiveness and increasing costs of sterilization, Korea's policy makers sought to stabilize the exchange rate by deregulating capital outflows. To this end, they loosened restrictions on domestic investors' portfolios of foreign securities. In 2006, the relaxation touched off a significant increase in

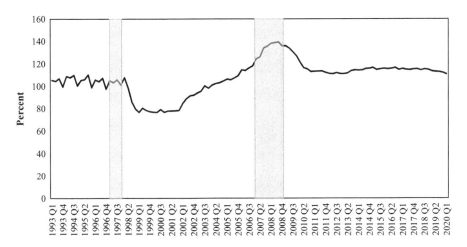

Figure 15.2. Loan-to-Deposit Ratio of the Banking Sector
Source: Economic Statistics System of the Bank of Korea.
Notes: The figure shows loans as a percent of deposits from Q1 of 1993 to Q4 2017. Shaded areas represent Q1 of 1997 to Q1 of 1998; Q1 of 2007 to Q4 of 2008.

investment in overseas bonds and equities. In the preceding year, Korea's portfolio investments abroad had risen to $67 billion.[1] This amount almost doubled in 2006 and soared again to $173.2 billion in the following year (Figure 15.3).

As shown in Table 15.1, over six years starting in 2005, other nonbank financial corporations, nonfinancial corporations, and households held on average almost 70 percent of total foreign stocks and more than 60 percent of bond investments.

The frenzy of investing in foreign securities was bound to stoke a sharp increase in the demand for U.S. dollars.[2] To make matters worse, private investors' hedging against the currency risk added to the growing demand as they entered into forwarding contracts. They took the short position

---

1. Korea's portfolio investments in foreign securities include overseas stocks and bonds as well as Korean paper such as convertible bonds, depository receipts, bonds with warrants, and certificates of deposit issued by local governments, banks, and companies in overseas markets.

2. There are only two foreign exchange markets in Korea: the won-dollar and won-yuan forward and swap markets. This means that private investors have to buy U.S. dollars before converting them into other currencies to invest in foreign securities that are not in U.S. dollars.

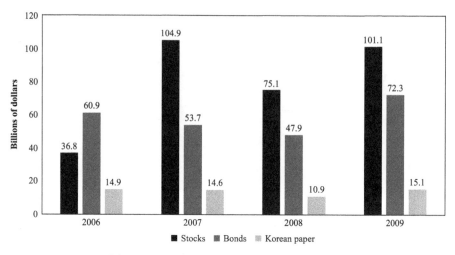

Figure 15.3. Portfolio Investments in Foreign Securities
Source: Bank of Korea.

in selling future proceeds of principals and interests paid on their bonds when they matured or of the sale of stock at future dates at a predetermined exchange rate.

The short selling was matched by a long position in the form of an agreement to buy the underlying dollar proceeds by banks as counterparties. Banks, though not required to do so, tend to maintain a square position in their holdings of foreign currency assets and liabilities to minimize the risks related to foreign exchange rates. Since banks hold a relatively small amount of foreign currencies, used mostly for day-to-day retail transactions, they had to borrow the same amount of U.S. dollars of the same maturity to cover their long positions. In this way, the currency mismatch was replaced by a maturity mismatch, which left Korea's banking sector vulnerable to the 2008 global financial crisis.

As in the case of domestic investors in foreign securities, Korea's shipbuilders took part in similar currency hedging operations. Since it takes several years to construct a ship, a standard order stipulates that the contract price will be paid in installments over the building period as advances. Shipbuilders usually enter into a forward contract with banks in which they agree to sell the advances at future dates at a given exchange rate. The short selling is then matched by a bank's long position. In 2007,

Table 15.1. Holdings of Foreign Bonds and Equities by Institutions
(billion dollars and percentages)

	Central Bank		Deposit-taking corporations		Other financial corporations		Nonfinancial corporations and households		Total	
	Stocks	Bonds	Stocks	Bonds	Stocks	Bonds	Stocks	Bonds	Stocks	Bonds
2005	0.0	10.4	5.1	3.8	8.8	24.1	1.9	1.3	13.9	38.2
	(0.0)	(26.3)	(32.3)	(9.6)	(55.7)	(60.9)	(12.0)	(3.3)	(100.0)	(100.0)
2006	0.0	13.8	12.2	7.2	24.6	39.9	4.6	1.2	36.8	60.9
	(0.0)	(22.2)	(29.5)	(11.6)	(59.4)	(64.3)	(11.1)	(1.9)	(100.0)	(100.0)
2007	2.5	16.6	8.3	7.2	94.0	29.9	14.3	2.2	104.9	53.7
	(2.1)	(29.7)	(7.0)	(12.9)	(78.9)	(53.5)	(12.0)	(3.9)	(100.0)	(100.0)
2008	10.3	6.3	2.5	4.2	35.0	16.8	5.5	1.6	47.9	27.2
	(19.3)	(21.8)	(4.7)	(14.5)	(65.7)	(58.1)	(10.3)	(5.5)	(100.0)	(100.0)
2009	20.8	7.5	2.1	3.6	49.4	17.7	5.5	2.3	72.3	28.8
	(26.7)	(24.1)	(2.7)	(11.6)	(63.5)	(56.9)	(7.1)	(7.4)	(100.0)	(100.0)
2010	32.5	11.2	2.7	4.1	46.8	15.0	5.9	2.4	81.9	30.3
	(37.0)	(34.3)	(3.1)	(12.5)	(53.2)	(45.9)	(6.7)	(7.3)	(100.0)	(100.0)
2011	35.7	9.7	2.9	5.2	33.0	16.9	4.9	2.8	71.7	31.8
	(46.7)	(28.0)	(3.8)	(15.0)	(43.1)	(48.8)	(6.4)	(8.1)	(100.0)	(100.0)

Source: Economic Statistics System of the Bank of Korea (https://ecos.bok.or.kr/EIndex_en.jsp).
Notes: Other financial corporations include insurance companies, pension funds, postal insurance, the Korea Securities Finance Corporation, and financial auxiliaries (defined in chapter 2). The numbers in parentheses are the percentages of total foreign equity investments (for stocks) and of total foreign bond investments (for bonds).

banks invested $60 billion in buying long-term forward dollar contracts from domestic shipbuilders.[3]

Because of the significant increase in investments in foreign securities and the shipbuilders' short sales, the demand for U.S. dollars soared at a time when the domestic supply was shrinking. The surplus on the current account was dropping. Still, Korea's policy makers continued sterilizing the surplus, adding more than $50 billion to expand the central bank reserves to $260 billion by the end of 2007.

---

3. Manufacturers of heavy industrial machinery entered into similar forward contracts.

After the 2008 global financial crisis broke out, many foreign ship buyers with contracts with Korean shipbuilders also suffered from the severe drop in shipping demand and a global liquidity drought, and they defaulted on their advance payments. As a result, on the delivery date, shipbuilding companies were forced to purchase U.S. dollars in the spot market to clear their short positions. This additional demand exacerbated the shortage of U.S. dollar liquidity when foreign investors were leaving the Korean market.

Much of the ensuing excess demand for U.S. dollar liquidity in the local foreign exchange market was eased by capital inflows, which consisted mostly of foreign bank loans secured by domestic banks from the branches of foreign banks.[4] The amount of short-term external funds raised by banks was $76 billion at the end of 2006. In the following year, this shot up by 37 percent, to $104 billion, and it increased by another 28 percent in 2008. The subsequent rise in the share of short-term foreign liabilities frightened foreign lenders and investors. Believing that a financial crisis was imminent, they hasten to leave the Korean market.

The growth of short-term foreign liabilities was certain to exacerbate the maturity and currency mismatches on bank balance sheets. Private investors purchase U.S. dollars to buy foreign securities in the won-dollar spot market through banks—which, as the leading suppliers, secure most of their short-term U.S. dollar funding from foreign bank branches in Korea. When the principal and interest are paid on their investments in foreign securities at their maturity dates, private investors sell their U.S. dollar proceeds back to banks for Korean won. Since the holding period of foreign securities that private investors own is likely to be longer than a year on average, while the maturities of banks' U.S. dollar liabilities are mostly short-term, banks incur a currency mismatch on their balance sheets.

For the three consecutive years beginning in 2005, a little over 60 percent of foreign currency assets held by banks consisted of foreign currency loans to domestic borrowers for their financing of long-term investments. As a result, banks—and, to some extent, other financial institutions—had growing maturity and currency mismatches on their balance sheets, making them vulnerable to a dollar liquidity shortage.

The risks associated with the substantial increase in short-term foreign liabilities were further compounded by the heavy losses incurred by Korean

---

4. Throughout this chapter, banks refer to depository corporations.

investors who bought large amounts of foreign securities when the global financial system plunged into turmoil. In 2008, more than 50 percent of the value of their investments evaporated, due mostly to the collapse of the financial markets they had entered. Worse yet, more than 80 percent of these investments were hedged against the currency risk. Because most private investors had bet that the won would appreciate, they ran up significant foreign exchange losses when the won weakened. This prospect of capital loss implied that there was a massive potential increase in Korea's foreign debt burden and a drain on its foreign exchange reserves.

The Ineffectiveness of Regulations

Having endured devastating consequences in the 1997 crisis, the prevention of the two balance sheet mismatches was at the top of regulatory reform. Korea's regulatory authorities had been watching the situation closely and introduced precautionary measures designed to fend off such mismatches. But the regulatory enforcement did little to make banks guard against the risks to which they might be exposed in managing assets and liabilities denominated in foreign currencies.

To mitigate the mismatch problems, the supervisory authorities implemented a regulation that required banks to relend in domestic currency to local borrowers up to a maximum of 15 percent of their total foreign currency funding maturing within three months and to relend up to a maximum of 85 percent in foreign currency. The local foreign currency loans also had to mature in less than three months.

These measures could prevent or moderate the pervasiveness of the two balance sheet mismatches, but they had the severe drawback of depriving banks of their role as asset transformers. Banks earn profits by engaging in debt-maturity transformation, borrowing short at low interest rates and lending long at higher interest rates. As Franklin Allen and Douglas Gale argue, the maturity mismatch "reflects the underlying structure of the economy in which individuals have a preference for liquidity, but the most profitable investment opportunities take a long time to pay off" (2007b, 59). A regulation for preventing mismatches weakens the competitiveness of domestic banks relative to their counterparts in other countries. If enforced strictly, domestic banks may not have incentives to move into international financial intermediation, implying that the regulatory restriction would be equivalent to another form of capital control.

Resolution and Consequences of the Crisis

It remains a mystery why Korea suffered more than any other Asian country from the 2008 global financial crisis. In the four months ending in November 2008, the Korean won lost 60 percent of its value against the U.S. dollar (Figure 15.4). The market was sending a clear signal that foreign investors were likely to accelerate the liquidation of their holdings of Korean assets, causing the exchange rate to spiral out of control and further undermining confidence in Korea's ability to weather the crisis.

By then, the Bank of Korea had spent more than a fifth of its foreign exchange reserves in defending the currency. The Korea Composite Stock Price Index had lost nearly half of its value, diving to 1,000 in November 2008 from 1,850 in May. Neither the reserve intervention nor the macroprudential supervisory reforms that were supposed to safeguard against a speculative attack were effective in reversing the pessimistic outlook.

Faced with the prospect of an implosion of the exchange rate and rapid depletion of foreign exchange reserves, on October 12, the government first issued a sovereign guarantee—for up to $100 billion in new foreign loans maturing before the end of June 2009. This guarantee was an at-

Figure 15.4. Changes in the Nominal Won-to-Dollar Exchange Rate, January 4, 2008–September 8, 2009
Source: Economic Statistics System of the Bank of Korea.

tempt to shore up foreign investors' confidence in the economy, as the government had done during the Asian financial crisis. Such guarantees had failed to allay fears of a financial meltdown at the beginning of the Asian crisis in 1997, and they failed again.

Only when Korea secured a swap line amounting to $30 billion from the Fed on October 30, 2008, did the foreign exchange market settle down somewhat. But that did not last very long. The exchange rate shot up to 1,513 won per dollar three weeks after the swap was announced. Foreign investors continued to leave the Korean market, as they were uncertain whether the $30 billion would be enough to turn back speculators. They also questioned whether the Fed would enter into swap transactions to make the swap proceeds available for servicing Korea's foreign loans. They thought that the Fed would be reluctant to do so, knowing that the country was saddled with a large amount of maturing Korean bonds held by foreign investors and international loans to be renewed in the first quarter of 2009.

Beginning in January 2009, the Bank of Korea began gradually withdrawing the funds provided by the swap with the Fed. For the next two months, the exchange rate was on a roller-coaster ride, reaching 1,573 won per dollar on March 3, 2009. Only after the seventh consecutive withdrawal from the swap did the won-dollar exchange rate begin appreciating gradually, reaching 1,300 won at the end of June 2009.

By the end of March 2009, the liquidity crisis was effectively over. Thereafter, Korea engineered an impressive recovery from the 2008 global economic crisis, ahead of many advanced and emerging economies. Against all the odds, the Korean economy grew 0.7 percent in 2009 after posting growth of 2.8 percent in 2008. In addition to registering a positive rate of growth, the current account balance returned to a surplus; the stock market managed a sustained rally, and the exchange rate gained vis-à-vis major currencies.[5]

---

5. Naohiko Baba and Ilhyock Shim (2011) present a somewhat different progression of the crisis. They estimate the deviation from covered interest parity—defined as the forward discount rate minus the interest rate differential—in the one- and three-month foreign exchange swap market. The deviations reached their peak in early December 2008 and then started to decline, which suggests that the tension in the U.S. dollar funding market peaked around the same time. They argue that the easing of the tension was primarily due to the Bank of Korea's U.S. dollar loan auctions that used the dollar proceeds from the swap transactions with the Fed, which reduced the difficulty Korean banks had in securing U.S. dollar funds thereafter.

In postmortems on the crisis, a series of analyses has searched for the reasons behind the relatively more significant damage Korea sustained compared to other emerging economies from the contagion of the U.S. subprime lending crisis. One could find fault with the inefficiency of Korea's policy regime in warding off the adverse external shocks. However, this study argues that Korea's inability to safeguard itself from such shocks had more to do with the absence of a global lender of last resort in an increasingly globalized financial system in which Korea was closely integrated.

Given the openness of its trade regime, the unprecedented collapse of global export markets in 2008–9 was bound to cause a deterioration of the current account and a massive fall in domestic aggregate demand. In moving ahead with financial market opening after the 1997 crisis, Korea had broadened and deepened its access to global financial markets, including those for short-term external debt.[6]

When the U.S. subprime lending crisis broke out, despite Korea's strong economic fundamentals, short-term external funding dried up quickly, and foreign investors—who were suffering from liquidity problems of their own—hurried to cash out. In the absence of a global liquidity safety net, there was little Korea's policy authorities could do to stop the ensuing liquidity crisis.

As Naohiko Baba and Ilhyock Shim (2011) point out, the Bank of Korea's loans, funded by the swap line with the Fed, were much more effective than its swaps using its foreign reserves. This evidence suggests that although vast foreign reserves could serve as self-insurance, once a country is faced with a speculative attack, nothing short of an intervention by the central banks of major reserve currency countries could stop a foreign liquidity run. As in the domestic economy, when a crisis is triggered by a market overreaction, it cannot be resolved without the intervention of a lender of last resort that is willing and able to provide an ample amount of liquidity. A close analogy applies to a country closely integrated into the global financial system.

---

6. Dani Rodrik and Andrés Velasco (1999), among others, have shown that countries with relatively well-developed financial sectors can and do access relatively large amounts of short-term external debt. However, even during the most difficult period following the collapse of Lehman Brothers, the volume of short-term foreign liabilities was less than the Bank of Korea's foreign exchange reserves. We return to this point below.

Comparative Analysis of the 1997 and 2008 Crises

To highlight the similarities and differences in the evolution and resolution of the two crises, this section of the chapter presents changes in many macroeconomic variables during the crises (Figures 15.5–15.10). In all six figures, period 0 refers to a period before the crisis picked up speed. For comparison, foreign exchange reserves and GDP are computed as indexes set to 100 at period 0 of each crisis, even though reserves and GDP were much larger in 2008 than in 1997.

EXCHANGE RATE AND FOREIGN
EXCHANGE RESERVES

During the first crisis, to meet the IMF's conditions for its loan, Korea moved to free-floating after having had a relatively rigid intermediate regime for years. Partly as a result of this abrupt regime change, the nominal exchange rate crashed slightly deeper in 1997–98 than in 2008–9 but recovered—ending up at about the same rate of depreciation. In both crises, the initial massive depreciation did not generate any expectations of a later appreciation. In fact, in the absence of reserve or other market

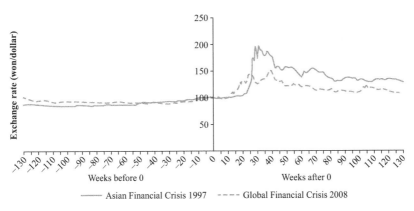

Figure 15.5. Changes in the Won-to-Dollar Exchange Rate, before and after the Financial Crises of 1997 and 2008
Source: Economic Statistics System of the Bank of Korea.
Notes: The 1997 crisis ran from the week of March 7, 1994 (-130) to the week of November 29, 1999 (+130), with the first week of June 1997 as week 0. The 2008 crisis ran from the week of March 7, 2005 (−130) to November 8, 2010 (+127), with the first week of June 2008 as week 0.

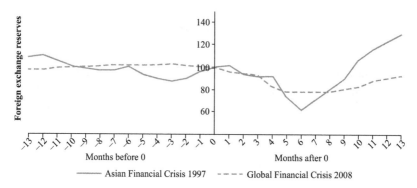

Figure 15.6. Foreign Exchange Reserves
Source: Economic Statistics System of the Bank of Korea.
Notes: The 1997 crisis rans from May 1996 to July 1998, with June 1997 as month 0. The 2008 crisis ran from May 2007 to July 2009, with June 2008 as month 0.

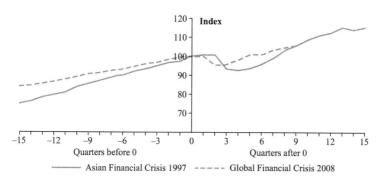

Figure 15.7. GDP
Source: Economic Statistics System of the Bank of Korea.
Notes: The 1997 crisis ran from the third quarter of 1994 to the first quarter of 2001, with the second quarter of 1998 as quarter 0. The 2008 crisis ran from the third quarter of 2004 to the third quarter of 2010, with the second quarter of 2008 as quarter 0.

interventions, the exchange rate could have moved onto an implosive path.

These reserves tell the same story because the amounts of reserve losses in the two crises were about the same, although 100 in 2008 corresponds to a reserve level 7.7 times larger than 100 in 1997. In 2008, Korea spent about $50 billion of its reserves to cope with the speculative attack. In 1998, it used about $60 billion, a sum equivalent to the $57 billion pledged by the IMF.

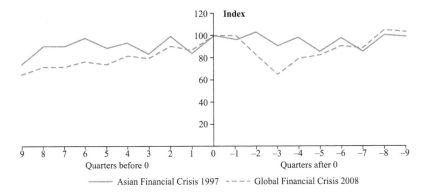

Figure 15.8. Exports
Source: Economic Statistics System of the Bank of Korea.
Notes: The 1997 crisis ran from the first quarter of 1995 to the third quarter of 1999, with the second quarter of 1997 as quarter 0. The 2008 crisis ran from the first quarter of 2006 to the third quarter of 2010, with the second quarter of 2008 as quarter 0.

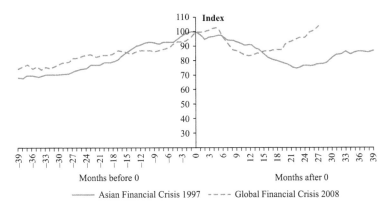

Figure 15.9. Inventory
Source: Economic Statistics System of the Bank of Korea.
Notes: The 1997 crisis ran from March 1994 to September 2000, with June 1997 as month 0. The 2008 crisis ran from March 2005 to September 2010, with June 2008 at month 0. The index was seasonally adjusted.

The won-dollar exchange rate recovered quickly in 1998, following the IMF agreement. So did the stock of reserves. A similar recovery took place in 2009 following the currency swap with the Fed (Figures 15.5 and 15.6). Both the IMF program and the Fed swap succeeded in turning the tide of capital outflows, whereas the use of reserves might not have achieved this result, no matter how large a stock of reserves Korea had.

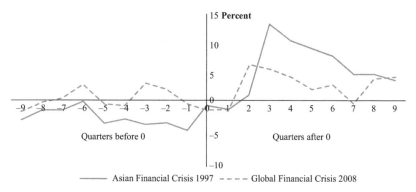

Figure 15.10. Current Account as a Percent of GDP
Source: Economic Statistics System of the Bank of Korea.
Notes: The 1997 crisis ran from the first quarter of 1995 to the third quarter of 1999, with the second quarter of 1997 as quarter 0. The 2008 crisis ran from the first quarter of 2006 to the third quarter of 2010, with the second quarter of 2008 as quarter 0.

GROWTH AND RECOVERY

Figure 15.7 shows that the decline in economic activity in terms of GDP was deeper in the earlier quarters of the 2008 crisis, compared to the 1997 crisis. But the economy rebounded earlier in the second crisis. This occurred because in the first crisis, the surge in export growth supported by a massive currency depreciation was not enough to compensate for the decline in investment demand. In contrast, once the stability of the financial system returned in the second crisis, domestic demand recovered—which offset much of the drop in export earnings.

Taken together, these changes mean that an expansion of exports (Figure 15.8) set off the recovery during the first crisis, whereas in the second crisis, it was domestic demand. In both cases, the crisis lasted about six months. By the end of the first quarter of 1998, the first crisis was over. The second was over by the end of the first quarter of 2009.

INVENTORY ADJUSTMENT

Figure 15.9 shows that the contraction in the inventory adjustment lasted much longer in the first than in the second crisis. In the 2008 crisis, firms had been piling up inventories before making a rather drastic cutback early in 2009. About six months later, firms resumed building up their inventories. This development suggests that recovery began earlier in the second crisis, which is consistent with the changes in GDP shown in Figure 15.7.

CURRENT ACCOUNT

In 1997, the large current account deficit that had been growing before the eruption of the crisis was perceived to be structural and one of the major causes of the financial meltdown. After the crisis, the current account exploded, generating a record high surplus. This was mostly due to a sharp cutback in imports, which in turn was caused by a decline in investment demand. In contrast, in the run-up to the 2008 liquidity crisis, the current account had been in surplus. It deteriorated for a short period before the crisis, due in part to a sustained real appreciation of the won. But once the won-to-dollar exchange rate began depreciating, it did not take long for the current account to produce a sizable surplus, though it was smaller than that of the 1997 crisis (Figure 15.10).

CHAPTER 16

The COVID-19 Pandemic and Financial Market Turmoil, 2019–20

A Financial Storm Brewing, 2018–19

There is a long-standing belief, which has become almost self-fulfilling, that Korea is destined to suffer a painful financial crisis every ten years. The country fell victim to a financial meltdown in 1997–98 and another debilitating crisis in 2008–9. In 2018, disturbing signs were emerging that the hedge fund industry was in disarray, with many of the firms suspending redemptions as losses stemming from questionable, some even fraudulent, investments mounted. Many hedge fund managers were implicated in investment scams and indicted.

Thus, COVID-19 reached Korea when the country was already struggling with slow growth and mounting financial imbalances. Korea has responded to the pandemic with the standard emergency measures of providing ample liquidity and supporting banks and other financial institutions. At this writing, in August 2020, the full effect and duration of the pandemic are still unknown. But in any case, the hedge fund fiasco is likely to aggravate financial uncertainties and imbalances and sustain the ten-year cycle of a financial crisis.

This chapter provides an overview of the effects of COVID-19 on the financial system. Because the pandemic hit just as problems with hedge funds were also affecting the financial system, the chapter begins with a summary of that emerging crisis.

An Emerging Crisis in the Private Equity Industry

Because of the continuing decline in the interest rate on deposits, Korean banks have been losing deposit customers to capital markets and nonbank financial institutions (NBFIs). To make up for the decline in revenue and profits, they have begun selling a variety of hedge fund products. These often are marketed with promised returns of 5 percent or more per year. To deliver such high returns, the banks took on much risk, selling very complicated products. Many of these products, created by dubious foreign asset managers, went bust.[1]

To sell more of these products, the banks falsified their credit evaluations of high-risk and high-return investments and marketed them as if they were safe and even guaranteed for redemption. As one commentator put it, "Bankers have perpetrated pirate banking rather than private banking" (Ki-hun Lee 2020). As more irregularities in the management of these funds were divulged, the demand for various products created by hedge funds evaporated, threatening the collapse of the private equity industry and thus posing a systemic risk for the entire financial system.

A consolidation of laws governing collective investment businesses—securities investment trusts and securities investment companies—created private equity firms in 2003. These private equity firms were to serve as needed by the institutions to facilitate corporate restructuring through mergers and acquisitions.

After Korea recovered from the 2008 global financial crisis, there was a growing demand for introducing hedge funds as a means of promoting capital market development by enlarging the menu of investment vehicles. As noted in chapter 8, Korea has been running persistent current account surpluses since the 1997 crisis. Since 2013 the financial account has also been in surplus. Hedge funds were seen as another channel through which these surpluses could be placed in external markets or invested domestically.

---

1. One of the funds, Lime Fund, which was registered in 2017, invested in other funds. One such fund was marketed by International Investment Group (IIG), based in New York. The U.S. Securities and Exchange Commission revoked IIG's license in 2018 on the grounds that it had been engaged in a Ponzi scheme. Although Lime was aware of the revocation and losses from Lime investments managed by IIG, it did not disclose the information to investors.

Thus, the government unveiled a Korean version of hedge funds in 2011. By the end of the year, twelve hedge funds had been introduced by nine asset management companies (see FSC 2012). They had a total committed capital of 149 billion won (US$135 million) (see FSC 2012).[2]

Initially, hedge funds were heavily regulated, and their formation required approval by the Financial Services Commission. They were required to hold a minimum of 40 billion won (US$36 million) in paid-in capital. The minimum investment per investor initially was set at 5 billion won (US$4.5 million), but this restriction meant that only institutional investors and wealthy individuals could invest. Subsequently, the minimum investment was lowered to 400 million won and then, in 2015, to 100 million won.

In 2015, the government initiated a new round of capital market deregulation. As a result, many restrictions on hedge funds were lifted. Practically anyone who could put up 1 billion won (US$900,000) as capital and who had at least three financial specialists as staff could register as a hedge fund. In setting up a fund, all the hedge-fund-type private equity firms had to do was to report the fund's establishment within two weeks of its setup.

In retrospect, it is clear that the extensive deregulation in the absence of adequate prudential supervision sowed the seeds of the collapse of the hedge fund industry. The demise has, in turn, further intensified financial instability. The deregulation has created opportunities to commit financial fraud and to bring in the shady industry operators to make, as one writer put it, private equity a "hotbed of crime" (see B. Kim 2020).

In 2016, there were 91 private equity firms with a total of 249.7 trillion won of committed capital (see FSC 2017). By May 2020, the number had jumped to 233, and the total committed capital of the firms had increased by more than 67 percent (see FSC 2020b). The number of funds created by these hedge fund firms rose to 11,734 from 7,734 in 2013 (see FSC 2020a). Many of these firms had fewer than ten specialists, including senior managers.

The hedge fund scandal became a major story just as COVID-19 was surfacing. On February 20, Reuters reported that prosecutors had begun a probe into Shinhan Investment and Lime Asset after regulators accused the companies of covering up losses at the hedge funds. On March 20,

---

2. Korean regulators have no formal definition of a hedge fund. Indeed, the term means different things to different people, and the meaning has evolved over time.

the CEO of Shinhan Investment resigned. Shinhan Investment is part of one of Korea's major financial groups.

From April through July 5, 2020, twenty-two private funds were unable to honor redemption requests from their investors. The redemption failure amounted to 5.6 trillion won (US$5.1 billion). Industry sources predict that the number of funds unable to meet redemption demand will increase.

A problem in Korea has been a conflation of hedge funds with private equity (venture capital). Financing new companies means a relatively long-term commitment, which generally would be made clear by not allowing redemption of funds for several years. Unfortunately, those marketing "hedge funds" in Korea promised liquidity that proved impossible to deliver. Although some of the funds may be outright Ponzi schemes, some of the underlying investments may prove successful with time.

One of the lessons of the hedge fund turmoil is how easy it is for well-intended financial market deregulation to cause havoc, especially in the absence of an efficient supervisory system.

The Economic and Financial Impacts of the COVID-19 Pandemic

From a health standpoint, Korea has been relatively unaffected by the pandemic. Active cases of COVID-19 peaked in March, and the number of daily deaths began to decline sharply in mid-April. As of August 3, 2020, there were fewer than 15,000 confirmed cases and 301 deaths in a country with a population of more than 51 million. Since the end of June, fewer than 50 new cases have been confirmed each day.[3] In contrast, however, the severity of the economic and financial disruptions and losses caused by the pandemic has been unprecedented.

The COVID-19 pandemic has proved to be the worst global shock to real activities and financial markets since the 2008 global financial crisis. The IMF (2020) reduced its global growth outlook for 2020 by a sizable margin (−4.9 percent) on June 24. With a projected growth rate of −2.1 percent in 2020, Korea was expected to fare better. Still, the Korean

---

3. Data are available at Worldometer database, https://www.worldometers.info /coronavirus/country/south-korea/; and Statistics Korea database, http://kostat.go.kr /portal/eng/pressReleases/8/10/index.board?bmode=read&bSeq=&aSeq=382775 &pageNo=1&rowNum=10&navCount=10&currPg=&searchInfo=&sTarget=title &sTxt=.

economy is already in recession, and the continuous decline in aggregate demand, in particular exports, foreshadows a further contraction that could be more significant if the pandemic persists.

This chapter first looks at the policy measures taken by the government to mitigate the adverse impact of the COVID-19 pandemic, and then analyzes the extent to which the effects of the pandemic have differed across industries and have been further aggravated by the preexisting financial vulnerabilities. Although it is too early to know the full effects of the pandemic, the analysis indicates that Korea will likely suffer another financial crisis, one much more severe than in 2008–9.

Policy Responses

FISCAL POLICY

To cope with the adverse effects of COVID-19, the government proposed, and the National Assembly passed, three supplementary budgets of 60 trillion won (US$54.5 billion)—about 20 percent of the total government budget for 2020. They cover an array of government spending, including the prevention and treatment of COVID-19 and issuing vouchers to help maintain consumption.

The first two supplemental budgets, amounting to 23.9 trillion won, were earmarked for financial support for the unemployed, low-income families, and small and medium enterprises (SMEs), as well as emergency cash, distributed virtually to all households. The third supplementary budget focuses on securing job market stability and the implementation of the Korean New Deal. The K-New Deal, as it is termed, was announced in mid-July. It is an overall stimulus plan with an emphasis on reshaping the post-pandemic economy.

MONETARY POLICY

The Bank of Korea (BOK) has been loosening monetary policy to cushion adverse impacts on the real economy and stabilize financial markets. It lowered the base rate twice in the first half of 2020, from 1.25 to 0.5 percent. In mid-May, it raised the ceiling on the Bank Intermediated Lending Support Facility by 5 trillion won to 30 trillion won to stimulate bank lending.

The central bank has not been shy about injecting a massive amount of liquidity whenever it is needed for recovery and at whatever amount. It initially did this through the regular repurchase agreement facility. However, the BOK concluded that the facility was not enough to supply liquidity to parts of the financial industry other than banking. Additionally, it has tapped into nonconventional channels of liquidity support, including purchases of treasury bonds (3 trillion won) and purchase agreements from NBFIs (3.5 trillion won).

The BOK also launched a new lending scheme, the Corporate Bond-Backed Lending Facility, to supply loans for up to six months to banks and NBFIs with high-quality corporate bonds as collateral. In July, the central bank undertook an unorthodox scheme of lending to the private sector by extending an 8 trillion won (US$6.64 billion) loan to a special purpose vehicle to be set up by the government-owned Korea Development Bank. The special purpose vehicle is set to start purchasing subprime corporate bonds and commercial paper that had been downgraded to junk status as a result of the COVID-19 pandemic.

FINANCIAL SUPPORT FOR SMES

On April 1, a government emergency financial relief package amounting to 12 trillion won for SMEs went into effect. It comprised loan maturity extensions and deferral of interest payments for six months. As part of the program, commercial banks have provided 3.5 trillion won of low-interest-rate loans to small business owners to a maximum of 30 million won at a fixed rate of 1.5 percent and a maturity of one year. Eligibility requires high credit ratings and an annual income of 500 million won or less.

The government finances the difference between the funding cost and low lending rates charged to SMEs, but banks have to shoulder credit risks associated with the subsidized loans. For this reason, only two of Korea's four largest commercial banks have lowered their average lending rates.

Growth and Current Account Development

Real GDP posted a steep fall of more than 3 percent during the second quarter of 2020, which is the worst loss per quarter since the global

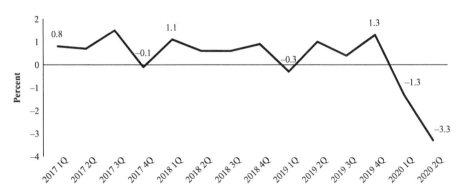

Figure 16.1. Quarterly GDP Growth Rate
Source: Economic Statistics System of the Bank of Korea.

financial crisis (Figure 16.1). On the demand side, private consumption was hit hard by social distancing and lockdowns, while exports have been contracting due to the collapse of external demand and disruptions in the global supply chain in many industries, including electronics and auto manufacturing (Figure 16.2). The deepening recession has also led to a drop in import demand, but less than that for exports, to realize a current account deficit, which is likely to expand.

Financial Markets

BOND MARKET

Figure 16.3 shows that both three-month KORIBOR (Korea Interbank Offered Rate) and three-year treasury bonds, representing short-term and long-term interest rates, respectively, have been trending downward due partly to the expansionary monetary policy. In the corporate bond market, spreads between AA- and BBB- jumped by about thirty basis points in mid-March, after which they have remained relatively stable. This increase in the spread reflected the market expectation that large corporations with a liquidity buffer would fare the pandemic better than SMEs with limited access to bank lending. This development is in stark contrast to what happened to spreads at the time of the global financial crisis. However, spreads have been less tightly linked to credit ratings since the government announced its liquidity support for firms with low credit ratings.

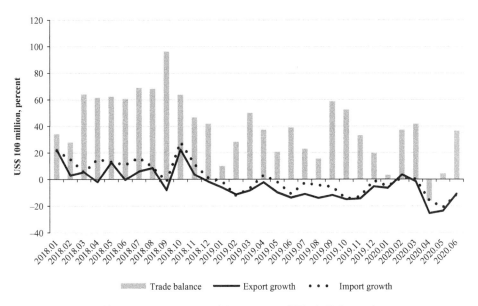

Figure 16.2. Changes in Exports and Imports, and Trade Balance (year-on-year growth)
Source: Customs Office.

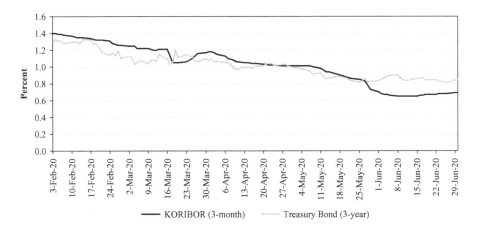

Figure 16.3. Trends of KORIBOR and Treasury Bond Rate
Source: Economic Statistics System of the Bank of Korea.

STOCK MARKET

The Korea Composite Stock Price Index (KOSPI) fell 36 percent in the months immediately following the first confirmed case of COVID-19 infection on January 20, 2020. It has bounced back since the implementation of expansionary monetary and fiscal policy and the signing of a US-Korea currency swap on March 19 (see Figure 16.4).

On the heels of the ample supply of liquidity and fiscal largesse, financial investors, including foreign groups, who believe that Korea has handled the pandemic better than some other parts of the world have swarmed the equity market, returning the index to its pre-pandemic level as of early August.

Developments in the stock price index, however, mask variations among industry and firms. The pharmaceutical, IT, and network service industries have led the stock market surge, with some firms registering an almost 60 percent increase in their stock prices. In contrast, stock prices of those firms whose production process is heavily dependent on global value chains, such as electronics and auto manufacturing, have underperformed.

The banking industry has been one of the worst-performing sectors in terms of stock prices owing to the combined effect of compressed net interest margins following extraordinary monetary easing and elevated credit risk associated with the onset of the private equity market crisis. Banks are also burdened by growing arrears among small business and

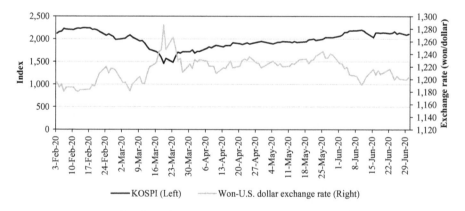

Figure 16.4. Trends of Stock Market Index (Jan. 4, 1980 = 100) and Exchange Rate
Source: Economic Statistics System of the Bank of Korea.

household borrowers to which the banks have been heavily exposed, as well as their exposure to the emerging hedge fund crisis.

FOREIGN EXCHANGE MARKET

In early March, when the pandemic began to take a heavy toll, the Korean won–U.S. dollar exchange began to soar as foreign investors started deserting the Korean market.

In the less than three weeks that the virus began to spread throughout the country in early February 2020, the stock market index fell by 36 percent and the Korean won–U.S. dollar exchange rate depreciated by more than 8 percent, reminiscent of what took place during the early period of the 2008 global financial crisis. If Korea's policy makers thought that the 2008 global financial crisis prepared the country for another financial crisis, the 2020 crisis was a rude reminder that they did not know how vulnerable the Korean economy still was to external shocks.

Frightened by the worsening prospect of an economic crisis, foreign lenders and investors began leaving the Korean market in droves for safety, creating shortages of U.S. dollar liquidity. It was clear that unless policy makers were able to secure substantial U.S. dollar liquidity, they could not stop capital outflows and hence a precipitous descent in stock prices and the value of the won against the dollar. Realizing the severity of the crisis, the Korean government, just as it did in 2008, approached the U.S. Federal Reserve Board (Fed) for a won-dollar currency swap.

As part of its currency swap system with nine countries active in international finance, the Fed injected fresh dollar liquidity into Korea's financial system through a won-dollar swap line amounting to $60 billion, doubling the size of the similar agreement in 2009. This swap line was enough to meet the surging demand for U.S. dollars and stopped speculation in the foreign exchange market. The subsequent return of foreign investors has also helped Korean financial assets to not only stage a comeback but also strengthen the won against the U.S. dollar beginning in late May.

It has done so for two reasons. One was that the swap agreement signaled to the financial market that the Fed was prepared to supply more dollar liquidity, if necessary, to sustain Korea's financial stability. As was the case during the 2008 global financial crisis, this implicit arrangement appears to have soothed the frayed nerves of market participants to believe that Korea would be out of the danger zone of a U.S. dollar liquidity crisis.

Table 16.1. Household Loans and Corporate Loans (changes during the period, trillion won)

	2018		2019		2020				Outstanding amount
	Year	May	Year	May	Jan-May	Mar	Apr	May	(end-May 2020)
Household loans	60.8	5.4	60.7	5.0	32.4	9.6	4.9	5.0	920.7
Bank loans	42.7	4.9	44.9	6.0	76.2	18.7	27.9	16.0	945.1

Source: Economic Statistics System of the Bank of Korea.
Note: Household loans and corporate loans are based on deposit money banks (including trust accounts).

This perception has slowed down capital outflows as it did during the global financial crisis. Another reason was that the return of financial stability backed by the currency swap gave Korea's policy makers confidence as well as room for a massive expansionary monetary and fiscal policy for reviving the economy. In the absence of liquidity support, Korea's policy makers would not have been as bold as they have in pursuing such loose macroeconomic policies for fear of deteriorating the current account and losing foreign exchange reserves.

Prospects of Recovery and Sustaining Financial Stability

Overall, Korea's economic policy has been geared toward preventing, or at least mitigating, a rise in unemployment and assisting hard-hit SMEs and the self-employed to stay afloat. It has done this by providing income support and short-term credit reprieve. Some of the macroeconomic data suggest that although Korea has slid into a deeper recession, the policy measures taken thus far have been relatively successful in preventing a free fall of the economy.

But the success has come with its own cost in the medium to long run. One of the growing concerns is that the expansionary policy has created a bubble in equity, housing, and other real asset markets. Since consumer price inflation is likely to remain low for the foreseeable future, the central bank may find it difficult to tighten monetary policy to tame asset inflation. Thus, monetary easing will continue to feed the bubble. This dilemma means that, as in many earlier incidences, policy makers will have to resort to direct price control and other administrative measures to burst the bubble.

But such a direct rupturing of the bubble poses a danger of touching off a full-scale financial crisis at a time when the financial system is quite vulnerable to both internal and external shocks. A large number of SMEs, which have been included in many government relief programs, are barely surviving. They would not be able to repay their loans even if the pandemic were brought under control soon. If the crisis in the hedge fund industry escalates, and is aggravated by a rise in the share of nonperforming loans, banks will lose much of their intermediation capacity and risk deterioration in their soundness and safety. Under these circumstances, the burst of the bubble will trigger a banking or debt crisis much more painful and costly than in 2008–9.

Another concern has been the growing pervasiveness of government intervention in the market. As long as the pandemic remains a public health threat, fiscal authorities will act as if there are no limits in government spending. They are not concerned with the consequential increase in the fiscal deficit as they believe that the share of government debt in GDP, which stands at below 43 percent, is low enough to sustain deficit financing without jeopardizing fiscal discipline.

At the same time, the central bank buys treasury bills and bonds and even low-rated private securities. Financial support for firms and industries, which falls into the realm of industrial policy, needs to be selective and targeted to save those firms with growth potential capable of competing in a rapidly changing global economy. These potential problems underscore the need to curtail government spending, or at least target spending so that markets play a more significant role in resource allocation.

Although these are serious policy issues, the general public will ignore them and policymakers will feel no pressure to change their stance on fiscal or industrial policy while the pandemic is ongoing. The question remains as to whether they will be prepared to rewind their crisis-mode policy regime once the pandemic ends.

As noted earlier, the BOK's rate cut, fiscal easing, and financial relief to small businesses have helped steady the financial sector and further contraction of the economy. But if Korea's major trading partners continue to drift away from trade liberalization and fail to mend the supply chains, Korea will experience a continuing contraction of its traditional export markets. This decline will prolong Korea's recession relative to countries that depend more on domestic demand, even after the pandemic is over.

CHAPTER 17

Summary and Conclusions

One of the most significant milestones in Korea's history of financial development has been the sweeping reform and liberalization following the 1997 Asian financial crisis. It ended a long period of repression dating back to 1945 when the country regained its independence. This study has analyzed the deepening of and structural changes in Korea's financial system since the early 1980s. The focus has been on the background and evolution of the reform to assess its effects on growth, efficiency, equity, and financial stability.

Until 1997, Korea had muddled through, with intermittent and half-hearted attempts at reform that often ended with relapses and regressions. If the past were any guide, Korea would not have launched such an epochal financial reform in the absence of external pressure. However, despite domestic opposition to and doubt about the effectiveness of the reform agenda, Korea's policy makers would have plowed ahead, building a relatively free and open financial system even if there were not any external pressures surrounding the 1997 financial crisis.

Financial Liberalization

The guiding principle of Korea's financial reform has been deregulation and the opening of financial industries and markets. The reform has led to a lifting of control over interest rates, the adoption of a free-floating exchange rate, overhauling of the system of risk management and governance at financial institutions, and revamping the financial market infrastructure—as well as creating an independent and unified financial regulatory agency. More importantly, the reform has dismantled the industrial policy regime of a developmental state that was characterized by a collusive arrangement among the government, the chaebol, and banks.

How successful has the reform been in achieving its objectives? There is clear evidence that financial liberalization has been the driving force behind the rapid growth of the financial system—in particular, the money and capital markets. Overall, the size of the financial sector more than tripled between 1985 and 2017 as measured by the ratio of total financial assets to GDP. In other respects, however, financial liberalization has fallen far short of initial expectations.

At its launching, reform advocates had little doubt about whether financial liberalization would create a control-free environment for intense competition among financial institutions and markets and thus enhance their efficiency. But more than two decades later, the banking sector is still characterized by an oligopolistic structure dominated by five large commercial banks. A few large firms also govern the securities and insurance industries.

Following the deregulation of foreign entry, a relatively large number of foreign securities and insurance firms ventured into the Korean market. Insurance firms have been most successful in gaining a significant market share, but securities firms have not fared as well. U.S.-based private equity funds acquired three ailing commercial banks for restructuring before selling them to other foreign or Korean banks. Only two foreign-owned banks remain, and their market shares make them almost irrelevant.

In underscoring the need for reform, Korea's policy makers brought financial liberalization to the fore as a pivotal strategy to strengthen the overall economic fundamentals, in the expectation of improving the allocative efficiency and resilience of the economy to withstand both domestic and external shocks better. Despite the impressive growth and diversification of the financial sector, there is no visible evidence to suggest that the reform has succeeded in this regard.

In the years since the 1997 crisis, Korea has endured deterioration in income distribution and suffered from a series of turbulent events in the financial market, including the 2008 liquidity crisis. These setbacks have raised doubt about the reform's effectiveness in laying a foundation for financial stability. There have been other adverse structural changes that have hampered efficiency and stability. But what has been disconcerting is that the favorable effects expected of financial liberalization have been rather inconsequential.

The limited effects of the reform may reflect the fact that Korea still has some distance to travel before completing the financial liberalization it began. However, Korea stands out as having had one of the most successful economies in the emerging world in implementing mandates to carry out financial liberalization. This evidence is shown in the IMF financial development index, which ranked Korea in fourth place, together with Australia, for a score of 87 in the July 2019 rankings. Switzerland was first with a score of 93, and the United States and Japan scored 88.

This high ranking may lend credence to the view that by the early 1990s, Korea had reached a mature stage of development with no more room to exploit the benefits associated with financial deepening. This study does not find any evidence suggesting that there has been "too much finance" in Korea.

Economic Efficiency and Growth: Why Has the Effect of Financial Deepening Been So Weak or Vanished?

A liberal reform of the financial system may influence savings and investment rates, total factor productivity, and hence GDP growth by reducing information and transaction costs and easing external financing constraints that face firms across different sectors of the economy. However, a casual observation of the raw data for the postcrisis period (1998–2017) does not show any positive association in Korea between financial growth on the one hand and the level of savings and investment as a proportion of GDP on the other hand.

The panel estimation in chapter 7 presents little—or at best, weak—evidence of a causal nexus from financial deepening (measured by the ratio of indirect finance to GDP) to the growth of real value added and total factor productivity of twenty-seven industries. A similar empirical examination also fails to find evidence that the shift to capital market financing at nonfinancial corporations has contributed to enhancing their growth or efficiency.

Between 2000 and 2017, annual GDP growth fell below 4 percent on average, less than half of what it had been over a similar period before the 1997 crisis. The long-term potential rate of growth, which had remained in the range of 6.4–6.7 percent between 1990 and 1999, declined to below 4.5 percent on average during the 2000–2009 period, before dropping to 3 percent after that. A sharp decline in the total factor productivity from 2.0 percent to 0.7 percent during the same period has been the leading cause of the fall.

No matter how rapidly the financial sector grows and how robust the finance-growth nexus is, financial deepening cannot counter fully or even partially the adverse consequences that originate from changes in various structural factors. Some of the limitations include the demographic changes of a declining birth rate and a rapidly aging population at a time when Korea is struggling with the high cost of catching up with rapid progress in developing new high-tech industries in advanced countries. This point is not in dispute.

From the perspectives of this study, and as far as the role of finance is concerned, perhaps one of the most serious constraints that have weakened the beneficial effect of financial deepening has been, and will continue to be, the growing weight of the service sector in GDP.

Adapting to the growing demand for services, a universal characteristic of economic development, nonfinancial firms have changed their growth strategy to augment their investment in various service industries. In addition, financial intermediaries and markets have allocated an increasing share of their lendable resources to service providers.

The productivity of the service sector has been anemic compared to that of manufacturing. Unless Korea's policy makers succeed in reforming the service sector to increase its productivity, given the tendency of finance to follow rather than lead industrial developments, the efficiency differential will continue to reduce the effects of financial development on enhancing the economy's growth and efficiency. Deregulation, opening, and diversification of financial institutions and markets will not solve this vexing problem.

The passive role of finance in economic development has a checkered history. By the early 2000s, it was evident that the era of catch-up growth was over. Korea had to join global technology leaders to remain competitive in the global market. In the face of changing comparative advantage, if the financial sector had looked to the future, it could have taken the lead in financing investments in innovative industries to increase Korea's industrial competitiveness.

However, this is not what has taken place. Conscious of laxity in risk management after the 1997 crisis, banks were determined to limit their exposure to lending to large corporations. As they were mandated to lower leverage, large corporations migrated to the stock market and began to rely much more on internal savings. The departure of large firms as borrowers gave banks more room to make loans to SMEs and households. It also coincided with deregulation that allowed banks and NBFIs to enter the consumer and mortgage loan markets. At the same time, the growing current account surplus creased opportunities for banks to engage in cross-border intermediation, through which they exported domestic savings to finance spending in foreign countries.

The deregulation of consumer lending unleashed a substantial pent-up demand for mortgage loans. In 2002 and 2003, household borrowing soared by more than 40 percent. This was bound to create a housing market bubble. The growth has slowed since then, but not enough to bring speculation in the housing market under control. Between 2003 and 2017, annual household loan growth averaged 7.3 percent, while a similar average (excluding the outlier years of 2007 and 2008) for large corporations was less than 2 percent. The expansion of housing loans has fed—and has, in turn, been fed by—housing speculation, creating an inflationary spiral in the housing market.

From the perspective of this study, there is the question of whether the shift in corporate financing has made any significant contribution to efficiency improvements and growth of corporate groups and large firms. Several pieces of evidence indicate that it has not. Nonfinancial corporations have also increased their holdings of bonds and equities and have enlarged their investments in various service industries. Most of all, the empirical examination in chapter 7 finds little difference in the growth performance of the two sectors—those relying heavily on the capital market and others relying on banks for external financing.

Financial Depth and Macroeconomic Stability

Economists do not agree on the potential effects of financial growth on the stability of output, consumption, or investment. Financial development relaxes constraints on the ability of firms to borrow, diversify risk, reduce the volatility of their revenues, and deflect the impact of internal and external shocks. Given these positive effects, financial deepening is likely to dampen the volatility of aggregate demand. Studies report that a more in-depth financial system, often measured by the ratio of private credit to GDP, is associated with greater macroeconomic stability.

Many studies also find that financial growth is positively correlated with output volatility, as financial development can either lead to more risk-taking by entrepreneurs and banks or facilitate overleveraging, both of which can increase volatility within the financial sector. According to some studies, when the ratio of private credit to GDP exceeds 100 percent, financial depth magnifies the volatility. The stability issue is, therefore, an empirical one.

In terms of the panel data on twenty-seven industries, this study examined the causal relationship between macroeconomic stability and financial deepening. As reported in chapter 7, the empirical results of the estimation of various hypotheses on the causal direction do not provide any evidence of the positive effects of financial growth on the stability of output or investment. One possible reason for the indeterminacy is the procyclicality of lending at banks and NBFIs, in which their lending increases the amplitude of the business cycle as financial institutions follow rather than lead real-sector developments.

Finance and Distributive Equity

Attempts to discover a causal nexus between financial depth and income distribution are inconclusive. This study assumes that at an early stage of development, financial deepening facilitates and increases low-income households' access to the organized financial system. This increase in the availability of relatively cheaper financing multiplies the opportunities for low-income families to undertake investments that are more productive and have a high return. That is, greater access enables poorer households to earn more than they did before, relative to households in higher income brackets, and thereby makes the distribution of income more equitable.

This positive effect may disappear when the financial sector crosses a threshold and becomes unable to generate benefits from financial deepening. Following this line of argument, this study conducts a two-stage analysis of the effects of financial growth on the distribution of income. Using data from the Korea Labor Institute household survey, this study first examines the impact of financial development on the access of households by income quintile to loans by banks and NBFIs. The second stage assesses the extent to which differences in the gain in access associated with financial growth (measured by the ratio of indirect finance to GDP) lead to differences in earnings by income quintile.

The results of the first-stage panel estimation over the 2001–16 period show that wealthy households benefit more in terms of bank loan access than they do from financial growth. The second-stage estimation reveals that the differential accessibility to bank loans leads to a significant increase in the income per household in the fourth and fifth income quintiles, in combination with a decrease in the lower-income quintiles.

Although the statistical significance is not as strong in the second-stage estimation as it is in the first-stage one, the result is robust enough for us to conclude that financial deepening has worsened distributive equity. Given the preferential treatment accorded to high-income households at banking institutions, this result is not surprising. It confirms what has become conventional wisdom (and a political issue)—that finance benefits only the rich in Korea.

Managing the 1997 and 2008 Financial Crises

The 1997 financial collapse, which was locally dubbed the "IMF crisis," awoke the nation to the need of arming itself lest it fall victim to a future crisis. In response, Korea's policy makers set to work to rectify the structural flaws in every sector of the economy and dismantle the interventionist policy regime.

Despite all of the precautionary measures Korea took in the wake of the 1997 financial meltdown, it was not able to deflect another financial crisis. The country succumbed to two idiosyncratic episodes of domestic origin in 2004 and 2011 and a liquidity crisis in 2008 that was reminiscent of the 1997 breakdown. To add to the crisis menace, starting in the early 2000s, Korea has endured the pain of a never-ending series of boom-and-bust cycles in the real property market.

Both in 1997 and 2008, Korea was overwhelmed by a crisis that had erupted elsewhere—the Thai crisis in the first case, and the U.S. subprime lending meltdown in the second. Some of the domestic factors that made Korea susceptible to the crisis and deepened it were much the same in both cases. A reversal in capital inflows triggered by ill-informed foreign investors' overreaction to the external crises elsewhere was the immediate cause both times.

In 1997, the exchange rate system was so rigid that it could not help reverse the massive capital outflows, but a flexible exchange rate system did not prevent or mitigate similar outflows in 2008. In both crises, a significant depreciation did not generate any expectations of a future appreciation. Instead, it shifted the exchange rate onto an implosive trajectory, as panic set in and triggered a destabilizing flight from the won.

In the run-up to the 1997 crisis, Korea depleted almost all of its reserves before going to the IMF. Afterward, realizing that the international community and the IMF would not come to the rescue—or at least not without making unacceptable conditions—Korea started accumulating foreign exchange reserves in case another crisis struck the country.

At the end of 2007, Korea held $260 billion in foreign exchange reserves, which was excessive, according to many experts. However, it turned out to be hardly enough to keep the speculators at bay. In 2008, more than 12 percent of the reserves had evaporated by September. If there was a lesson to be drawn from the 2008 liquidity crisis, it is that no amount of foreign exchange reserves can guarantee immunity from a financial crisis.

Korea's experiences with the crises point to the inherent difficulty that small open and emerging economies have in moderating and adjusting to a high degree of volatility in capital flows. This difficulty stems from the fact that even well-managed economies with few structural frailties in a globalized financial system can easily fall victim to the effects of a crisis elsewhere. This resembles a domestic banking crisis in which healthy banks succumb to a liquidity drought as a result of a run on deposits at an insolvent bank. Similarly, when a market overreaction in the domestic economy triggers a crisis, it cannot be resolved without the intervention of a lender of last resort that is willing and able to provide an ample amount of reserve currency liquidity.

To large foreign private and institutional investors, exposure to an individual economy like that of Korea's often accounts for a small share of their total portfolio. However, in the case of a small economy with shallow and illiquid domestic financial markets, their investments are frequently significant enough to overload the markets' absorptive capacity. In many cases, investments in local financial markets and changes in portfolios determine the direction of change in and volatility of the exchange rate. When foreigners pull out for whatever reason, nothing short of direct capital controls can stop a run on reserves.

On managing a capital account crisis, this study shows that there is a limit to which micro- and macroprudential regulations can protect banks and NBFIs from a reserve currency liquidity crisis. In emerging economies, banks that are active in international intermediation often rely on short-term funding in foreign currency for their long-term lending in local currency to domestic borrowers. This risks the development of both maturity and currency mismatches and exposure to a liquidity crisis, which often provokes a bank run.

Banks in emerging economies are likely to find it challenging to comply with the various regulatory restrictions aimed at precluding the two mismatches. This is because if the restrictions are strictly enforced, they limit the scope and competitiveness of banks' lending operations, relative to counterparts from advanced or reserve-currency countries that are not subject to a similar constraint on currency mismatch.

The Economic and Financial Consequences of the COVID-19 Pandemic

The COVID-19 pandemic reached Korea at the same time that a financial storm was brewing and signs of a recession were on the horizon. It was such a virulent epidemic that the contagion of the virus virtually brought the economy to a standstill, with millions of people placed under lockdown and a rapidly growing number of businesses forced to close, leading to mass layoffs.

In the less than three weeks that the virus began to spread throughout the country in early February 2020, the stock market index fell by 36 percent and the Korean won–U.S. dollar exchange rate depreciated by more than 8 percent, reminiscent of what took place during the early period of the 2008 global financial crisis. If Korea's policy makers thought that the 2008 global financial crisis prepared the country for another financial crisis, the 2020 crisis was a rude reminder that they did not know how vulnerable the Korean economy still was to external shocks.

Frightened by the worsening prospect of an economic crisis, foreign lenders and investors began leaving the Korean market in droves for safety, creating shortages of U.S. dollar liquidity. It was clear that unless policy makers were able to secure substantial U.S. dollar liquidity, they could not stop capital outflows and hence a free fall of stock prices and the value of the won against the dollar.

Realizing the severity of the crisis, the Korean government, just as it did in 2008, approached and secured a won-dollar currency swap line from the U.S. Federal Reserve Board (Fed) amounting to $60 billion, doubling the size of the similar agreement in 2009.

The announcement of the swap agreement on March 19 rallied financial markets to bring about a measure of financial stability and slowed down capital outflows. The additional liquidity also gave Korea's policy makers confidence as well as room for a massive expansionary monetary and fiscal policy as it dissipated much of the fear of deteriorating the current account and losing foreign exchange reserves.

In retrospect, the COVID-19 pandemic has not been a significant health issue in Korea in terms of the number of deaths and cases. By the first week of April, the pandemic was brought under control. As of August 3, 2020, there were 301 deaths and fewer than 15,000 cases in a country with a population of 51.64 million. In contrast, however, the economic impact has been unprecedented, in both breadth and depth. During the second quarter of 2020, the economy shrank by 3.3 percent after a decline of 1.3 percent in the preceding three-month period. It was the sharpest fall in GDP since the 2008–9 global financial crisis.

The expansionary policy measures were likely necessary in order to prevent a free fall of the economy. But they have come with their own cost in the medium to long run. One of the concerns is that the massive liquidity poured into the economy has created and will continue to feed a bubble in equity, housing, and other real asset markets. As before, when the bubble bursts, a banking crisis will ensue, further aggravating the hedge fund industry fiasco. Korea would be continuing the pattern of the once-a-decade financial crisis that is analyzed in this study. Another concern is that the vast deficits from pandemic mitigation spending have increased government debt substantially. Some dismiss this concern, whereas others see it as a future problem.

Korea is very dependent on its role as a key player in the global supply chain. Thus, how soon and how well Korea recovers from the pandemic and the hedge fund scandal depend very much on how quickly the rest of the world recovers. Slow global recovery will put intense pressure on the financial viability of Korean firms, and thus on their banks and investors.

Financial Regulatory Reform

Before the 1997 crisis, Korea's financial supervisory system was organized into four independent institutions, one each for deposit money banks, securities firms, insurance companies, and NBFIs. The postcrisis reforms allowed financial firms to move into the traditional territories of other service providers by offering composite products that combine features of deposits, insurance, and investments in securities.

This made the precrisis system inefficient and outdated. The conglomeration and diversification of financial services provided by banks and NBFIs made it necessary to have close cooperation and coordination and to facilitate information exchange among the separate regulatory institutions. Realizing the need to consolidate the institutions, the government thus created a unified system consisting of the Financial Services Commission (FSC) as a policy-making body and the Financial Supervisory Service (FSS) as the FSC's executive arm.

The unified system is viewed as lacking in statutory independence and has been criticized for disregarding consumer protection. The division of labor and legal status of the FSC and FSS has not been specified. Moreover, the twin structure has been criticized for a potential conflict of interest arising from the fact that the FSC has two functions: to supervise the financial sector and to make financial policy. Not surprisingly, the system has been subjected to repeated restructuring ever since it was established.

Despite the apparent need to correct the structural flaws—and public pressure to do so—the governments that came to power in 2008 and 2013 did not want to undertake any major restructuring. This was because they were unable to find a compromise among different proposals. The exception was a 2008 proposed law to enhance the protection of consumers of financial services. However, the law remains only a proposal more than a decade later.

Criticisms about the role of the current system have been directed at its failure to avert the credit card and savings bank debacles. When a financial crisis is of domestic origin, as those two were, domestic regulatory and liquidity interventions could have served as the first line of defense. The credit card lending boom and bust was a classic case in which a combination of moral hazard and laxity in regulation escalated an insolvency problem in a small financial industry into a crisis, posing systemic risks that threatened the stability of the entire financial system.

Many believed that democratization and market liberalization, together with various checks and balances created over the past two decades, had rooted out much corruption in the public and banking sectors as well as the business community. The savings bank crisis in 2011 shattered this perception. The reality was that bankers, regulators, and politicians were conspiring to falsify books and conceal losses to keep zombie savings banks in operation. One important lesson to be learned from Korea's experience with financial regulation is that no matter how sophisticated the regulatory apparatus is, it is of no avail if regulators are corrupt or succumb to political influence.

In the aftermath of the 2008 global financial crisis, there has been a growing movement led by the G20 toward strengthening financial regulations at the global level for the prevention and better management of crises. Korea has taken steps to accommodate new regulatory proposals, such as Basel III. It remains to be seen whether these measures could help reestablish the proper role of the financial supervisory system.

Lessons and the Way Forward

The benefits of constructing a freer and open financial system have been much less in Korea than theories, and the experiences of other countries suggested would be the case. This assessment does not mean that Korea would be better off moving back to a more repressive and closed regime. Indeed, turning back the clock would be self-defeating. For an economy as open as Korea's is, and for one classified by the IMF as among the other advanced economies, it would be too costly to close the country's financial markets to foreign borrowers, lenders, and service providers. Instead, Korea would be better advised if it addresses structural deficiencies of its financial system to remain active in international finance.

One such weakness is that Korea has been lagging behind the United States and the European Union in adapting to the rapidly changing financial environment ushered in by the financial technology revolution.

Korea has been toward the back of the pack in the digitalization of finance. But now, financial industries are moving to catch up by embracing and investing heavily in new technologies. Digitalization could herald a more competitive and dynamic financial system. It could improve the efficiency of financial institutions and markets, as well as produce a host of new products and services tailored to the needs of savers and investors. The emergence of a large number of variegated fintech firms could change the financial landscape, putting pressure on incumbent banks, insurance firms, and securities companies to improve their competitiveness.

Digitalization has already contributed to a breakdown of the separation of banking from commerce, with the emergence of new entrants such as big tech companies. Although nominally administered by traditional financial institutions, companies such as Amazon issue credit cards, and alternative payment methods such as Apple Pay mean many people use neither cash nor checks.

Digitalization is thus sure to raise a host of issues on financial supervision and regulation. Uncertain about the future of fintech, there is the danger that financial supervisory authorities may lean toward a reactive, rather than proactive, policy stance in responding to technological changes in finance. It is imperative that regulatory ability evolve apace with digitalization.

At the same time, the COVID-19 pandemic is forcing the global economy to undergo fundamental changes in how the industrial, trade, and financial sectors are structured. Social distancing may become the new norm, and thus personal interactions between financial institutions and clients will carry even higher costs, which favors digitalization.

References

Abiad, Abdul, Enrica Detragiache, and Thierry Tressel. 2008. "A New Database of Financial Reforms." IMF Working Paper WP/08/266, International Monetary Fund, Washington, December.

Aggarwal, Raj, and John Goodell. 2009. "Markets and Institutions in Financial Intermediation: National Characteristics as Determinants." *Journal of Banking and Finance* 33 (10): 1770–80.

Aghion, Philippe, Geroge-Marios Angeletos, Abhijit Banerjee, and Kalina Manova. 2010. "Volatility and Growth: Credit Constraints and the Composition of Investment." *Journal of Monetary Economics* 57 (3): 246–65.

Aghion Philippe, and Patrick Bolton. 1997. "A Theory of Trickle-Down Growth and Development." *Review of Economic Studies* 64 (2): 151–72.

Ahn, Sanghoon, Joon-Ho Hahm, and Joon-Kyung Kim. 2008. "External Finance and Productivity Growth in Korea: Firm Level Evidence before and after the Financial Crisis." *KDI Journal of Economic Policy* 30 (2): 27–59.

Allen, Franklin, and Douglas Gale. 1997. "Financial Markets, Intermediaries, and Intertemporal Smoothing." *Journal of Political Economy* 105 (3): 523–46.

———. 1999. *Corporate Governance and Competition.* Philadelphia: University of Pennsylvania Press.

———. 2007a. "Systemic Risk and Regulation." In *The Risks of Financial Institutions*, edited by Mark Carey and Rene Stulz, 341–76. Chicago: University of Chicago Press.

———. 2007b. *Understanding Financial Crises.* Oxford: Oxford University Press.

Altonji, Joseph, and Rosa Matzkin. 2005. "Cross Section and Panel Data Estimators for Nonseparable Models with Endogenous Regressors." *Econometrica* 73 (4): 1053–102.

Arcand, Jean Louis, Enrico Berkes, and Ugo Panizza. 2015. "Too Much Finance?" *Journal of Economic Growth* 20 (2): 105–48.

————. 2016. "Too Much Finance or Statistical Illusion: A Comment." Graduate Institute of International and Development Studies Working Paper No. 12/2015, Graduate Institute of International and Development Studies, Geneva.

Aspachs Oriol, Charles Goodhart, Miguel Segoviano, Dimitrios Tsomocos, and Lea Zicchino. 2006. "Searching for a Metric for Financial Stability." LSE Financial Markets Group Special Paper 167, London, May.

Baba, Naohiko, and Ilhyock Shim. 2011. "Dislocations in the Won-Dollar Swap Market during the Crisis of 2007–09." BIS Working Paper No. 344, Bank for International Settlements, Geneva, Switzerland, April.

Baek, Chulwoo, YoungGak Kim, and Heog Ug Kwon. 2009. "Market Competition and Productivity after the Asian Financial Crisis: Evidence from Korean Firm Level Data." CEI Working Paper No. 2009-12, Institute of Economic Research, Hitotsubashi University, Tokyo (in Japanese).

Baier, Scott, Jeffrey Bergstrand, and Michael Feng. 2014. "Economic Integration Agreements and the Margins of International Trade." *Journal of International Economics* 93 (2): 339–50.

Baily, Martin, Charles Hulten, and David Campbell. 1992. "Productivity Dynamics in Manufacturing Plants." *Brookings Papers on Economic Activity: Microeconomics*, 187–267.

Banerjee, Abhijit, and Andrew Newman. 1993. "Occupational Choice and the Process of Development." *Journal of Political Economy* 101 (2): 274–98.

Bank of Korea. 2004. "Current Status of Bank Governance Structure and Remaining Tasks." *Bank of Korea Information*, April (in Korean).

————. 2012. *Financial Institutions, Markets and Infrastructure in Korea*. April.

————. 2017. *Financial Markets in Korea*. https://www.bok.or.kr/viewer/skin/doc.html?fn=FILE_201803300855131511.pdf&rs=/webview/result/E00024 10/201708.

————. 2018. *Financial System in Korea*. https://www.bok.or.kr/eng/bbs/E0000743/view.do?nttId=10050214&menuNo=400226&pageIndex=1.

Banker, Rajiv, Hsihui Chang, and Seok-Young Lee. 2010. "Differential Impact of Korean Banking System Reforms on Bank Productivity." *Journal of Banking and Finance* 34 (7): 1450–60.

Beck, Thorsten. 2012. "The Role of Finance in Economic Development–Benefits, Risks, and Politics." In *Oxford Handbook of Capitalism*, edited by Dennis C. Mueller, 161–203. New York: Oxford University Press.

Beck, Thorsten, Elena Carletti, and Itay Goldstein. 2015. "Financial Institutions, Markets and Regulation: A Survey." Mimeo, http://www.coeure-book.ceu.edu/FinancialMarkets.pdf.

Beck, Thorsten, Hans Degryse, and Christiane Kneer. 2014. "Is More Finance Better? Disentangling Intermediation and Size Effects of Financial Systems." *Journal of Financial Stability* 10 (C): 50–64.

Beck, Thorsten, Asli Demirgüç-Kunt, and Ross Levine. 2007. "Finance, In-equality and the Poor." *Journal of Economic Growth* 12 (1): 27–49.

Beck, Thorsten, Asli Demirgüç-Kunt, and Maria Soledad Martinez Peria. 2006. "Banking Services for Everyone? Barriers to Bank Access and Use around the World." World Bank Policy Research Working Paper 4079, World Bank, Washington, December.

Beck, Thorsten, and Ross Levine. 2002. "Industry Growth and Capital Alloca-tion: Does Having a Market- or Bank-Based System Matter?" *Journal of Fi-nancial Economics* 64 (2): 147–80.

Beck, Thorsten, Ross Levine, and Norman Loayza. 2000. "Finance and the Sources of Growth." *Journal of Financial Economics* 58 (1–2): 261–300.

Bekaert, Geert, Campbell Harvey, and Christian Lundblad. 2006. "Growth Vol-atility and Financial Liberalization." *Journal of International Money and Fi-nance* 25 (3): 370–403.

Bencivenga, Valerie, and Bruce Smith. 1991. "Financial Intermediation and En-dogenous Growth." *Review of Economic Studies* 58 (2): 195–209.

Bernanke, Ben, and Mark Gertler. 1989. "Agency Costs, Net Worth, and Busi-ness Fluctuation." *American Economic Review* 79 (1): 14–31.

Bernanke, Ben, Mark Gertler, and Simon Gilchrist. 1999. "The Financial Ac-celerator in a Quantitative Business Cycle Framework." In *Handbook of Mac-roeconomics*, edited by John Taylor and Michael Woodford, 1: 1341–93. North Holland, Netherlands: Elsevier.

Black, Bernard, Woochan Kim, Hasung Jang, and Kyung Suh Park. 2005. "How Corporate Governance Affects Firm Value: Evidence on Channels from Korea." Finance Working Paper No. 103/2005, European Corporate Gover-nance Institute, Brussels.

Blanchard, Olivier. 2009. "Emerging Market Countries in the Crisis." Keynote address at the Annual Bank Conference on Development Economics Seoul, June 22–24.

Blanchard, Olivier, Giovanni Dell'Ariccia, and Paolo Mauro. 2010. "Rethink-ing Macroeconomic Policy." IMF Staff Position Note No. SPN/10/03, Inter-national Monetary Fund, Washington, February 12.

Board of Audit and Inspection of Korea. 2001. *An Audit Report on Management and Oversight of Public Funds.* Seoul.

Bolton, Patrick, Tano Santos, and Jose Scheinkman. 2016. "Cream-Skimming in Financial Markets." *Journal of Finance* 71 (2): 709–36.

Borio, Claudio. 2003. "Towards a Macroprudential Framework for Financial Su-pervision and Regulation?" BIS Working Paper No. 128, Bank for Interna-tional Settlements, Basel, Switzerland, February.

———. 2009. "Implementing the Macroprudential Approach to Financial Regulation and Supervision." Financial Stability Review No. 13, Banque de France, Paris, September.

Borio, Claudio, Craig Furfine, and Philip Lowe. 2001. "Procyclicality of the Financial System and Financial Stability: Issues and Policy Options." BIS Working Paper No. 1, Bank for International Settlements, Basel, Switzerland, March.

Borio, Claudio, and Philip Lowe. 2002. "Asset Prices, Financial and Monetary Stability: Exploring the Nexus." BIS Working Paper No. 114, Bank for International Settlements, Basel, Switzerland, July.

————. 2004. "Securing Sustainable Price Stability: Should Credit Come Back from the Wilderness?" BIS Working Paper No. 157, Bank for International Settlements, Basel, Switzerland, July.

Boyd, John, and Bruce Smith. 1998. "The Evolution of Debt and Equity Markets in Economic Development." *Economic Theory* 12 (3): 519–60.

Brei, Michael, Giovanni Ferri, and Leonardo Gambacorta. 2018. "Financial Structure and Income Inequality." BIS Working Paper No. 756, Bank for International Settlements, Basel, Switzerland, November.

Brunnermeier Markus, Thomas Eisenbach, and Yuliy Sannikov. 2012. "Macroeconomics with Financial Frictions: A Survey." NBER Working Paper No. 18102, National Bureau of Economic Research, Cambridge, MA, May.

Carletti, Elena. 2008. "Competition and Regulation in Banking." *Handbook of Financial Intermediation and Banking* 126 (5): 449–82.

Cecchetti, Stephen, and Enisse Kharroubi. 2012. "Reassessing the Impact of Finance on Growth." BIS Working Paper No. 381, Bank for International Settlements, Basel, Switzerland, July.

————. 2015. "Why Does Financial Sector Growth Crowd Out Real Economic Growth?" CEPR Discussion Paper No. DP10642, Centre for Economic Policy Research, London.

Chakraborty, Shankha, and Tridip Ray. 2006. "Bank-Based versus Market-Based Financial Systems: A Growth-Theoretic Analysis." *Journal of Monetary Economics* 53 (2): 329–50.

Chang, Soon-Taek. 2010. "Mortgage Lending in Korea: An Example of a Countercyclical Macroprudential Approach." Policy Research Working Paper No. 5505, World Bank, Washington, December.

Chang, Woo Hyun. 2016. "Is Korea's Public Funding for SMEs Achieving Its Intended Goals?" KDI Focus no. 63, Korea Development Institute, Sejong.

Chinn, Menzie, and Hiro Ito. 2006. "What Matters for Financial Development? Capital Controls, Institutions, and Interactions." *Journal of Development Economics* 81 (1): 163–92.

Cho, Sungbin. 2005. "Interdependence of Corporate Control Mechanisms and Firm Performance." KDI Policy Study, Korea Development Institute, Sejong (in Korean).

————. 2006. "A Study on Korean Firms' Agency Costs." KDI Policy Study, Korea Development Institute, Sejong (in Korean).

Cho, Yoon-Je, and Joon-Kyung Kim. 1995. "Credit Policies and the Industrialization of Korea." World Bank Discussion Paper No. 286, World Bank, Washington.

Choi, Byung-Sun. 1993. "Financial Policy and Big Business in Korea: The Perils of Financial Regulation." In *The Politics of Finance in Developing Countries*, edited by Stephan Haggard, Chung H. Lee, and Sylvia Maxfield, 23–54. Ithaca, NY: Cornell University Press.

Choi, Doo Yeol. 2001. "The Weaknesses in the Financial Supervisory and Regulatory System of Korea's Merchant Banks before the Currency Crisis of 1997." Research Report 01-06, Korea Economic Research Institute, Seoul (in Korean).

Choi, Young-joon, Joon Choi, and Min-ryul Park. 2011. "The Effects of Capital Inflows on Economic Growth." *Monthly Bulletin* (June), Bank of Korea (in Korean).

Chun, Byung-chul, and Hyo-sung Kwon. 2008. "An Evaluation of the Competition of the Banking Industry," *Monthly Bulletin* (August), Bank of Korea (in Korean).

Chung, Duck-Koo, and Barry Eichengreen. 2004. *The Korean Economy beyond the Crisis*. Cheltenham, UK: Edward Elgar.

Chung, Jin Yeong, Sungjean Seo, and Jong-Hyun Kim. 2019. "Class/Collective Actions in South Korea: Overview." Thomson Reuters Practical Law. Online.

Claessens, Stijn. 2017. "Global Banking: Recent Developments and Insights from Research." *Review of Finance* 21 (4): 1513–55.

Claessens, Stijn, Asli Demirgüç-Kunt, and Harry Huizinga. 2001. ""How Does Foreign Entry Affect Domestic Banking Markets?" *Journal of Banking and Finance* 25 (5): 891–911.

Clarke, George, Lixin Colin Xu, and Heng-fu Zou. 2006. "Finance and Income Inequality: What Do the Data Tell Us?" *Southern Economic Journal* 72 (3): 578–96.

Clement, Piet. 2010. "The Term 'Macroprudential': Origins and Evolution." *BIS Quarterly Review*, March.

Cline, William. 2015. "Too Much Finance, or Statistical Illusion?" Peterson Institute for International Economics Policy Brief No. PB15–9, Peterson Institute for International Economics, Washington, June.

Committee on the Global Financial System. 2010. "Macroprudential Instruments and Frameworks: A Stocktaking of Issues and Experiences." CGFS Paper No. 38, May.

Crockett, Andrew. 2000. "Marrying the Micro- and Macro-Prudential Dimensions of Financial Stability." Remarks at the Eleventh International Conference of Banking Supervisors, Basel, Switzerland, September 20–21.

Dabla-Norris, Era, Erasmus Kersting, and Geneviève Verdier. 2010. "Firm Productivity, Innovation and Financial Development." IMF Working Paper No. 10-49, International Monetary Fund, Washington, February.

Dabla-Norris, Era, and Narapong Srivisal. 2013. "Revisiting the Link between Finance and Macroeconomic Volatility." IMF Working Paper No. 13-29, International Monetary Fund, Washington, January.

Demirgüç-Kunt, Asli, Erik Feyen, and Ross Levine. 2013. "The Evolving Importance of Banks and Securities Markets." *World Bank Economic Review* 27 (3): 476–90.

Demirgüç-Kunt, Asli, and Ross Levine. 2009. "Finance and Inequality: Theory and Evidence." *Annual Review of Financial Economics* 1 (1): 287–318.

Demirgüc-Kunt, Asli. and Vojislav Maksimovic. 1994. "Capital Structures in Developing Countries: Evidence from Ten Countries." Policy Research Working Paper No. WPS 1320, World Bank, Washington, July.

———. 1998. "Law, Finance and Firm Growth." *Journal of Finance* 53 (6): 2107–37.

Economist, The. 2009. "Domino Theory." Economic Focus, February 26.

Efron, Bradley, and Robert Tibshirani. 1993. *An Introduction to the Bootstrap.* Boca Raton, FL: Chapman and Hall.

European Central Bank. 2007. "Financial Stability Review." December.

Fair Trade Commission. 2007. "Company Belonging to Enterprise Group Subject to Limitations on Mutual Investment." Press release, Fair Trade Commission, Seoul, April 12.

———. 2017. "Company Belonging to Enterprise Group Subject to Limitations on Mutual Investment." Press release, Fair Trade Commission, Sejong, May 1.

Favara, Giovanni. 2003. "An Empirical Reassessment of the Relationship between Finance and Growth." IMF Working Paper No. 03/123, International Monetary Fund, Washington, June.

Financial Services Commission. 2012. "First Annual Status Report on the Hedge Fund Industry." Press release, Financial Services Commission, Seoul, December 6.

———. 2017. "2016 Fund Market Activities and Trends." Press release, Financial Services Commission, Seoul, February 8 (in Korean).

———. 2020a. "Measures for Improving Regulatory Framework on Private Equity Funds." Press release, Financial Services Commission, Seoul, April 27 (in Korean).

———. 2020b. "FSC to Inspect Fraud-prone Sectors for Financial Consumer Protection." Press release, Financial Services Commission, Seoul, July 2.

Financial Supervisory Service. 2001. "New Measures to Present Excess Competition in Solicitation for Credit Card Membership and to Strengthen Financial

Supervision." News release, Financial Supervisory Service, Seoul, February 27 (in Korean).

————. 2019. "Digital Transformation Status of Financial Firms in Korea." News release, Financial Supervisory Service, Seoul, May 15 (in Korean).

Fintech News. 2019. "South Korea's Banks Commit US$492.7 Million to Digitisation," June 5. https://fintechnews.hk/9486/fintechkorea/south-korea-bank -digitisation/.

Fisman, Raymond, and Inessa Love. 2003. "Financial Dependence and Growth Revisited." NBER Working Paper No. 9582, National Bureau of Economic Research, Cambridge, MA, March.

"Former Top Financial Regulator Indicted over Savings Bank Scandal." 2011. *Korea Herald*, November 2. http://www.koreaherald.com/view.php?ud =20111102000896.

Galati, Gabriele, and Richhild Moessner. 2011. "Macroprudential Policy—A Literature Review." BIS Working Paper No. 337, Bank for International Settlements, Basel, Switzerland, February.

Galindo, Arturo, Fabio Schiantarelli, and Andrew Weiss. 2007. "Does Financial Liberalization Improve the Allocation of Investment? Micro-Evidence from Developing Countries." *Journal of Development Economics* 83 (2): 562–87.

Galor, Oded, and Joseph Zeira. 1993. "Income Distribution and Macroeconomics." *Review of Economic Studies* 60 (1): 35–52.

Goldstein, Morris. 2003. "IMF Structural Programs." In *Economic and Financial Crises in Emerging Market Economies*, edited by Martin Feldstein, 363–458. Chicago: University of Chicago Press for the National Bureau of Economic Research.

Goldstein, Morris, and Philip Turner. 2004. "Currency Mismatches at Center of Financial Crises in Emerging Economies." Washington: Peterson Institute for International Economics.

Goldstein, Morris, and Daniel Xie. 2009. "The Impact of the Financial Crisis on Emerging Asia." Peterson Institute for International Economics Working Paper No. 09-11, Washington, October.

Gollier, Christian. 2001. "Wealth Inequality and Asset Pricing." *Review of Economic Studies* 68 (1): 181–203.

Goodhart, Charles. 2004. "Some New Directions for Financial Stability." Per Jacobson Lecture, Zurich, June 27.

Greene, William. 2004. "The Behaviour of the Maximum Likelihood Estimator of Limited Dependent Variable Models in the Presence of Fixed Effects." *Econometrics Journal* 7 (1): 98–119.

Greenwood, Jeremy, and Boyan Jovanovic. 1990. "Financial Development, Growth and the Distribution of Income." *Journal of Political Economy* 98 (5): 1076–107.

Habermeier, Karl, Annamaria Kokenyne, and Chikako Baba. 2011. "The Effectiveness of Capital Controls and Prudential Policies in Managing Large Inflows." IMF Staff Discussion Notes, No. 11/14. International Monetary Fund, Washington.

Hall, Maximilian, and Richard Simper. 2013. "Efficiency and Competition in Korean Banking." *Applied Financial Economics* 23 (10): 881–90.

Hannoun, Hervé. 2010. "Towards a Global Financial Stability Framework." Speech delivered at the 45th SEACEN Governors' Conference, Siem Riep, Cambodia, February 26–27.

Hong, Gwangheon, and Bong Soo Lee. 2011. "The Trading Behavior and Price Impact of Foreign, Institutional, Individual Investors and Government: Evidence from Korean Equity Market." *Japan and the World Economy* 23 (4): 273–87.

Hoshi, Takeo, Anil Kashyap, and David Scharfstein. 1991. "Corporate Structure, Liquidity, and Investment: Evidence from Japanese Industrial Groups." *Quarterly Journal of Economics* 106 (1): 33–60.

Huybens, Elisabeth, and Bruce Smith. 1999. "Inflation, Financial Markets and Long-Run Real Activity." *Journal of Monetary Economics* 43 (2): 283–315.

Igan, Deniz, and Heedon Kang. 2011. "Do Loan-to-Value and Debt-to-Income Limits Work? Evidence from Korea." IMF Working Paper No. WP/11/297, International Monetary Fund, Washington, December.

Igan, Deniz, Ali Kutan, and Ali Mirzaei. 2016. "Real Effects of Capital Inflows in Emerging Markets." IMF Working Paper No. 16/235. International Monetary Fund, Washington, December.

Illing, Mark, and Ying Liu. 2003. "An Index of Financial Stress for Canada." Bank of Canada Working Paper No. 2003-14, Ottawa, June.

International Monetary Fund. 2018. "The IMF's Annual Macroprudential Policy Survey—Objectives, Design, and Country Responses." Policy Paper Series, IMF, Washington, April.

———. 2019. *Financial Soundness Indicators: Compilation Guide*. Washington: IMF.

———. 2020. "A Crisis Like No Other: An Uncertain Recovery." World Economic Outlook Update, June. Washington: IMF.

Jwa, Sung-Hee. 2003, "In Search of 'Global Standards': The Fallacy of Korea's Corporate Policy." *Harvard Asia Quarterly* 7 (2): 45–52.

Kahou, Mahdi, and Alfred Lehar. 2017. "Macroprudential Policy: A Review." *Journal of Financial Stability* 29 (C): 92–105.

Kang, Dongsoo. 2004. "Key Success Factors in the Revitalization of Distressed Firms: A Case of the Korean Corporate Workouts." *Journal of Restructuring Finance* 1 (2): 331–38.

———. 2005. "Reforms on SME Credit Guarantee System." In *Medium-term Policy Priorities and Fiscal Management*. Research Monograph 2005–

06, edited by Youngsun Koh. Korea Development Institute, Seoul (in Korean).

Kang, Hwan-Koo, Do-Wan Kim, Jae-Hyun Park, and Jin-Hyun Han. 2016. "The Estimation of the Potential Growth of the Korean Economy." *Monthly Bulletin* (January). Bank of Korea (in Korean).

Kang, Joung Ku. 2017. "The Effects of Household Debt on Consumption and Economic Growth." *Economic Analysis (Quarterly)*, 23 (2), 28–57 (in Korean).

Kang, Tae Soo. 2011. "The Role of Macroprudential Policies in Asia: Case in Korea." PowerPoint presentation at the Asian Regional Conference on Banking Supervision and Regulation, Bank of Korea, Seoul, February.

Kang, Tae Soo, and Guonan Ma. 2007. "Recent Episodes of Credit Card Distress in Asia." *BIS Quarterly Review*, June: 55–68.

Kim, Bongsoo. 2020. "Structural Problems and Improvement Measures of Korean Hedge Funds." Keynote address at conference organized by National Assembly member Chang Hyun Yoon, July 23, 2020.

Kim, Eun Mee, Joon-Kyung Kim, and Jun-Il Kim. 2000. "Restructuring of the *Chaebols* and Financial Sector in Korea: Progress and Assessment since the Financial Crisis." ICSEAD Working Paper No. 2000-23, International Centre for the Study of East Asian Development, Kitakyushu, Japan, December.

Kim, Han-Ah. 2003. "The Relationship between Economic Growth and Financial Liberalization and Development." *KDIC Financial Stability Studies* 4 (2): 5–30 (in Korean).

Kim, Jaehoon, and Hwa Ryung Lee. 2015. "Outside Directors on Corporate Boards: Background and Behavior." KDI Focus, October, Korea Development Institute, Sejong.

Kim, Joongi. 2008. "A Forensic Study of Daewoo's Corporate Governance: Does Responsibility for the Meltdown Solely Lie with the *Chaebol* and Korea?" *Northwestern Journal of International Law and Business* 28 (2): 273–340.

Kim, Joon-Kyung. 1999. "Chaebol's Ownership of Financial Institutions and the Related Problems." KDI Research Report No. 99-18, Korea Development Institute, Seoul (in Korean).

———. 2004. "Assessment of Progress in Corporate Restructuring in Korea since the 1997–98 Crisis." *Journal of Restructuring Finance* 1 (2): 289–310.

Kim, S., and H. Lim. 2017. "Bank-Reorganizations for Additional Re-Rating." *Daily News*, August 3. Shinhan Investment Corporation.

Kim, Seungwon. 2010. "The Effects of Foreign Capital Inflows on Economic Growth." BOK Working Paper No. 421, Economic Research Institute, Bank of Korea, Seoul.

Kim, Soyoung, Doo Yong Yang, and Jubeom Oh. 2014. "Impacts of Capital Control and Prudential Measures on Capital Flows in Korea: Estimation of

Capital Liberalization Index." *Panel Analysis in Korean Economy* 20 (3): 57–101 (in Korean).

Kim, Won-kyu. 2017. "Productivity Analysis of Korean Economy and Policy Implications." Issue Paper No. 2017-419, Korea Institute for Industrial Economics and Trade, Sejong (in Korean).

Kim Woo-Choong. 1992. *Every Street Is Paved with Gold: The Road to Real Success.* New York: Morrow.

Kim Yung Do. 2018. "Analysis of the Impact Channel of Mortgage Regulations on Housing Prices." *Journal of Money and Finance* 32 (4): 1–35 (in Korean).

King, Robert, and Ross Levine. 1993. "Finance and Growth: Schumpeter Might Be Right." *Quarterly Journal of Economics* 108 (3): 717–37.

Ko, Moonsoon. 2015. "Investing in Startup Food Stand." *Money Today,* November 30. https://news.mt.co.kr/mtview.php?no=2015112716272081661.

Korea Development Institute. 2017. *Forecasting Macroeconomic Variables for the Estimation of National Pension Finance in Korea.* Jeonjoo: National Pension Research Institute (in Korean).

Korea Productivity Center. 2019. *International Comparison of Total Factor Productivity.* Seoul: Korea Productivity Center (in Korean).

Kose, Ayhan, and Eswar Prasad. 2012. "Capital Accounts: Liberalize or Not?" In *Finance and Development,* edited by Camilla Andersen. Washington: International Monetary Fund.

Kose, Ayhan, Eswar Prasad, and Marco Terrones. 2009. "Does Openness to International Financial Flows Raise Productivity Growth?" *Journal of International Money and Finance* 28 (4): 554–80.

Kwak, Do Won, and Yung Chul Park. 2019. "Financial Growth and Distribution of Income: Evidence from Household Survey data." Unpublished manuscript.

La Porta, Rafael, Florencio Lopez-de-Silanes, Andrei Shleifer, and Robert Vishny. 2000. "Agency Problems and Dividend Policies around the World." *Journal of Finance* 55 (1): 1–33.

Lancaster, Tony. 2000. "The Incidental Parameter Problem since 1948." *Journal of Econometrics* 95 (2): 391–413.

Lane, Timothy. 1999. "The Asian Financial Crisis: What Have We Learned?" *Finance and Development* 36. (3): 44–47.

Lee, Benjamin Joon-Buhm. 2017. "Saving the Korean Class Action." *University of Pennsylvania Journal of International Law* 39 (1): 247–92.

Lee, Chong-hee. 2016. "Proliferation of Illicit Wealth by the Family Members of the Controlling Shareholders through Tunneling, 6th Report (2016)." Economic Reform Report No. 2016-13, Economic Reform Research Institute, Seoul (in Korean).

Lee, Jungyeoun, and Yang Su Park. 2015. "The Korean Financial Cycle." *Economic Analysis* 21 (3): 137–55 (in Korean).

Lee, Keun. 2003. "Global Standards vs. Local Specificity in Corporate Reform in Korea." Unpublished manuscript. Seoul National University (August).

Lee, Ki-hun. 2020. "We Want Honest Bankers." *The Chosun Ilbo*, May 28. https://news.chosun.com/site/data/html_dir/2020/05/27/2020052704679 .html.

Lee, Min Hwan, and Mamoru Nagano. 2008. "Market Competition before and after Bank Merger Wave: A Comparative Study of Korea and Japan." *Pacific Economic Review* 13 (5): 604–19.

Lee, Sangwoo, Kwangwoo Park, and Hyun-Han Shin. 2009. "Disappearing Internal Capital Markets: Evidence from Diversified Business Groups in Korea." *Journal of Banking and Finance* 33 (2): 326–34.

Lee, Seok-Young. 2012. "Efficiency Analysis of the Korean Banking Industry." *Korean Journal of Accounting Research* 17 (4): 249–76 (in Korean).

Lee, Soonghee. 2014. "South Korea: Class Action Lawsuit Act Discussions." *International Financial Law Review*, April 24.

Lee, Y., and S. Lee. 2018. "A Study on the Effects of Macroprudential Policies Using Panel VAR Model—With Focus on the Apartment Prices of the Seoul Metropolitan Area." *Journal of Financial Regulation and Supervision* 5 (2): 123–58.

Lensink, Robert, and Niels Hermes. 2004. "The Short-Term Effects of Foreign Bank Entry on Domestic Bank Behaviour: Does Economic Development Matter?" *Journal of Banking and Finance* 28 (3): 553–68.

Levine, Ross. 1997. "Financial Development and Economic Growth: Views and Agenda." *Journal of Economic Literature,* 35 (2): 688–726.

———. 2002. "Bank-Based or Market-Based Financial Systems: Which Is Better?" *Journal of Financial Intermediation* 11 (4): 398–428.

———. 2005. "Finance and Growth: Theory and Evidence." In *Handbook of Economic Growth*, edited by Philippe Aghion and Steven Durlauf, 1: 865–934. Amsterdam: Elsevier.

Levine, Ross, Norman Loayza, and Thorsten Beck. 2000. "Financial Intermediation and Growth: Causality and Causes." *Journal of Monetary Economics* 46 (1) 31–77.

Levine, Ross, and Sara Zervos. 1998. "Stock Markets, Banks, and Economic Growth." *American Economic Review* 88 (3): 537–58.

Lim, Kyung-Mook. 2008. "Impacts of Increasing Volatility of Profitability on Investment Behavior." *Korea Development Review* 30 (1): 1–31 (in Korean).

Lim, Youngjae. 2002. "Hyundai Crisis: Its Development and Resolution." *Journal of East Asian Studies* 2 (1): 261–83.

Lim, Youngjae, et al. 2003. "Developing and Measuring an Evaluation Index for Market Reform." Korea Development Institute. Unpublished manuscript. Mimeo.

Lombardi, Marco, Madhusudan Mohanty, and Ilhyock Shim. 2017. "The Real Effects of Household Debt in the Short and Long Run." BIS Working Paper No. 607, Bank for International Settlements, Geneva, Switzerland, January.

Ma, Yong, and Ke Song. 2018. "Financial Development and Macroeconomic Volatility." *Bulletin of Economic Research* 70 (3): 205–25.

McKinnon, Ronald. 1973. *Money and Capital in Economic Development.* Washington: Brookings Institution.

Ministry of Finance and Economy. 1998. *Korea's Economic Reform Progress Report.* Seoul: Ministry of Finance and Economy.

Mundy, Simon. 2013. "Foreign Banks Struggle in South Korea." *Financial Times,* September 18.

Naceur, Sami Ben, Robert Blotevogel, Mark Fischer, and Haiyan Shi. 2017. "Financial Development and Source of Growth: New Evidence." IMF Working Paper No. 17/143, International Monetary Fund, Washington, June.

Naceur, Sami Ben and Ruixin Zhang. 2016. "Financial Development, Inequality and Poverty: Some International Evidence." IMF Working Paper No. 16/32, International Monetary Fund, Washington, February.

Nam, Il Chong, Soo-Geun Oh, and Joon-Kyung Kim. 1999. "Insolvency Mechanisms in Korea." KDI Working Paper No. 9917, Korea Development Institute, Sejong, December.

Noh, J. Y. 2018. "Reducing Rate Differences between Large Firms and SMEs." *Kyunghyang Biz,* April 17. http://biz.khan.co.kr/khan_art_view.html?artid =201804172216005&code=920100.

Organization for Economic Cooperation and Development. 2004. *OECD Economic Surveys: Korea 2004.* Paris: Organization for Economic Cooperation and Development.

Ostry, Jonathan, Atish Ghosh, Karl Habermeier, Marcos Chamon, Mahvash Qureshi, and Dennis Reinhardt, 2010. "Capital Inflows: The Role of Controls." IMF Staff Position Note No. SPN/10/04, International Monetary Fund, Washington.

Padoa-Schioppa, Tommaso. 2003. "Central Banks and Financial Stability: Exploring the Land in Between." In *The Transformation of the European Financial System,* edited by Vitor Gaspar et al., 269–310. Frankfurt: European Central Bank.

Pagan, Adrian. 1984. "Econometric Issues in the Analysis of Regressions with Generated Regressors." *International Economic Review* 25 (1): 221–47.

Panzar, John, and James Rosse. 1987. "Testing for 'Monopoly' Equilibrium." *Journal of Industrial Economics* 35 (4): 443–56.

Park, Donghyun, and Kwanho Shin. 2015. "Economic Growth and Financial Development, and Income Inequality." ADB Economics Working Paper No. 441. Asian Development Bank, Metro Manila, Philippines, August.

Park, Jungsoo, Hail Park, Yung Chul Park, and Junghwan Park. 2018. "Finance and Growth in Korea: Financial System Inefficiency and Excessive Finance." *Journal of Korean Economic Analysis* 24 (1): 107–72.

Park, Kang H. 2009. "Has Bank Consolidation in Korea Lessened Competition?" *Quarterly Review of Economics and Finance* 49 (2): 651–67.

Park, Kang H., and William Weber. 2006. "A Note on Efficiency and Productivity Growth in the Korean Banking Industry, 1992–2002." *Journal of Banking and Finance* 30 (8): 2371–86.

Park, Yung Chul. 1998. "Financial Liberalization and Opening in East Asia: Issues and Policy Challenges." Korea Institute of Finance, No. 1998, 3–69.

———. 2006. *Economic Liberalization and Integration in East Asia: A Post-Crisis Paradigm.* Oxford: Oxford University Press.

———. 2010. "Global Economic Recession and East Asia: How Has Korea Managed the Crisis and What Has It Learned?" Bank of Korea Working Paper No. 409, Economic Research Institute, Bank of Korea, Seoul.

———. 2011a. "Reform of the Global Regulatory System: Perspectives of East Asian Emerging Economies." In *Annual World Bank Conference on Development Economics 2010 (Global): Lessons from East Asia and the Global Financial Crisis,* edited by Justine Yifu Lin and Boris Pleskovic. Washington: World Bank.

———. 2011b. "The Role of Macro Prudential Policy for Financial Stability in East Asia's Emerging Economies." In *Asian Perspectives on Financial Sector Reforms and Regulations,* edited by Masahiro Kawai and Eswar Prasad, 138–63. Washington: Brookings Institution Press.

Park, Yung Chul, and Jong Wha Lee. 2002. "Financial Crisis and Recovery: Patterns of Adjustment in East Asia, 1996–99." ADBI Research Paper No. 45, Asian Development Bank Institute, Metro Manila, Philippines, October.

Philippon, Thomas. 2010. "Financiers versus Engineers: Should the Financial Sector Be Taxed or Subsidized?" *American Economic Journal: Macroeconomics* 2 (3): 158–82.

———. 2015. "Has the US Finance Industry Become Less Efficient? On the Theory and Measurement of Financial Intermediation." *American Economic Review* 105 (4): 1408–38.

Public Fund Management Committee of Republic of Korea. 2009. "White Paper on Public Fund Management." Public Fund Management Committee Information, September (in Korean).

Quadrini, Vincenzo. 2011. "Financial Frictions in Macroeconomic Fluctuations." *Economic Quarterly* 97 (3): 209–54.

Radelet, Steven, and Jeffery Sachs. 1998. "The Onset of the East Asian Financial Crisis." NBER Working Paper No. 6680, National Bureau of Economic Research, Cambridge, MA, August.

Rajan, Raghuram. 2006. "Has Finance Made the World Riskier?" *European Financial Management* 12 (4): 499–533.

Rajan, Raghuram, and Luigi Zingales. 1998. "Financial Development and Growth." *American Economic Review* 88 (3): 559–86.

———. 2003a. "The Great Reversals: The Politics of Financial Development in the Twentieth Century." *Journal of Financial Economics* 69 (1): 5–50.

———. 2003b. *Saving Capitalism from the Capitalists: Unleashing the Power of Financial Markets to Create Wealth and Spread Opportunity.* New York: Crown Business.

Ro, Young-Jin, and Jin Woong Kim. 2014. "A Study on the Investment Behavior of Manufacturing Companies in Korea." *Journal of the Korean Official Statistics* 19 (2): 56–72.

Rodrik, Dani, and Andrés Velasco. 1999. "Short-Term Capital Flows." NBER Working Paper No. 7364, National Bureau of Economic Research, Cambridge, MA, September.

Sahay, Ratna, Martin Cihak, Papa M. N'Diaye, et al. 2015. "Rethinking Financial Deepening: Stability and Growth in Emerging Markets." IMF Staff Discussion Note No. SDN/15/08, International Monetary Fund, Washington, May.

Samphantharak, Krislert. 2006. "Internal Capital Markets in Business Groups." Unpublished manuscript.

Schinasi, Garry. 2004. "Defining Financial Stability." IMF Working Paper No. 4-187, International Monetary Fund, Washington, October.

Shaw, Edward. 1973. *Financial Deepening in Economic Development.* New York: Oxford University Press.

Shin, Dong Jin, and Brian H. S. Kim. 2011. "Efficiency of the Banking Industry Structure in Korea." *Asian Economic Journal* 25 (4): 355–73.

———. 2013. "Bank Consolidation and Competitiveness: Empirical Evidence from the Korean Banking Industry." *Journal of Asian Economics* 24, 41–50.

Shin, In-seok, et al. 2000. *The 3 Year IMF Programme in Korea.* Seoul: Financial Services Commission (in Korean).

Shin, Yong-Sang, and Wankeun Oh. 2005. "Financial Dependence, Growth Opportunities, and Industrial Growth in Korea." *Kyungjehak Yeonku* (Journal of Korea Economic Association) 53 (3): 49–76 (in Korean).

Shleifer, Andrei, and Robert Vishny. 2010. "Unstable Banking." *Journal of Financial Economics* 97 (3): 306–18.

Suh, Jung-ho. 2016. "Competition in the Korean Banking Market and Its Policy Implications." KIF Financial Analysis Report No. 2016-04, Korea Institute of Finance, Seoul (in Korean).

United Nations Conference on Trade and Development. 2008. *Trade Development Report 2008*. New York: United Nations.

White, William. 2004. "Making Macroprudential Concerns Operational." Speech delivered at the Financial Stability Symposium Organized by the Netherlands Bank, Amsterdam, October, 25–26.

Wi, Pyeong Lyang. 2018. "Concentration of Economic Power in the Hands of the Chaebol." Economic Reform Report No. 2018-02, Economic Reform Research Institute, Seoul (in Korean).

Wooldridge, Jeffrey M. 2005. "Fixed-Effects and Related Estimators for Correlated Random-Coefficient and Treatment-Effect Panel Data Models." *Review of Economics and Statistics* 87 (2): 385–90.

———. 2010. *Econometric Analysis of Cross Section and Panel Data*. 2nd ed. Vol. 1. Cambridge, MA: MIT Press.

———. 2016. *Introductory Econometrics*: *A Modern Approach*. Boston: South-Western Cengage Learning.

World Bank. 2008. *Finance for All? Policies and Pitfalls of Expanding Access*. Washington: World Bank.

———. 2018. "Global Financial Development Report 2017/2018: Bankers without Borders." November 9. Washington: World Bank.

———. 2019. "Global Financial Development Database (GFDD)," October. Washington: World Bank.

Yellen, Janet. 2010. "Macroprudential Supervision and Monetary Policy in the Post-Crisis World." Speech delivered at the Annual Meeting of the National Association for Business Economics, Denver, Colorado, October 11.

Yun, Seong-Hun. 2004. "Impact of Direct Regulations on the Korean Credit Card Market and Consumer Welfare." Bank of Korea Economic Paper No. 42, Bank of Korea, Seoul, August.

Zhang, Ruixin, and Sami Ben Naceur. 2019. "Financial Development, Inequality and Poverty: Some International Evidence." *International Review of Economics and Finance* 61 (May): 1–16.

Index

Page numbers for figures and tables are in italics.

Harvard East Asian Monographs
(most recent titles)